NJÁLS SAGA:
A LITERARY MASTERPIECE

NJÁLS SAGA:
A LITERARY
MASTERPIECE

By
EINAR ÓL. SVEINSSON

Edited and translated by
PAUL SCHACH

With an introduction by
E. O. G. TURVILLE-PETRE

UNIVERSITY OF NEBRASKA PRESS · LINCOLN

Publishers on the Plains

UNP

Copyright © 1971 by the University of Nebraska Press
International Standard Book Number 0–8032–0789–1
Library of Congress Catalog Card Number 70–128914

Manufactured in the United States of America

Contents

    I. Transient events the roots of creative art of permanent value. *Njáls saga* the work of one man. 7. — II. An example of the "elements" of *Njála:* Flosi's dream about Járngrímur and its sources. 12. — III. Archeological evidence in support of the burning of Njáll. 16. — IV. Oral sources: stories about events identical with or similar to those which *Njála* deals with. 18. — V. Written sources for events related in the saga: *Kristni þáttur, Brjáns saga,* the genealogical record. Historical validity of *Njála.* 21. — VI. Icelandic saga writing, its development and its influence on *Njáls saga.* Clerical language. The influence of the matter and the character depictions of earlier sagas. 28. — VII. The influence of contemporary times: laws, ideas, artistic taste. Individual events and persons similar to those depicted in *Njála* and other connections between the saga and contemporary times. 34. — VIII. Summary. 39.

Contents

Foreword

Professor Einar Ólafur Sveinsson is the foremost contemporary interpreter of *Brennu-Njáls saga*, the mightiest of the Sagas of Icelanders and one of the great classics of world literature. This is reason enough for making available to English readers his perceptive and penetrating treatise *Á Njálsbúð, bók um mikið listaverk* (*At the Site of Njál's Assembly Booth, A Book about a Great Work of Art*). There are, however, two additional reasons for doing so. The first is a professional one. In recent years the "Icelandic school" of saga research has incurred the displeasure of certain scholars outside of Iceland—not, as one would expect, because of its conservatism in regard to the importance of oral traditions in saga composition, but rather because of its repudiation of simple a priori answers to complicated questions of saga literature such as the "free prose" doctrine as espoused by Andreas Heusler. In all fairness to our Icelandic colleagues who choose to write in their native tongue, a selection of their scholarly production should be made available to scholars and laymen not conversant with Modern Icelandic so that they can judge the merit of these publications for themselves. The second reason is a more personal one: the publication of this American adaptation of *Á Njálsbúð* is a small token of gratitude and appreciation for the pleasure and profit I have derived both from reading Professor Einar's many studies and editions of Icelandic sagas as well as from the many conversations about Icelandic civilization I have enjoyed with him and his gracious wife, Kristjana Þorsteinsdóttir, in their home in

Reykjavík and at such historical sites as Þingvellir, Oddi, Hlíðarendi, and Bergþórshvoll.

A few words must be said about the background and sources of the present volume. During the spring semester of 1942 Professor Einar lectured on *Njáls saga* at the University of Iceland. These lectures were incorporated into the book *Á Njálsbúð*, which was published the following year. In 1954 his monumental edition of *Njáls saga* appeared as volume 12 of the series *Íslenzk fornrit*, and in the autumn of that year Professor Einar delivered three guest lectures in Danish at the University of Bergen dealing with the genesis, the art, and the life attitudes of *Njála*. In revised form these lectures were published in Swedish translation in *Scripta Islandica* (Isländska sällskapets årsbok 12) in 1961. In 1959 Professor Ludvig Holm-Olsen brought out his condensed Norwegian translation of *Á Njálsbúð* under the title *Njáls saga, kunstverket*.

The present adaptation of *Á Njálsbúð* was completed at the National Library of Iceland (Landsbókasafn) during the winter of 1966 and revised during the summer of that year with the help of Professor Einar. It is based primarily on the original Icelandic book, but substantial portions were taken from the Norwegian rendition with the kind permission of Professor Holm-Olsen and the Bergen-Oslo University Press. The Danish lectures, the article in Swedish, and the introduction and notes of Professor Einar's edition of *Njála* were also consulted. All changes from the original work of Professor Einar were made with his approval. Three appendices are included: Appendix A gives excerpts from the *Dialogues* of St. Gregory as the source for Flosi's dream; Appendix B summarizes some of the interpretations of the character of Hallgerður; and Appendix C explains the spelling and pronunciation of Icelandic proper names.

Quotations from the saga are from Professor Einar's edition, and therefore differ at times from those in *Á Njálsbúð*. In the translation of these saga quotations, the Latin translation by Jón Johnsonius (1809) was frequently consulted. My repeated reading of other translations, especially the German one by Heusler (Sammlung Thule IV, 1914) and the English translations of Hollander and Bayerschmidt (American-Scandinavian Foundation, 1955) and of Magnus Magnusson and Hermann Pálsson (Penguin Classics, 1960) has left its mark upon my own work. May I suggest that in reading this volume, one should constantly consult either one or both of these English translations. For those not acquainted with *Njáls saga*, it would be advisable to read a translation before reading Professor Einar's perceptive interpretation of it.

Grants from the American Philosophical Society and the Research Council of the University of Nebraska and a Woods Humanities Fellowship enabled me to devote two semesters and the intervening summer (1966) to research in Iceland. As noted above, it was during this time that the present translation was made. I wish to express my gratitude to Professor Turville-Petre for consenting to write an introduction to this volume in the midst of pressing duties.

Introduction

Dr. Einar Ól. Sveinsson, Professor in the University of Iceland and Director of the Manuscript Institute of Iceland, has been recognized as the foremost authority on *Njáls saga* ever since 1933, when he published his learned treatise *Um Njálu* (*Concerning Njáls Saga*).[1] In that book Dr. Einar examined in minute detail all major problems about this, the greatest, although one of the latest, of the Icelandic sagas. He studied its structure, sources, and age. Some of his conclusions were, at that time, revolutionary, but most of them stand unchallenged at the present day. Dr. Einar's studies of *Njáls saga* have continued since his first work on it was published, culminating in 1954 with an edition of the saga.[2] This edition contains the first critical text to be published for many years, besides copious notes on textual variants, linguistic niceties, and subject matter. Dr. Einar reexamined problems in the light of the most recent research. He considered numerous manuscripts, discussing the relationship between them, and was thus able to present a text as nearly authoritative as any which we are likely to see. He dealt carefully with general questions about the saga, its sources, age, and place of origin, and he searched cautiously for its author. The literary value of the saga was discussed, as well as its value as history, partly in the light of recent archeological finds.

The volume which is now offered for the first time in English translation was first published in Icelandic in 1943 under the title *Á Njálsbúð*

1. *Um Njálu*, I Bindi, Reykjavík: Bókadeild Menningarsjóðs, 1933.
2. *Brennu-Njáls saga*, Íslenzk fornrit XII, Reykjavík: Hið íslenzka fornritafélag, 1954.

(*At the Site of Njál's Assembly Booth*). It is in many ways unlike Dr. Einar's other works on the subject. He has distilled his deep knowledge of *Njáls saga* and shown his readers how to value it as a work of art. He does not confine himself to technical problems, but thinks especially of the aesthetic qualities of the saga. He studies the chief characters as, historically or not, the author of the saga portrays them. One of the most puzzling figures is Hallgerður, the wife of Gunnar. She is thievish and seemingly treacherous, betraying her noble husband in his last battle. She refuses to give him a lock of her beautiful hair to replace his broken bowstring. Dr. Einar is able to regard this woman with a certain sympathy: *tout comprendre c'est tout pardonner*. Other important characters, Skarphéðinn and Njáll himself, complicated as they are, are also studied closely. One of the most interesting chapters is the last, in which Dr. Einar explains the philosophical outlook of the author of *Njáls saga*, his views on morals, justice, fate.

This is an unusually personal and sensitive work, such as could be written only by a scholar who had lived with *Njáls saga* for many years, even since childhood. It is worth noting that Dr. Einar began his life in the wild regions of southern Iceland, not far from the scenes of some events described in the saga. I may add that, in 1948, Dr. Einar published a scholarly volume on the original settlement of the southern districts.[3] He began with the Irish hermits (*Papar*), and passed on to the Norse settlers, their origins, legal practices, and religion; he made full use of the evidence of place names, as well as of literary sources.

I need say no more of the present volume, for it will speak for itself. I would like, however, to say something of Dr. Einar's works on subjects other than *Njáls saga*. His interests are wide and his output immense. He has published critical editions of several of the major sagas, *Laxdæla*, *Eyrbyggja*, *Vatnsdæla*, as well as of some of the minor ones.

3. *Landnám í Skaftafellsþingi*, Skaftfellinga Rit II, Reykjavík: Skaftfellingafélagið, 1948.

All of these editions bear the stamp of a master. They are furnished with thorough, penetrating introductions, as well as copious explanatory notes on the subject matter and idioms in the prose. These volumes also include remarkably lucid notes on the intricate verses embedded in some of the sagas, the so-called skaldic verses.

Among other important works I would mention the perceptive *Sturlungaöld* (Reykjavík, 1940), which may be read in the English translation of Jóhann S. Hannesson, *The Age of the Sturlungs*.[4] This is a study of the civilization of Iceland in the thirteenth century. Among many topics Dr. Einar describes class structure, vices and virtues, the position of the Church and her priests. In a less well known, but not less important, work, *Um íslenzkar þjóðsögur* (*Concerning Icelandic Folk Stories* [Reykjavík, 1940]), Dr. Einar discusses Icelandic folk stories of all ages, analyzing beliefs in trolls, the hidden people, ghosts, second sight, and magic.

Some years ago, I was happy to translate from manuscript an instructive work by Dr. Einar entitled *Dating the Icelandic Sagas, an Essay in Method* (London: Viking Society for Northern Research, 1958). In this book it was shown how difficult it was to assign individual sagas to a given date confidently as former scholars had often done. There was evidence enough, although much of it was treacherous. Dr. Einar showed, however, that certain evidence could be trusted. It was sometimes possible to see, for instance, that one saga had been influenced by another, or by some historical work, such as *The Book of Settlements* (*Landnámabók*) in one version or another. Some sagas contained archaic words or word forms which indicated ancient origin. The influence of historical events of the thirteenth century had also to be considered. *Laxdæla saga*, to take one example, was written at a time when trial by ordeal was still legal in Iceland, although it was apparently abolished

4. Published in *Islandica*, Vol. XXXVI, Ithaca, New York: Cornell University Press, 1953.

in 1248. *Laxdæla saga* was, therefore, written before that date, although evidence suggested that it was not written many years earlier. Dr. Einar was also able to date *Njáls saga* about 1280. His evidence was manifold, partly that of extant manuscripts and partly traces of the influence of other sagas upon *Njáls saga*. The most important evidence of all was the influence of the law book *Járnsíða*, introduced into Iceland in 1271 and current for the next decade. A revised, augmented edition of *Dating the Icelandic Sagas* has been published under the title *Ritunartími Íslendingasagna* (Reykjavík: Hið íslenzka bókmenntafélag, 1965).

The most ambitious of all Dr. Einar's works is not yet complete, but it will cover the whole of Icelandic literature from its beginnings until the close of the fourteenth century. Only the first volume, a substantial one of over five hundred pages, has yet been published.[5] It deals especially with the oldest poetry, that of the *Edda* and comparable collections. There are separate chapters on each of the major Eddaic lays, establishing as far as possible their sources, ages, and places of origin. There are also more general chapters, two of which are particularly interesting for me. One of these is on metrics, and it includes studies of the various measures used in the Eddaic lays, as well as of the far more complicated skaldic measures, with their strict syllable count, internal rhyme and half rhyme. Another chapter is about poetic diction, a subject which, I am sure, Dr. Einar will develop further in his next volume. I am glad to say that a translation of this first volume is now being prepared in English.

Dr. Einar has written many essays, some of which were collected in a volume published in 1956.[6] Among the most interesting is one, first published in 1947, on the diction of the skalds. I have read no more lucid and humane account of the kennings and other skaldic devices than this one.

5. *Íslenzkar bókmenntir í fornöld*, I, Reykjavík: Almenna bókafélagið, 1962.
6. *Við uppspretturnar*, Reykjavík: Helgafell, 1956.

To sum up, it may be said that Dr. Einar is a profound scholar, but he is not a pedant; he is also a thinker and a man of deep aesthetic sense. He is well versed in literature, not only of Iceland, but also of other European countries. His life has been devoted to literature.

I would like to say a word about the present translation by Professor Paul Schach. I mentioned earlier that the book is an unusually personal one. The style is also personal and unusual, difficult enough for most who are not native Icelanders, even perhaps for some who are. Dr. Schach has succeeded in conveying much of the tone of the original in his translation. This is not, in fact, a straightforward translation, but it has been edited and brought up to date, partly by the author and partly by the translator. It will thus be valuable even for those who are able to read the original text.

E. O. G. TURVILLE-PETRE

Oxford

NJÁLS SAGA:
A LITERARY MASTERPIECE

1. Overture: At the Site of Njál's Assembly Booth

I

Ruins. A wall half sunken into the earth, so that only the blue-gray, moss-covered tops of the stones project—Njál's booth, people say. And round about grows marsh grass, through which breezes sigh all summer long. The sighing of the wind blends with the muffled roar of the waterfall, and it seems as though this eternal song were one with time itself as it passes by.

Overhead the gray sky arches, a sky with clouds that seem to have existed forever, changeless, yet always changing, with rifts and rents half hidden in this endless grayness pregnant with a singular cold earnestness. The clouds cast a cool, blue-gray tranquillity over Ármannsfell and Hrafnabjörg; thus have these mountains stood since the dawn of time.

Or else the sun shines upon Þingvellir, shrouding the landscape in a veil of mystery. The earth takes on a strange luster from the glittering blades of grass, and this patch of marsh grass expands into a vast plain. The mountains are far, far away, and the islands out in the lake are fairylands. Time seems to lose its course in the sunlight. *Now* and *then* coalesce into an eternal moment. The life of man seems to become as transparent as glass. The walls separating man from man disappear, and we become involved in all of life, in its grief and joy, its anguish and bliss.

Memories of ages past are no longer dead letters in an old book; the ruins are no longer sunken, half-covered heaps of stones. The booths again stand all over the Assembly area, just as they did in ancient times, and men and women stroll among them. The teeming life of the

Assembly has risen again, and it is strange to see and experience it all. Here are uprooted farmers who have fled from their ancestral homes; here are Vikings who never knew any other home than the sea, who cared for nothing but fame and deeds of prowess and adventure. All of them are trying to put down roots in a new land, a bare and rugged land which yields them only a harsh existence. In due time they begin to frequent this place for their assemblies; they enter into fellowship with each other and become one people. The unsociable dweller in a remote fjord, who is discomfited when first summoned to testify before the Assembly, here becomes more cosmopolitan, and the Viking is driven by necessity to accept the laws and adapt himself to the customs of a civilized country. He continues to dream of fame and exploits and adventure and of his own merit, but these dreams do not break loose from their firm moorings in the earth—the farmer sees to that. Yet their dreams lift spirit and deed up from the dust, and these men rise to a higher level of development than their conditions of life would give reason to expect. Their impulse toward heroic deeds bears fruit. They are destined to have the good fortune of being able to use their powers in a manly fashion. For this reason the characteristic stamp of the men who lived here in the first centuries is so easily discernible.

To those who prefer to sit snugly in their warm, sheltered nooks the good fortune of these men may seem questionable. For their sagas deal with what people are wont to call misfortune, adversity, and tragic events. Most of the saga heroes are not conquerors, but men who are hunted and pursued until finally they are killed. The hero has not fully proved himself until he has shown that he knows how to die. The high point of a saga is the death of the hero. In that moment he gains his victory over the whole world.

But no one takes this road knowingly and willingly. Every living being wants to live, and every creature endowed with feeling desires happiness. Men seek to avoid disaster, and are reluctant to pass through the gates of death. But human strength avails little, and man is bound with countless bonds which drag him, willingly or unwillingly, along with the stream. The life of man is filled with mystery and wonder; tears and laughter are blended in a strange and terrible manner. The sage Njáll gazes at this mystery for a long time until finally he is able to see through it in its entirety. It is just as though his eye had thawed an opening in the frost-covered window of the future. Should he not through his prescience be able to intervene decisively in this drama and influence its outcome in accordance with his will?

II

At this place stood the great sage, Njáll of Bergþórshvoll, gazing with clairvoyant eyes at the throngs of people attending the Assembly, with those keen eyes which sometimes beamed with good will and warmheartedness and lighted up with pleasure, but which at other times were as hard and cold as steel or were darkened by anguish of heart. Beside him stands a splendid, noble-looking man who has sought advice from Njáll regarding the collection of some property belonging to a kinswoman of his: but what far-reaching consequences are to result from that counsel—the fortune and misfortune of many men, life and death, and finally the death of these two men themselves! Up there on the hillside among the shimmering gold patches of dew cups we see Gunnar of Hlíðarendi again. Now he is conversing with Hallgerður. The sorcery of her eyes robs him of his peace of mind, and before the sun sets over the Plains of the Assembly he has pledged his troth to her—and with her to misfortune, which clings to him until the end of his days and drags after it another train of disaster leading to the death of Njáll. We see Njál's eldest son; behind the mask of his face glow volcanic fires, and the cast of his forehead reflects the solitude of desolate tracts of sand and glacial rivers. We see the other sons of Njáll and his sons-in-law and kinsmen of Gunnar, and how they all come to play their parts in the tragedy, and it is impossible to determine whether the force of circumstances or their own characters are the stronger. Should not the peace-loving sage be able to bring about peace? Certainly he exerts all of his wisdom and strength to this end, but nevertheless the final result of his endeavors, the outcome of his counsels, is that his farmstead goes up in flames around himself and his sons, and he perishes with them in the fire.

Into this drama are drawn a multitude of people, both at the Assembly and at their homes throughout the countryside. There on the plain and up under the hill by the Law Rock we can see the entire Assembly engaged in battle. They are all there: Kári, Ásgrímur, Gizur inn hvíti, Þorgeir skorargeir; and the enemies: Flosi, the sons of Sigfús, the chieftains from the East Fjords. We can see where each one fights and how the battle surges out across the Assembly site. Over there is where Snorri goði stood when he exchanged words with Flosi. Up there, coming from the bridge, went Hallur of Sída and his son Ljótur in an effort to part the combatants. And there is where Ljótur stood as the fatal spear flew toward him. . . .

III

These mental images which arise before us seem to be reality itself, so clear and lifelike is everything about them. And yet these events never took place in the way we picture them. Perhaps Njál's Assembly booth is in the same class as Juliet's grave. To be sure, there are the remains of an old building here, but could not the name "Njál's booth" derive from a literary work of such compelling artistry that people could see before them everything it related and therefore felt impelled to discover the place itself? For everything that we have recalled and imagined here comes from this great literary masterpiece, *Brennu-Njáls saga*. Everything that seers and clairvoyants of later times have conjured up from this saga—they never realized how deeply influenced they were by it. It has even led scholars astray.

Almost seven hundred years ago the author of this literary masterpiece stood at this spot. He walked among the booths, he went up to the Law Rock, he stood on the upper brink of the Almannagjá, from which he gazed out over the Assembly site. The sun shone down on the fields, a gentle wind sighed through the foliage, the grass on the roof of the Þingvellir farmstead swayed in the breeze—it was the same sun as now. The author's thoughts wandered back, and time strayed from its course in the sunshine. Events that had occurred three centuries before rose up before his inner eye.

What were these events like? About that we know almost nothing except for a few isolated facts. What were the sources of the author, the roots of the saga? About this we know considerably more. But we will not see the light of day until we turn our backs on such questions and surrender ourselves to the power of this work of narrative art as it is revealed to us on the pages of the book itself.

Here we will see a whole world filled with those wondrous things which the human mind is wont to brood over. We will encounter many notable persons, men of all walks of life, from the chieftain to the thrall, each with his own personality, each one pursuing his peculiar, singular destiny. There is laughter in the world of this saga, but most often the laughter veils bitter suffering; this whole world is spattered with blood. With heavy heart the author sees how deeds of bravery and virtue beget venom and depravity and destruction. How can this be? With heart and mind this man seeks to discover some design or order in this merciless confusion. He shapes this chaos into artistic form: he creates his literary masterpiece. Sometimes he depicts the waxing and waning of this envenomed, infectious tragedy. Sometimes he tries to soothe his wounds with the cold tranquillity of fatalism. Finally his suffering opens up to him a new world, a new life. It becomes clear to him that in spite of everything there must be a loving hand which governs. He gains freedom, independence, and serenity of soul. It would not have been difficult for him to go with Lear and Cordelia into imprisonment:

> ... So we'll live,
> And pray, and sing, and tell old tales, and laugh
> At gilded butterflies.

IV

In the following pages I shall try to give an account of this great work of literature as I see and interpret it. I shall try to explain more

precisely much which was briefly touched on here. My methods and
points of view will be discussed when necessary, but for the most part
they will be revealed most clearly in the study itself.

There is one matter which I think I should clarify at the outset. I do
not presume to set myself up as some sort of apologist for *Njáls saga*,
as some persons do. This work does not need my defense or that of
anyone else. Nor is it necessary to gloss over its flaws or cover up its
faults. This saga will live on the basis of its own merits and not through
an attempt to conceal its defects. If I am found to say more about the
good qualities of the saga than about its weak points, it is not because
I want to make a defense for it, but for altogether different reasons. To
be sure, mistakes in the saga such as anachronisms and errors in legal
procedure are not unworthy of note; but there are other things which
are much more noteworthy, and it is these which I feel should be
emphasized. The difficulty of interpreting *Njáls saga* is considerably
lessened by the fact that my previous study of this work has laid the
foundation for the present essay.

Literary research changes with the times and is soon consigned to
the past and forgotten except by a few scholars. The great literary
masterpieces themselves, however, possess eternal vitality and validity.
Odysseus, Don Quixote, Prince Hamlet—all have survived the ravages
and vicissitudes of time and will continue to do so. Even a little poem
can be preserved and continue to live, like the verse Horace wrote two
thousand years ago about the wolf which fled from him even though
he was unarmed:

> A wolf, with mouth-protruding snout,
>   Forth from the thicket bounded—
> I clapped my hands and raised a shout—
>   He heard—and fled—confounded.[1]

And *Njáls saga*, too, will live on as long as the Icelandic tongue is known.

1. This free translation of the third verse of Horace's "Integer Vitae" is by
John Quincy Adams, sixth president of the United States.

2. The Roots

I

In ancient Icelandic annals there is entered under the year 1010 the word *Njálsbrenna*—that is to say, the burning of Njáll in his home. I do not know what sources the annals are based on here, but I am convinced that they refer to an event which really took place at about that time. Strife breaks out and leads to arson; as a consequence, fighting later erupts at the General Assembly. These events must have made a deep impression upon the age in which they took place; a few individuals who experienced them perhaps felt that their entire world was on the verge of collapse. But time heals all wounds, and soon the fire at Bergþórshvoll and the ensuing battles belonged to the past and left behind no more than most quarrels and hostilities and wars do: legends which live on in the memory of the people and notations made by scholars in old books. But scarcely three centuries after these events occurred, something singular happens: a man decides to write a saga about them, a saga which not only has become a major monument in the literature of an island people poor and few in numbers, but also is one of the great masterpieces in the literature of the world. This is *Brennu-Njáls saga*, as it is called in Icelandic, or *Njála*, as it is often known in our time. It is with this literary masterpiece that the present study is concerned, and not with events from the saga age on which it is based. But since many persons tend to confuse the saga with its sources, or else are curious about its origin, it will be necessary to devote this chapter to a discussion of the roots and the genesis of *Njáls saga*.

Selma Lagerlöf tells somewhere how *Gösta Berlings saga* came into existence. She says:

Once there was a saga which wanted to be told and to be launched out into the world. This was quite natural, since it was aware of the fact that it already was practically finished. Many people had participated in creating it by their extraordinary deeds; others had contributed to it by telling of those deeds again and again. The only thing that was lacking was for the parts to be joined together somewhat here and there so that the saga could conveniently journey about the country. It was still not much more than a swarm of stories, a shapeless cloud of adventures, which drifted back and forth like a swarm of bees that had gone astray on a summer day and did not know where they would find someone who could gather them into a hive.

After this, the author goes on to a more detailed account of the development from a "shapeless cloud of adventures" to the literary work, and it is evident that she put it much too simply when she spoke of how this work of art came into being. What took place was something quite different from a mere joining together of separate parts.

When we study the Icelandic sagas, we would welcome a similar authentic account of their genesis; this, unfortunately, we do not have. We must painstakingly scrutinize each individual saga in order, if possible, to arrive at a clear understanding of its sources and origin.

Perhaps some people will say that the investigation of sources, of models, and of the author's life in reality often leads away from a work of art. The scholar may believe that he has completed his task when he has established the individual components of which a literary work is composed. This does not mean, of course, that the investigation of the genesis of a work of art is in itself unnecessary, but simply that the scholar who limits his investigation in this manner has stopped at the halfway mark. As far as the Icelandic sagas are concerned, the reader, as a rule, will naturally enough ask about their historical truth and how they came to be; and it is necessary, whether one wants to or not, to try to provide an answer for these questions before proceeding to other matters which in themselves are more important.

For many of those who write about the sagas, things are quite simple. Some consider the sagas a faithful reflection of events and people in the saga age; others characterize them without more ado as novels with little or no historical foundation. The author of this book is not one of those happy people. I have always, in my investigation of the sagas, encountered complications; and I think that instead of looking for a simple, striking label for "the Saga," as some persons like to express it, one ought to examine the individual sagas. When this has been done, and after one has gotten out of the realm of hypothesis and down onto solid ground, one can search for a label—if by then it still seems worthwhile. Instead of trying to prove some preconceived hypothesis, one should try to find objective criteria with which to work. The method is that which Goethe somewhere calls *eine tätige Skepsis: "Eine tätige Skepsis ist die, welche unablässig bemüht ist, sich selbst zu überwinden und durch geregelte Erfahrung zu einer Art von bedingter Zuverlässigkeit zu gelangen."* ("An active skepticism is one which endeavors unceasingly to overcome itself and, through ordered experience, to arrive at a kind of conditional certainty.")

Everyone who has read *Njála* knows its illusory stamp of reality. We know the saga age itself, the tenth century and first half of the eleventh, not from contemporary sources, but chiefly from the sagas, which date from a much later period; and the picture of the saga age in *Njála* appears at first glance to be much the same as that of the other sagas. Therefore it is not surprising that people for centuries should have thought that this saga presented an authentic picture of historical facts. To be sure, Árni Magnússon had pointed out that the Icelanders were praised far too highly in the sagas, as if they were far superior to the people of other nations: "Above all others, the author of *Njáls saga* knew no modesty in this respect." For the most part, however, people were in agreement far into the nineteenth century that *Njáls saga* was history.

In 1856 Guðbrandur Vigfússon published his famous treatise on the chronology of the sagas, "Um tímatal í Íslendinga sögum i fornöld," which appeared in the first volume of *Safn til sögu Íslands*. He had discovered various difficulties with the chronology in *Njála*, but did not investigate those problems more closely and did not arrive at any conclusions regarding them. This he did, however, in his later writings. In 1883 there appeared the book by Karl Lehmann and Hans Schnorr von Carolsfeld, *Die Njálssage*, in which it is pointed out that not a few things in the saga indicate a late origin, and it is shown there that the legal procedures in the saga are constructed and based on written laws. As early as the nineteenth century there also appeared the first studies of the saga as a work of art. Special mention should be made of Carsten Hauch's excellent treatise, "Indledning til Forelæsninger over Njals-saga," printed in *Afhandlinger og æsthetiske Betragtninger* (1855), and A. U. Bååth's *Studier öfver kompositionen i några isländska ättsagor* (1885). In both of these studies the saga's artistic unity is emphasized; and, what is no less important, the way is cleared for an understanding of the saga's poetical elements, which it owes to *one* author. These ideas were advocated by a number of scholars of the twentieth century, including W. P. Ker, Andreas Heusler, Sigurður Nordal, Sigurður Guðmundsson, and Paul V. Rubow.

At the close of the last century Finnur Jónsson set forth his theories concerning *Njáls saga* in *Den oldnorske og oldislandske Litteraturs Historie*. He was well aware of everything that indicates that the saga, as we have it, is fairly late, and that there is not a little in it which is unhistorical. His demonstration of the nonclassical features of the saga is of enduring value. But Finnur Jónsson was, as is known, a champion of the view that tradition is historical, and he tried to save as much as possible to support this view. He adopted a hypothesis, which was current, to the effect that *Njála* had come into existence through the piecing together of two old, classical, and historically reliable sagas, now lost: *Gunnars saga* and *Njáls saga*. At the time they were pieced together, their texts were supposedly revised; still later the complete saga which had come into existence in this manner was supposed to have been interpolated, not once but several times. In this way all the unhistorical, nonclassical, and late elements in the saga are supposed to have gotten into it. In a treatise from the year 1904 and in his edition of the saga (1908) Finnur Jónsson modified his hypothesis to the extent that he allowed for the possibility that there never had existed an old *Gunnars saga*. The first part of the saga would then be a later addition to the hypothetical older *Njáls saga*.

In my book *Um Njálu* (Reykjavík, 1933) I undertook to show that this hypothesis is untenable, and I shall not repeat all the arguments which can be assembled against it. A few will be cited only briefly here.

All the manuscripts derive from the same original, in which the saga must have existed in the form it now has; and fragments have been preserved from not less than a score of medieval manuscripts. The arguments put forth to show that the saga was interpolated prove upon closer examination to be specious; the passages in question are found to have good connection and continuity with the remaining parts of the saga. Thus we return to the whole saga as we have it now; and if we examine its characteristic features, such as composition, style, ideas, delineation of character, etc., it becomes clear that we are dealing with a distinctive work by one author, an artistic unity of unusually firm cast. The pieces of evidence concerning recentness which Finnur Jónsson and others have found are important. One of the most important is Lehmann's demonstration of the influence of the Norwegian-influenced law book *Járnsíða*, which was introduced into Iceland in 1271. Between that year and the time of the oldest preserved manuscript (about 1300) the saga was written, perhaps in the years between 1280 and 1285. But it was precisely the last few decades of the thirteenth century which were fateful in the development of Icelandic literature. The spirit of the age of the Commonwealth and of the classical saga was coming to an end. *Njála* appears to have been written by a man who was brought up in the school of the classical sagas, but who was not able to avoid being influenced by his own time.

That which is old in the saga, and which points toward the time of the classical saga or even farther back—is it of such a nature that one must presuppose one or more older sagas about Njáll and Gunnar, supposedly incorporated into our saga? I do not think so. That which

especially gives the impression of being old, such as a large part of the
names of the characters and the main events, can easily stem from other
sources. But the description of the individual events, the motivation,
and the continuity give, upon closer inspection, the impression of
blinding poetic illusion rather than simple preservation of old traditions.
As an example the saga's legal procedures may be cited, but other
things could just as well be brought out. On the whole it appears
improbable, upon closer examination, that the hypothetical "original"
sagas ever existed.

II

Then what sources does *Njáls saga* have? For although it is the work
of one man, it was not created from nothing. All things are made of
some substance, as Snorri Sturluson expressed it; *Njáls saga* has its
sources and models like every other literary work. Let us look at chapter
133 in the saga, where we have an excellent example of how involved
the process of the genesis of the saga was. The chapter deals with a
dream that Flosi had the winter after the fire at Bergþórshvoll:

> One night at Svínafell Flosi was restless in his sleep. Glúmur Hildisson
> roused him from his sleep, but it was a long time before he awoke. Flosi
> asked him to fetch Ketill of Mörk.
>
> When Ketill came there, Flosi said: "I want to tell you my dream."
>
> "Do so!" said Ketill.
>
> "I dreamed that I was at Lómagnúpur," Flosi said. "I went outside and
> looked up toward the cliffs, and they opened up, and a man came out. He
> was wearing a goatskin cloak and had an iron staff in his hand. He went about,
> shouting and calling to my men, several at a time, and summoning them by
> name. First he called my kinsman Grímur inn rauði and Árni Kolsson. Then
> a strange thing seemed to happen: I thought he summoned Eyjólfur Bölverks-
> son and Ljótur the son of Hallur of Síða, and some six other men. Then he
> was silent for a while. Then he called five more of our band, and among them
> were the sons of Sigfús, your brothers. Then he called another five men, and
> among them were Lambi and Móðólfur and Glúmur. Then he called three
> men, and last of all he called Gunnar Lambason and Kolur Þorsteinsson.

"After that he came up to me. I asked him the news, and he said that he would tell me. Then I asked him his name, and he said it was Járngrímur. I asked him where he intended to go, and he replied that he was going to the Assembly.

"'What will you do there?' I asked.

"He answered: 'First I shall clear the jury, then the court, and then I shall clear the field for battle.'

"After that he spoke this verse:

> 'A great warrior
> Will rise above the land;
> Men will see the ground
> Strewn with many skulls.
> The din of the clash of swords
> Will echo in the hills;
> The dew of blood
> Will spatter the limbs of men.'

Thereupon he struck the ground with his staff, and there was a great crash. Then he walked back into the cliffs, and I was seized with dread. Now I want you to tell me what you think this dream means."

"I have a premonition," said Ketill, "that all those who were called are doomed men. It seems advisable to me that we tell no one of this dream for the time being."

Flosi agreed that they should not.

I am sure that most people will agree that this is an excellent dream story. The account of the witch ride which appeared to Hildiglúmur (chapter 125) and some of the apparitions in *Brjáns þáttur* (chapters 156–57) are, to be sure, more dramatic, but Flosi's dream is almost as impressive. It also seems to be all of one piece and uncompounded. For this reason it may seem strange that I should think it possible to see how this account was constructed and what its "elements" are. But there is scarcely an episode in the saga which, in my opinion, is as completely transparent in this respect. Let us look more closely at its individual elements.

Flosi sees the mountain Lómagnúpur open up, and a man clad in a goatskin (i.e., a cloak made of goatskin), with an iron staff in his hand, come out. The inhabitant of the mountain chants a verse which warns that hostilities are in store, and then goes back into the mountain. Here we are dealing with a figure from popular belief, which is known both from old sources and from folk tales of later times. *Njála* itself speaks several times of mountain dwellers. The chieftains at the General Assembly once say that Skarphéðinn looks like a troll and another time that he looks as if he had come out of mountain crags. In chapter 123 reference is made to the Svínafell Troll, and in chapter 119 Skarphéðinn speaks of Eydís járnsaxa and Steðjakollur, who abduct human women. In *Landnámabók* we read about a cliff dweller who appears in a dream to Hafur-Björn, a giant who causes volcanic fire, and about a troll who sits on cliffs and kicks out into the sea so that the breakers roar and speaks a verse about ships and men that perish in the breakers. In other places we are told of a troll with an iron staff in his hand and with clothes of the same fashion as the goatskin cloak in Flosi's dream. The saga undoubtedly builds upon popular tales here, and the author perhaps heard such folklore concerning the mountain Lómagnúpur. This we do not know. But certainly we have here an example of the use of oral tradition.

That is, however, not the only source. If we look further at the story, we notice a unique feature. The mountain dweller calls out the names of Flosi's men. He calls them in groups. In the midst of this he is silent for a while, and then he calls again. Ketill and Flosi understand that all those he has called are going to die.

Among all the many tales I have read about dreams and tidings of death, there is only one which especially resembles this one. Those marked for death are called by name, and there is a moment of silence in the middle of the summoning. This tale is found in the *Dialogues* of Pope Gregory the Great. A monk, Anastasius, founded a monastery beneath a high *rupes*, a steep and towering cliff. Then it happened one night that Anastasius heard a voice from the mountain: "Come, Anastasius!" After that seven other friars were called by name. Then there was a moment's silence, after which an eighth one was called. The monks understood immediately that this meant that they were soon to die; and they did die, in the same order in which they had been named. But the eighth monk died somewhat later than the others.

Pope Gregory's *Dialogues* existed in Icelandic in the twelfth century, and there is a similarity between the wording of the tale of Anastasius and the account of Flosi's dream. The author of *Njála* must have been familiar with the story in the *Dialogues*, which were widely read in Iceland. And now we come to an interesting situation. In the Arnamagnæan collection of manuscripts in Copenhagen there is a fragment of the translation of Gregory's *Dialogues* which Árni Magnússon procured in 1699 from the church at Kálfafell, a few miles west of Lómagnúpur. Thus it is quite probable that the story about Anastasius was to be found in the near vicinity of Lómagnúpur at the time the author of *Njála* was alive. Here we have an example of a written source for the saga.[1]

Flosi asks the mountain dweller what his name is. His name is Járngrímur. Where is he going? To the Assembly. He is going to clear away the jury and the judges, and afterwards the place of battle for the fighters. We also meet a Járngrímur in *Sturlunga saga*, just after the battle at Örlygsstaðir (1238). A man named Guðmundur was outside walking in the dark. Then a big, powerful man wearing a hooded cloak and with his hat down over his face came toward him. Guðmundur asked what his name was, and he said it was Járngrímur. "Where are you going?" said Guðmundur, and Járngrímur named a place where a man was killed that same evening. Here we are dealing with influences upon the saga from contemporary times.[2]

But it still remains for us to point out the innermost core of the tale;

1. See Appendix A.
2. *Sturlunga saga*, ed. Jón Jóhannesson, Magnús Finnbogason og Kristján Eldjárn, Reykjavík: Sturlungaútgáfan, 1946, Vol. I, p. 441. If I remember correctly, it was Steinn Dofri who first commented in print on this parallel between *Njála* and *Sturlunga saga* (*Saga* II [1926], p. 18).

and that core is the awe-inspiring mountain Lómagnúpur itself, which no one can forget once he has seen it. In the saga it lies shrouded in night and soundless autumn darkness, which suddenly is filled with crashes and terror. Now and then episodes in the saga are of such a nature that the reader immediately feels that the author must once have stood at that very place. The story of Lómagnúpur is one of them. The author of *Njála* certainly saw the mighty mountain, gazed up at it from the farm below, and perhaps felt the inexplicable terror which can grip a person when he looks out of the world of men and into the giant world of nature. He had been brought up with stories of trolls and mountain dwellers, whether he actually heard a legend concerning this particular mountain or not. Perhaps it was on a farm in the vicinity that a cleric read or told to him the story of Anastasius and the mountain Suppentonia. Perhaps he heard here the account of Guðmundur and Járngrímur. We do not know; but it is Lómagnúpur and the mysterious light which in the mind of the author hovers over this mountain that unites the elements in the dream and fuses them into a whole.

Thus there are found in this dream all the elements of which the saga is constructed: oral tradition, written sources, influence from contemporary times, and the author's life experience.[3]

We will first discuss the question of oral traditions. In former days they were assumed a priori; now people are more cautious. When one attempts to demonstrate tradition, he is dealing with three factors: features in the saga which appear to derive from oral transmission, independent written sources which make mention of incidents in the saga, and the testimony of archeology. We shall begin with the last factor.

III

Both *Njála* (chapters 61–63) and *Landnámabók* (part 5, chapter 5) relate that Gunnar fought with Egill at Sandgil, near Knafahólar, or in

3. In connection with the next three sections of this chapter see *Um Njálu*, section IV, and *Íslenzk fornrit*, Vol. XII, pp. v ff.

the vicinity of the river Rangá. Long ago the wind blew away grass and sand at this place; graves, human bones, the tip of a spear, and various other objects were unearthed. It is tempting to connect these findings with Gunnar's battle; this has also been done, but there are certain difficulties involved, including some of an archeological nature.

At the farm Bergþórshvoll, extensive excavations have been made, especially in the years 1927–28 and 1951–52. The first of these was led by Iceland's national antiquarian, Matthías Þórðarson. He excavated a large area west of the present farmhouse, and made discoveries which showed that at that place one group of farm buildings had been built right after another, ever since the time of the sagas. He found definite signs of a fire at only one place, at a depth of 2.3 meters, 2.8 meters west of the farmhouse. The area of the fire extended from north to south and was 7.5 meters long and 2.8 meters wide at the north end. Here it seems to be a question of a building which was located to the rear of the main buildings. Remains of these were found, layer upon layer downward, which show that they were laid out in a row from east to west. The burned-out area in the rear building was almost coal black and quite distinct, full of charred pieces of wood, and in some places there were ashes. There was also found a considerable amount of burned barley and straw. The grain was certainly Icelandic, and the building was used for the drying of grain—a so-called *sofnhús*.

Directly west of this strip, 17 meters from the edge of it, on the west slope of the hill where the farm is located, Kristján Eldjárn, formerly national antiquarian and now president of Iceland, found remains of buildings in the most recent excavation; and again there were buildings on top of one another. In the lowest layer, down on the sand bottom itself, so to speak, there was a strip which had been burned. It proved to be the remains of two buildings which obviously had burned down. One was a cow stable, about 4.2 meters wide and 14.2 meters long. The other was a small shed on the south side of the cow stable, near the door. The stable had obviously been built of turf. Along the middle of the floor of the stable there were to be seen traces of a floor drain, about one meter wide, and the stalls were approximately 1.5 meters long. They had been separated by birch logs. Along each wall there had been room for fifteen stalls, such that there could have been thirty animals in the stable. The little shed could have been a barn.

That there are no traces of fire to be found where the main buildings must have been situated is only what one could expect. The Icelandic turf structures must be renovated after a relatively short time, and it is possible—even probable—that the continual rebuilding of the farmstead has wiped out all definite traces of the fire in the center of the group of buildings, while on the outside edges we are more likely to find remains of the fire intact. This hypothesis, which Kristján Eldjárn has advanced, seems to me to be very plausible.

If one regards the burned buildings from a stratigraphic point of view, one comes to the conclusion that they date from the first 100 to 150 years after the settlement of Iceland. The same result was obtained in a carbon-14 test undertaken in the National Museum in Copenhagen in 1959; the charred birch remains were demonstrated to have been from trees fully grown about 940, but with a margin of error of 100 years either way (840–1040). A second carbon-14 test was undertaken at the University of Saskatchewan, Canada, this time of the charred botanical remains; the result pointed to the year 1039, plus or minus 60 years. Thus the findings of these tests are in agreement with the statements of the saga.[4]

IV

The surest evidence that there have existed oral traditions concerning the events *Njála* tells about is found, naturally enough, in written sources. Most of the people in the saga are mentioned in other places, among them "Brennu-Flosi" and "Brennu-Kári" or "Sviðu-Kári";

4. On the archeological excavations made at Bergþórshvoll see especially Sturla Friðreksson, *Árbók fornleifafélagsins* (1960), 64–75; Kristján Eldjárn, *Árbók* (1961), p. 154; and *Íslenzk fornrit*, Vol. XII, pp. v ff.

and Snorri Sturluson, who in his youth at the end of the twelfth century lived in the region which is the scene of *Njála*, mentions "Brennu-Njáll" and quotes a verse of his which is not found in the saga. For the most part, *Landnámabók* is probably the most important source. Now—especially after Jón Jóhannesson's investigation—we feel certain that we know considerably more about the textual history of *Landnámabók* than was known before.⁵ There is a probability which approaches certainty that this work existed in one form or another in the first half of the twelfth century.⁶ In a section which apparently was included in the oldest version of *Landnámabók* a reference is made to Njáll, who was burned to death at Bergþórshvoll together with seven (another manuscript has eight) others, an account which was probably written only a century after the fire is supposed to have taken place. The reference reads as follows:

> Þórólfur, an illegitimate brother of Ásgerður, took land at her suggestion to the west of Fljót, between the two rivers named Deildará, and lived afterwards at Þórólfsfell. With him was reared Þorgeir gollnir, the son of Ásgerður, who lived there afterwards. He was the father of Njáll, who was burned to death in his house together with seven (eight) other persons at Bergþórshvoll.

This reference shows that memories of the burning of Njáll lived on at places other than the one where the saga was written.

Furthermore, mention is made of several events in Gunnar's life in various recensions of *Landnámabók*: his battle at Knafahólar, mentioned above, the battle with Otkell, and Gunnar's death. But if we compare the short notes of *Landnámabók* with the account of the saga, we find a considerable number of discrepancies. In connection with Gunnar's final battle *Landnámabók* states that Gunnar had a grown man with him on his farm. But in the saga narrative this man would have been a

5. *Gerðir Landnámabókar*, Reykjavík: Félagsprentsmiðjan, 1941.
6. The best discussion in English of the problem of the date and genesis of *Landnámabók* is by E. O. G. Turville-Petre in his book *Origins of Icelandic Literature*, Oxford: Clarendon Press, 1953, pp. 96–108.

disturbing factor. From an artistic point of view it was necessary for Gunnar to face the overwhelming odds alone. It is generally assumed that the account in *Landnámabók* is based on the oldest tradition; and if this assumption is correct, we have here a good example of the tendency of the saga to idealize. What we do not know for certain is whether the author of *Njála* was here following an independent tradition later than that of *Landnámabók*.

And in addition, there are tales in *Landnámabók* from the districts around Njál's home which are similar to episodes in the saga but are connected with different individuals. Thus, for example, *Landnámabók* tells about Ásmundur *skegglausi* ("the Beardless"), the son of Ófeigur grettir, and about Þorbjörn *kyrri* ("the Quiet"), an uncle of Njáll, who was presumably, like his nephew, "fond of ease." This historical work also tells of supernatural powers and witchcraft, as in the account of Dufþakur and Stórólfur or that of Loðmundur of Sólheimar, and of prescient men such as Þorsteinn rauðnefur; it tells of sages and men clever at litigation, such as Mörður gígja (who also plays an important part in *Njála*), and Christian saga heroes such as Ásólfur alskik and the people of Kirkjubær. And there was no dearth of tales about battles and killings. From this it can be seen that all around the stories of *Njála* there was a swarm of related oral tales which dealt with similar events or depicted men somewhat like those in that saga.

There are some works of literature in which one can almost feel the oral sources behind them; the content of such works is formed in accordance with the laws of oral tales. Sometimes we can distinguish variants, and sometimes we find blind motifs, that is, remnants of fuller accounts which are no longer understandable. But the author of *Njáls saga* has such a mastery over his material that little or nothing of this kind is discernible. Bååth has said of him that he had the last line of his story in mind when he wrote the first one. The one exception is found in the story of Gunnar, where we can distinguish two "layers"; according to one, Gunnar's death is attributed to his hubris, while in the other, Hallgerð's hair plays a major part. Much more palpable are tales associated with places or place names in the saga; in the mountain called Þríhyrningur there is a valley in which Flosi concealed himself; on the knoll near the farmhouse at Bergþórshvoll is a small hollow where Flosi and his men (according to the saga) concealed themselves and tied their two hundred horses; the ford Þorgeirsvað is named for Þorgeir Otkelsson because he was slain there, etc. But perhaps even more can be learned from the poetry in the saga. In the first part there are a considerable number of verses, which are found only in some of the manuscripts (and in some editions); but these are rather mediocre as poetry and are doubtless younger than the saga itself. The remaining verses seem to be from various times, some of them probably going back to the saga age and some of them being of more recent origin. To the extent that they are older than the saga, these verses are valuable as evidence that traditions concerning the events which the saga relates did exist. But there is nothing in these few verses which suggests a rich tradition. A closer comparison with the concise notes of *Landnámabók*, referred to above, seems to indicate a far more thorough and reliable knowledge in this work. Still, the author of *Njála* appears to have known most of the chief characters and the most important events from tradition; and even though this tradition was not rich, it may well have been inspiring to him.

V

At the time when *Njáls saga* was written, these oral tales about various events were three centuries old and therefore unreliable from the standpoint of historical truth. From this point of view it would doubt-less be of considerable importance if it were possible to move backward somewhat in time and to obtain written documents based on oral traditions as they existed, let us say, a century earlier, at the time when the writing of sagas about Icelandic heroes was in its infancy and when people were perhaps more concerned with the memory and recollection of such matters than they were later on. I am not speaking here of the possibility of still older evidence, let us say 150 years old, which would be only 150 years removed from the events themselves and would presumably not have undergone so great a degree of transformation as it had 50 or 150 years later. But this brings us to the question of written sources.

Since *Njála* was written about 1280, there is reason to believe that the author knew a number of sagas which were written before that time. And this seems to have been the case. The most important criterion for determining this is a similarity of style and phraseology together with the identity of motifs between *Njála* and the older sagas. From the older sagas the author of *Njála* could learn various things as far as the content itself is concerned. From *Laxdæla saga* he could get information about the family of the people of Laxárdalur—about Höskuldur, Hrútur, Hallgerður, etc. From *Eyrbyggja saga* he knew the distinctive character of Snorri goði, and in addition he could read there about the death of Gunnar, although this was probably not necessary. In *Ljósvetninga saga* he could find information concerning the conflict between Guðmundur inn ríki and Þorkell hákur—and at one place in his story he obviously acts as a critic of that saga.[7] From the lost saga about Gaukur Trandilsson, the former existence of which has been convincingly demonstrated, he could have learned about Ásgrímur Elliða-Grímsson and his kin.[8] From the saga of Hróar Tungugoði, excerpts of which Sturla Þórðarson included in his recension of *Landnámabók*, he could have gotten information concerning the people in the Skaftafells district, whom he seems to know so much about. And from an account about the people of the Rangá district, an excerpt of which also occurs in Sturla's *Landnámabók*, he could have read about Mörður gígja. It is interesting to see how the author of *Njála* used the fame of this great lawyer to enhance both Njáll and Gunnar by demonstrating how they surpassed him in both cleverness and hardihood. And thus we could continue.

7. See *Íslenzk fornrit*, Vol. X, pp. xlviii ff.
8. On this see Jón Helgason, "*Gauks saga Trandilssonar*," *Heiderskrift til G. Indrebø*, 1939, pp. 92–100; reprinted in *Ritgerðarkorn og ræðustúfar*, 1959, pp. 100 ff.

Twice the author inserted extracts or abbreviated accounts from older writings into his story. One of them was a treatise on the introduction of Christianity, which was based on the *Íslendingabók* of Ari inn fróði and perhaps on a document by the monk Gunnlaugur Leifsson. This was an ecclesiastical work of history, which would have seemed dry if its spirit had not been so martial. The author of *Njála* made a very detailed summary of this treatise, a summary on which he nevertheless left his own individual stamp in several places. From this document he could have learned all sorts of things about events and especially about people in the saga. The description of Hallur of Síða, of Gizur inn hvíti, and of Hjalti Skeggjason come to mind. The other document is an old story about the Irish king Brjánn and the Battle of Clontarf. This was a learned piece of writing, full of marvelous and poetically colored stories, which the author of *Njála* took great delight in. Both of these documents may well have been almost a century older than the saga, and the sections which they underlie have a character different from the rest of the saga.

And then we have the saga's genealogies, which are both long and stately. It is impossible to imagine that they could originate with an author writing about the year 1280. They contain far too much old and genuine material for that. They are not derived from any recensions of *Landnámabók* which have come down to us. I believe that the only possible conclusion is that they must derive from an old written source. Nor can they be interpolations in the saga, as several scholars at the end of the last century supposed; for the genealogies are reflections of one of the saga's most important sources, a document which must have resembled *Landnámabók* insofar as it contained, in addition to genealogical lists, brief notes on historical events which related to persons mentioned in the genealogies. The fact is that we find here and there in the saga's genealogies such notes about individuals, and a few times even notes about events in the saga. These notes were included inadvertently; the master neglected to omit them. But from them we can conclude that this document referred to a number of the most important events related in the saga. A few examples will be cited here. In chapter 77 mention is made of Hróaldur, the son of Geir goði: "He was an illegitimate son and his mother was Bjartey, a sister of Þorvaldr inn veili, who was killed at Hestlækur in Grímsnes." The slaying of Þorvaldr is described more fully in chapter 102, and it violates the customary practice of the saga to allude in such a way to an event which is to be related later. It is conceivable, however, that this might well happen inadvertently if the author was using a written source. In chapter 96, in the genealogy of Síðu-Hallur, mention is made of his brother Þorsteinn breiðmagi: "His son was Kolur, whom Kári killed in Bretland." In chapter 159, near the end of the saga, we find this statement about Kári: "Flosi gave to Kári in marriage his niece Hildigunnur, *who had been the wife of Höskuldur Hvítanessgoði. To begin with (fyrst)* they lived at Breiðá." This is followed by the account of how Flosi died, and then the author continues: "These were the children of Kári and Helga Njálsdóttir: Þorgerður and Ragneiður, Valgerður and Þórður, who was burned to death at Bergþorshvoll. The children of Kári and Hildigunnur were the sons Starkaður and Þórður and Flosi. . . ." The author of *Njála* sometimes refers briefly to events which have already been related, and it cannot be said that the phrase *who had been the wife of Höskuldur Hvítanessgoði* is out of keeping with his narrative practice even though it is unnecessary (for which reason the scribe who wrote manuscript *Y* thought fit to omit it). But the word *fyrst (to begin with)* doubtless indicates that the author was in possession of additional information, and the listing of the children also shows this. I think that the author here was following a written document, and I see no reason for not regarding this document as the source of his genealogies.

These examples appear to have been derived from a written source (a genealogical document) in such a manner that some of the phraseology and subject matter of the source was inadvertently included in the narrative of the saga, where it is somewhat out of place. It is not to be expected, however, that this would often happen with a writer as skillful as the author of *Njála*. He would, on the contrary, endeavor to eliminate all such unsuitable traces in the process of transforming his source material into a living, dramatic narrative. I feel certain that this genealogical source must have contained references to a considerable number of incidents, and there seems to be little doubt about it insofar as the above interpretation of the final chapter of the saga is correct. It is astonishing how much story material is contained *in nuce* in the concise passages of *Landnámabók* or the terse account of *Íslendingabók*. I believe that a large number of the characters of *Njála* were mentioned in the genealogical source, and consequently the genealogical information of the saga is more worthy of note than might be expected. A very large number of the secondary characters must have been mentioned there, to say nothing of the main characters. And I think that a very large number of events related in the saga were mentioned there. It is easy to understand that people are in the dark concerning what incidents were mentioned in addition to the main events.

If this interpretation is correct, this lost genealogical document helps to bridge the gap between the events themselves and their portrayal in *Njáls saga* and thus reduces the period of oral transmission by possibly a century or more. Hence it follows that there may be more truth, more facts, preserved in the saga than would otherwise be likely. On the other hand this interpretation does not lend support to the assumption that individual traits, the dialogues, and the external trappings (descriptions of clothing, weapons, etc.) in the saga are old. It must also be assumed that this genealogical source provided little information about the connection of the individual events. Here the author had to supply a great deal in order to transform his material into the great "drama." Some of that which the author had to supply could be based on older written sagas and on oral tales which were current in his day. But it seems likely that the explanation of how and why this or that was done, that is, the causal connection of the events and their motivation, was the product of the author's own imaginative ingenuity.

And finally there is the question of the legal formulas and procedures in *Njála*. Guðbrandur Vigfússon was probably the first scholar to suggest that the author of *Njála* must have made use of a written legal document when he composed his saga. Lehmann set forth arguments in favor of this view, and various other scholars supported it. Still others, however, including Vilhjálmur Finsen, challenged it. Nevertheless, I think there is no doubt that the former view is correct. There are several passages in the saga which are clearly based on written laws and which can scarcely be explained otherwise.

People were taken by surprise when Lehmann presented evidence to show the use of a written legal code in *Njála*. But actually nothing could be more natural than that. No sensible man would fail to make use of the best source for the laws of the time of the Commonwealth. There are no indications that any memories were preserved regarding the legal procedures in individual episodes, either in oral tradition or in written documents, and therefore the author had to furnish such material himself. Most of the legal material can be traced back to the law code known as *Grágás;* several details are in disagreement with this code, but parallels exist in the laws in effect during the Sturlung Age (for example, monetary compensation for manslaughter), while almost none of it preserves traces of older laws.

If *Njála* is compared with other sagas, it can be seen that it is concerned much more with laws, to say nothing of the many legal formulas employed. This shows that the author was fascinated by the subject, once he had become absorbed in it. But his fascination far exceeded his knowledge. There is nothing that indicates that he had been trained in the law. But when he began to make preparations for his saga, he also began to give serious attention to the laws of the Commonwealth and for this purpose procured a legal code. In one passage (chapter 73) a number of manuscripts preserve a clause which shows the author thinking aloud, as it were. Contrary to the conventions of saga style and composition, he cannot resist explaining (for the reader or for himself) why Gizur hvíti did not ask witnesses *at*

bera sakartökuvætti ("to bear testimony to the taking up of the suit").
But his study of this document was made well before the writing of the
saga was finished, and therefore a large number of errors of various
kinds crept into it. Lehmann has written extensively about this, and
even though he went too far, Finsen's critical comments in his treatise
Fristatens Institutioner (pp. 105–106 and especially 112) show that despite
a quite different approach to the saga, Finsen was in many respects in
agreement with Lehmann. But the author's imaginative power was so
vigorous that the laws were transformed into life and action. No one
else could have succeeded as he did in transforming the legal paragraphs
and formulas of chapter 142 into effective and impressive saga material.

Some people might think they were hitting the nail on the head by
labeling *Njála* a historical novel. But that really does not bring us much
closer to the essence of the matter, for the expression "historical novel"
can be used to designate quite different things. Some authors of historical novels or dramas fabricate almost everything, while others
undertake careful preparatory research with the result that their works
are half-history. Guðmundur Kamban's four-volume *Skálholt* was
preceded by many hours of study in the Arna-Magnæan Foundation,
and Schiller's Wallenstein tragedy was preceded by his history of the
Thirty Years' War. In more recent times writers have centered their
endeavors on recapturing the spirit of the age they are writing about,
and many of them carefully avoid subjects which great literary masters
of former times have already dealt with—presumably because they feel
that such subjects offer them too little freedom. It seems to me that
Njála is more closely related to certain historical plays of an earlier
period, whose authors had little concern for the spirit of the age they
were dealing with, but confined themselves to tracing the events as
they are described in the best historical sources at their disposal and
transforming them into dramas. This is the way Shakespeare proceeded
in his historical plays (the chronicle plays, in which he followed Holin-
shed primarily, and the Roman plays, which are based on Plutarch).
I do not think it is far-fetched to mention *Njála* in this respect in the

same breath with *Henry IV* or *Antony and Cleopatra*, even though the
sources are very different in nature. These authors pay very close
attention to historical truth as it is revealed to them in their sources.
Their main concern, however, is the search for truth of a different
kind, the truth about human life, and they endeavor to portray that
truth in such a way as to make it clearly evident.

VI

When *Njáls saga* was written, the thirteenth century was nearly at
an end. Almost a century had passed since the first major saga about
Icelandic heroes was written: *Víga-Styrs saga ok Heiðarvíga*. This saga
represents an attempt to create a story that in form would be in keeping
with the contemporary kings' sagas, which were at that time develop-
ing from synoptic histories of limited scope into long and entertaining
(and sometimes not too trustworthy) biographies, such as those of
Oddur Snorrason and Gunnlaugur Leifsson. The narrative acquires a
certain breadth. The style still retains traces of the clerical language of
the twelfth century, and the mode of thought at times is clerical; but
the secular spirit, the native Icelandic manner of thinking, which was
an undercurrent during the twelfth century, now breaks forth and
comes to the surface. The secular spirit grows more powerful and
eventually becomes dominant. This is not yet the case in clerical writings such as *Kristni þáttur* and *Brjáns saga*, which we know from *Njála*,
but this secular spirit appears sooner than one might expect in one work
after another. Time passes, sufficient for the sagas to develop from
infancy to maturity, and then we can see how this outlook dominates
the genre—in such works as *Egils saga*, *Eyrbyggja*, and *Víga-Glúms saga*.
Here we find the same fullness of presentation. The style has become
free of clerical vocabulary and the sentence structure remarkably flex-
ible. The phraseology is vigorous yet refined; the narrative is such that
the reader or listener can visualize what is related. The characters and
events are portrayed without too much explanation; a great deal is
expected of the reader; he must often draw his own conclusions.

Everywhere there prevails a remarkable impartiality, understanding, realism, sobriety, and strict self-discipline on the part of the author: he must conceal himself within and behind his work; he is not permitted to give free rein to his sympathies and antipathies, nor to extend a finger to point out to the reader how his work is to be interpreted. The point of view is completely human, the ideals are secular, and the chief concern is man, the individual human being.

Again a period of time passes, and soon innovations in saga writing become noticeable. In *Laxdœla saga* the influence of medieval romanticism makes its appearance, with its fondness for beauty and finery, courtesy and nonmartial virtues, a predilection for stylistic elegance and rhetoric, and for poetic and romantic matter. At the same time another change becomes apparent, which grows increasingly more important: the impartiality, realism, and self-discipline of the author begin to lessen, and the element of fiction increases rapidly. This can be detected in almost everything that is written after this time.

At about the same time another work is written which is no less of an innovation: *Bandamanna saga*. Here too the reins are held quite loosely. *Bandamanna saga* is a comedy or satire which is probably pure fabrication except for the frame, that is, the beginning and end of the story. The dialogue is remarkably vigorous and brisk. A coarse and vulgar and mischievous, plebeian humor runs rife in this satire, together with a delight in grotesque descriptions and glibness of tongue. Both of these have their roots or parallels in older works. It will suffice in this connection to refer to *Hreiðars þáttur heimska*, one of the finest humorous tales of our ancient literature. *Hreiðars þáttur* is very old, and in time a different taste came to prevail, the refined and restrained, ambiguous irony of Snorri's *Edda* and *Eyrbyggja saga*. But now the plebeian spirit again erupts through the prevailing restraint of saga style, the plebeian taste, which fills *Bandamanna saga* with scathing satire against the power of the aristocrats.

Shortly after this the *riddarasögur* (prose translations and adaptations of Continental romances) begin to inundate the country, and they inspire all those innovations which characterize *Laxdæla*. And now too the first of the *fornaldarsögur* (stories dealing with legendary and historical Scandinavian and Germanic heroes before the settlement of Iceland) are written; these tales preserve the style of the classical sagas of Icelanders, but repudiate their spirit. But with the advent of both genres, the *riddarasögur* and the *fornaldarsögur*, the door is opened for fantastic tales of adventure and extravagant exaggeration; it is as though the ability to appreciate reality diminishes, as though a vital nerve were degenerating.

At this stage of literary history *Njáls saga* is written, and in this saga we can detect traces of all previous forms of Icelandic literature: the author remembers them just as people recall the weather of days long past. Pictures from them have engraved themselves on his mind, and he is familiar with their manner of presentation. The genealogical lore of the twelfth century appears in the genealogies of his saga, the native clerical literature in the episodes dealing with the conversion (*Kristni þáttur*) and the battle of Clontarf (*Brjáns saga*). His chief models, however, are the classical sagas such as *Egils saga* and *Eyrbyggja*—their literary taste and narrative method, their goals and ideas. This was the primary initiation of the author, and the impression it made on his mind was so deep that it held in check the influences from other forms of literature even though these cannot be said to have been slight. The author of *Njála* had a thorough knowledge and a keen appreciation of *Laxdæla saga*. From it more than from any other saga he learned to develop anticipations of future events into a constant feeling of foreboding of coming events on the part of the reader. This saga taught him to appreciate beautiful descriptions, finery and coats of arms, and to depict nonmartial character traits with sympathetic understanding. The author of *Njála* acquired a trace of the derision of *Bandamanna saga*, but this influence, whether it came directly or indirectly, is tempered and blended with the refinement of the classical sagas, and the irony of *Njála* thus becomes the richest and most artistic to be found in any literary work from ancient times. The *fornaldarsögur* have lent color to

Njála; their adventurous element is reflected in the episodes of voyages abroad. Tales about sorcery, clairvoyance, and dreams, which entranced the mind of the author, abound everywhere about him, and are enlisted to serve his dramatic purpose. All of this is evident in the saga, but it is kept within definite limits, sometimes within quite narrow limits, and above and beneath and throughout *Njála* there hovers the spirit of the classical sagas.

The style of *Njála* too is modeled on that of the classical sagas, but through the influence of other genres the sentences assume a peculiar richness and color. Sometimes the wording becomes sensitive or even sentimental; sometimes it is informed by an inner fire. What here may appear to be unclassical in taste and style can for the most part be traced to the influence of clerical language. When Flosi visits Hildigunnur after Höskuld's death, she receives him with these words (chapter 116): "*Ok er nú fegit hjarta mitt tilkvámu þinni*" ("My heart rejoices at your coming"). This has been attributed by some scholars to influence from the chivalric sagas, but it is obviously and doubtlessly biblical language. It is easy to find in a moment a half-dozen or more examples of this expression in the Bible: "*hjarta mitt (þitt) fagnar*" ("my [thy] heart rejoices"); in the Vulgate: "*lætatum est cor meum, gaudeat* or *exultat cor meum,*" etc.). At the General Assembly following Höskuld's slaying (chapter 122) Njáll declares that when he learned of this terrible deed "it was as though the sweetest light of my eyes had been extinguished." The expression "*ljós augna minna*" ("*lumen oculorum meorum* or *nostrorum*") occurs in the *Book of Tobit* (X, 4) and in the sagas of saints.[9] These and similar expressions lend richness and variety to the language of *Njála* without, in my opinion, impairing it, for they are used with discretion and moderation.

There is no doubt that memories and images from older sagas became fixed in the mind of the author of *Njála.* They provided the raw material for his imagination and ultimately the phraseology, the incidents, and the events of his own saga. In this regard I am not far from

9. See *Um Njálu,* p. 340.

my former views, and this is an interpretation at which quite a few individuals have strongly taken umbrage. But I see no reason for going into the matter in greater detail here. If the author did not get the material for his story from those sources, he got it from some other sources. For all things *are* made of some substance, and no one other than God Almighty has ever been known to create something from nothing. Human originality is of a different nature. It can be compared with the art of the alchemist, who transformed lead into gold. And this is what the author of *Njála* knew how to do.

The information and inspiration which could be derived from the narrative skill, the artistic methods, and the character portrayal of older sagas were certainly not restricted to individual events or episodes. Let us consider, for example, the matter of character depiction. In *Eyrbyggja* Snorri goði was described in such a manner that nothing needed to be added to his portrait; the author of *Njála* merely had to see to it that this character did not lose its vitality in his hands. Þórarinn spaki in *Heiðarvíga saga*, Gestur Oddleifsson in *Laxdæla*, and Þórhallur spámaður in *Þiðranda þáttur ok Þórhalls* excited his imagination, and he created a whole host of prophet-seers, each one different from the others. Oddur Kötluson in *Eyrbyggja* was as challenging to him as an unsolved puzzle; he studied this character, sought for the inner motives of his actions, and a new man, Skammkell, appeared in his mind's eye. Þiðrandi Síðu-Hallsson fascinated him, and he began anew and created Höskuldur Hvítanessgoði.

All of these character portraits from the older sagas possess certain qualities of excellence, not the least of which is their uniqueness. They are such great portraits of individuals that the author of *Njála* was inspired not to copy them, but rather to create new individuals which, to be sure, possess a certain family resemblance to the older character descriptions, but yet are independent. For the most part they have been created with even more sensitive and deliberate art.

The comparison of individual examples of character description in *Njála* with those of older literary works—of individual parallels—casts much light on a noteworthy situation. But such a comparison will remain one-sided unless the basis of comparison is broadened. Scarcely any of the character portraits in *Njála* have been based on a single source (with the possible exception of Snorri goði and the heroes connected with the introduction of Christianity), and even though we can sometimes detect a close relationship between individuals in *Njála* and those of older writings, it is not possible to gain a complete view of the roots of its character descriptions unless we have a comprehensive knowledge of Old Icelandic literature in its totality—and some idea of the oral tales which existed in swarms around and beyond those which found permanence on parchment. And then it is as if the critic were able to discern distinct family traits, which can be traced from ancient times: sometimes the descendant is aware of his family relationship, and sometimes he is not. Some artist or other catches a vision, and this mental picture is preserved in stories and tales, preserved and transformed according to the spirit of the times or the interpretation of other men. Thus Baldur the Good becomes Þiðrandi Hallsson and Höskuldur Hvítanessgoði. Often the trail is difficult to follow: Njáll bears the family mark of Oðinn, but this family line is difficult to trace, and Njáll has many characteristics which can be derived from elsewhere. Skarphéðinn can be numbered among the not inconsiderable group which may be called the dark-haired heroes: they are, to be sure, each unlike the other, but nevertheless share certain characteristics in regard to the essentials of their temperaments and their destinies. In the same way Gunnar belongs to the group of light-haired heroes. I have already mentioned how Oddur Kötluson may well have been of value to the author of *Njála* when he created his portrait of Skammkell: in this character he became acquainted with groundless dishonesty and malice without reason—and when the portrait of Skammkell was finished, there was a bit left over of Oddur, something bold but at the same time slick and slippery, which appears in the character of Hrappur. But the likeness of Hrappur is to be seen elsewhere—perhaps it too is a family likeness. In this connection it is well to recall the observation of Hans

E. Kinck: "I believe that the legends about the Loki-figure with its metamorphoses and the like may have made a contribution to this truly excellent character portrait."[10]

VII

The author of *Njála*, as we have seen, made use of oral tales and written sources, and so we come to Járngrímur to complete the account, and Járngrímur means contemporary times. For, of course, *Njála*, like other works of art, bears the mark of its own time.

Let us first consider a matter which is both simple and commonly known. *Njála* was written after *Járnsíða*, the new legal code from Norway, had been introduced into Iceland (1271). The author, who took great delight in cogitating about laws and legal complexities, procures an old legal codex from the time of the Commonwealth for the purpose of demonstrating to his contemporaries the laws and juridical procedures of former times. He copies from this codex to his heart's content, but his enthusiasm exceeds his knowledge (apparently he himself had little experience in litigation during the time when the laws of the Commonwealth were in effect); consequently various oddities and even downright mistakes creep into his work, including words from the Norwegianized legal terminology of his own day. All this is a great stumbling block for those who like to regard the saga primarily from a historical point of view. The reader who is ignorant of such matters, on the other hand, probably is often impressed and amazed at how much life has been injected into the dry matter of jurisprudence through the wizardry of the author.

Much more noteworthy is the author's relation to the mode of thought and the life views of his own age. Here we do not have to grope in the dark so much, for a great deal is known about the culture of the Icelanders in the thirteenth century. I have attempted to give an

10. *Mange slags kunst*, p. 16. On this problem see also "Tvær kvenlýsingar," *Helgafell* II (1943), 16–31; reprinted in *Við uppspretturnar* (pp. 91–114) under the title "Klytæmestra og Hallgerður."

account of my views about this matter in my book *Sturlungaöld* (*The Age of the Sturlungs*), and it is not difficult to draw lines of connection between Icelandic culture of that period and *Njáls saga*.

Let me mention several examples of the relationship of the saga to the age in which it was written. I shall not go into this problem in detail here, since I have reserved it for a later chapter on the ideas and ideals expressed in the saga. The Sturlung Age is characterized by a fierce struggle between foreign and native ethical ideals. The essence of the native attitude is the honor and the dignity of the individual. This involves the ideal of noble-mindedness (*drengskapur*), the spirit of emulation (*kappgirni*), the duty of blood vengeance, and armed conflict. The foreign ideals are directed toward love, peace, and reconciliation among men as well as humility and submission to a foreign institution, the authority of the Universal Church. In *Njála* too there is a struggle between the ideal of honor and the desire for peace, and in the end peace is sealed by the Pope in Rome. The native spirit created for itself a sort of philosophy based on belief in fate and the concepts of fortune and misfortune; Christianity, on the other hand, proclaimed faith in providence: this conflict can be regarded as the basic element of the attitude toward life in the saga. Medieval Christianity made penance a sacrament; in the saga too such an idea becomes apparent.

At the time when the saga was written, there were many men living who grew up during the time of the Commonwealth and retained something of its spirit. The author of *Njála* must surely have been such a man. On the other hand, he does not completely lack appreciation for the romanticism of his own time. And it is true that here and there we can distinguish traces of the popular taste of the times, which increases by leaps and bounds as the middle class becomes impoverished and the number of tenant farmers increases, and as correspondingly the spirit of freedom which characterized the people of the Commonwealth gradually declines and people begin to grow accustomed to oppression: the strength to rise above it is lacking.

Far be it from me to attribute all points of similarity between the

saga itself and the events and the spirit of the times exclusively to the
latter. That would scarcely be reasonable, in view of the fact that there
is so much that we do not know about the saga's sources, especially the
oral ones. I do not doubt that there was a significant difference between
people, between warlike men and benevolent sages during the time of
paganism. This has always been true, regardless of what kinds of ethical
views prevailed. And at that time people also had an appreciation of
splendor and stateliness, no less so than during the chivalric age. And
so we could continue. What I have in mind is this: whether these
various elements or incidents are ancient or recent in origin is irrelevant;
the important thing is that some of them have acquired something of the
atmosphere and the conflict of the author's day. These were the problems with which the minds of men were wrestling, and which sometimes seemed to threaten to overwhelm them, and it is this which
endowed such passages with warmth and life.

If my interpretation of Flosi's dream is correct, we have here an
example of how an individual incident from the author's time served
as a model for an episode in his saga. Might there not be more such
examples? This seems very probable. At least it is easy to find events
in the saga which are similar to those described in contemporary historical records. It is much easier, however, to point out relationships
between contemporary events and incidents in the story than to
demonstrate a literary connection between historical records of the
thirteenth century and the saga. I shall mention a few of the many
examples, chosen at random.

Almost constantly throughout the ninth decade of the thirteenth
century there were poor seasons and scarcity of food. At about this
time *Njála* was written, and I am convinced that these conditions are
reflected in the description of the bad season in the episode of the saga
in which Gunnar goes to Kirkjubær in an attempt to buy food and hay
(chapter 47). But it would be useless to insist that this is so since it is
impossible to prove it.

I have confidence in those characters and pedigrees in the saga which

are based on the author's written genealogical source, but those characters who were not included there or about whom there are no special
sagas are much more doubtful. (We must not forget that the events
related in the saga occurred three centuries previously.) Among the
latter are foreign skippers who play only minor roles in the story. They
bear such names as Hallvarður hvíti, Högni hvíti, Bárður svarti, Kolbeinn Arnljótarson, Eyjólfur nefur, Kolbeinn svarti, etc. It so happens
that around the middle of the thirteenth century there were Norwegian
travelers in Iceland named Kolbeinn svarti, Eysteinn hvíti, Skeggi
hvíti, Þórhalli hvíti, Eyjólfur auðgi, Hallvarður gullskór, and Ívar
Arnljótarson. The question of such names in *Njála* does not seem
difficult to solve; they were either borrowed or invented by a process
of combination.

When the priest Guðmundur Arason had been elected bishop at a
meeting held at Viðimýri, Kolbeinn Tumason himself prepared the
seat of honor for him for the evening meal and spread a cloth before
him on the table; but when it came time to begin supper, it was seen
that the cloth was full of holes. Kolbeinn made apologies for this, but
Guðmundur replied with a smile (and with his smile he concealed his
great displeasure): "There is no need to find fault with the tablecloth,
but my bishopric will fare accordingly: it will be as full of holes as the
tablecloth." Kolbeinn blushed at these words, but he made no reply.[11]
This event, which was commonly known, is reminiscent of the seat of
honor and the torn towel at Vorsabær and of the displeasure of Flosi,
which is dramatically revealed when he refuses to dry his hands on the
towel. Both Guðmundur and Flosi interpret the torn cloth symboli-
cally, and whatever else may be the case, this story about Guðmundur
at least serves to shed light on the account in *Njála*.

People have expressed surprise at the fact that Flosi attends divine
services before he sets out on his expedition to burn Njáll and his
family; he also has his followers go to the church at Kirkjubær to pray.

11. *Guðmundar saga Arasonar*, chapter 43, in *Byskupa sögur*, ed. Guðni Jónsson,
Reykjavík: Íslendingasagnaútgáfan, 1953.

Yet Ögmundur Helgason does the same thing at Kirkjubær before he sets out to slay the sons of Ormur.[12]

It would be easy to continue to enumerate such parallels between *Njála* and events from contemporary times, but I shall limit myself to one more example: the burnings during the Age of the Sturlungs. In various ways they have points of similarity with the burning in *Njála*, and this, of course, is just what we might expect.[13]

In a similar manner it is easy to detect this or that point of similarity in conduct or appearance between the historical personages in *Sturlunga saga* and the characters in *Njáls saga*. Sometimes we can detect in the saga a peculiarly strong sympathy or antipathy for various characters, and we can well imagine that it is due to certain personal reasons on the part of the author. Or there is a strange connection between the saga and the people of that day. Nietzsche speaks of "*die ewige Wiederkunft*," the eternal recurrence. By some strange coincidence a man by the name of Njáll lived shortly before the time of the author—a remarkable man, who was of the same family as the Njáll in the saga. That Njáll had a contemporary named Þorgeir, who lived at Holt. During the author's own lifetime (and surely he must have known them) there lived two men west of the river Þjórsá named Gizur and Hjalti (Gizur Þorvaldsson and Hjalti biskupsson). I am strongly inclined to believe that the author was not ill-disposed toward Gizur Þorvaldsson. It has long been asserted that it was to Flosi's advantage and not to his disadvantage that he was of the family of the Svínfellingar. Who knows but what the same might be true of Njáll and his kinsmen? The similarity between Skarphéðinn and Sæmundur Ormsson is scarcely accidental: each of them is pale and has fine eyes and an ugly mouth—and this is of great importance in the portrait of Skarphéðinn.

---

12. *Svínfellinga saga*, chapter 10 (= *Sturlunga saga*, Vol. II, p. 98).
13. One such burning is described in *Guðmundar saga dýra*, chapter 14 (= *Sturlunga saga*, Vol. I, pp. 189–92). For an English translation see Jacqueline Simpson, *The Northmen Talk*, London and Madison: University of Wisconsin Press, 1965, pp. 93–96. See further *Íslenzk fornrit*, Vol. XII, p. cxv.

It is, of course, possible to arrange all of these parallels between the saga and the time in which it was written in such a way that they form a connected whole. This I did in an article entitled " *Njála* og Skógver-jar" published in the journal *Skírnir* (1937), in which I suggested that *Njála* was somehow connected with the family of the Skógverjar in the south of Iceland. It would be possible to add to the arguments set forth there as well as to counter the objections made to them. But that is really nothing more than a sort of scholarly game of building card houses, and this applies no less to similar constructions made by other scholars in this question.

There is one thing I wish to emphasize regarding the relationship of *Njála* to the age in which it was written: I regard it as highly inadvisable to treat the saga as a sort of *roman à clef*, a reproduction of a definite complex of events from contemporary times including the individuals involved, in which the function of the author consists chiefly in assigning new names to people and events.[14] I regard this view as a complete misunderstanding of the nature of the saga.

Regardless of whether a larger or smaller number of the events of *Njála* have their roots in the thirteenth century, it is certain that this saga sprouted and grew in the spirit of that age. It was from this age that the author acquired his understanding of human nature and the human soul, the life experience and manifold wisdom which characterize his work.

VIII

And now we can summarize. The author of *Njála* heard tales about Gunnar, Skarphéðinn, and Njáll. I am inclined to think that it happened during his youth. I visualize it this way: men sit by the fire in a hall, but the lamps have not yet been lighted. An old man tells stories of

14. This was done by Barði Guðmundsson in a series of essays reprinted in the posthumously published book *Höfundur Njálu*, Reykjavík: Bókaútgáfa Menningarsjóðs, 1958. For a refutation of these views see *Íslenzk fornrit*, Vol. XII, pp. cviii–cxi.

former times. For the boy who sits listening, the narrative is blended with the flickering light and the shadows on the walls and the ceiling. The twilight stimulates his imagination, and these legends ever afterward remain a vitalizing force even though details of them become obscure. They are responsible for what happens later, when in the mind of the author the dead knowledge acquired from his genealogical source is transformed into pulsating life. Time passes, and the times change. The author of *Njála* is deeply moved by the works of the masters who created the chief Icelandic sagas before and during his own lifetime. Before he is aware of it, what he has heard and read coalesces and becomes blended with his own life experience and spiritual struggles. We meet him at the foot of the mountain peak Lómagnúpur. We find him among the mirages on the sandy plains of Kringlumýri. We see him on the flats along the river Markarfljót, gazing enraptured at the lovely slopes of Hlíð, with their golden grain fields and new-mown hay. And we meet him at Þingvellir on the brink of Almannagjá, where Flosi and Eyjólfur Bölverksson sat in deliberation after the burning of Njáll: from this point one has a wide view. Some of what he learned from the old stories is forgotten, much is understood in a different way than formerly, most of it is changed. Fragments of stories have merged with the literary creations of other masters; memories of a richer age have been colored by bright dreams and bitter experience. From the simple tales of the old storyteller there emerges this great tragedy, brilliant in its narrative art, radiant with human understanding, and trembling with the love and hatred of human life.

And when the saga is completed, it is no longer the author's; it becomes the possession of unknown men far from him in time and space. He himself must pay the debt which all men have to pay. Within a short time he has disappeared like the snows of yesteryear. But his literary masterpiece lives on.

3. The Literary Masterpiece

The assistance which literary history affords the reader who desires
to gain a deeper appreciation of a work of literature is sometimes,
unfortunately, not unlike the information given to a man who intended
to take a hike in the mountains in a region where he had never been
before. He asked a friend of his what paths to take, both to avoid
dangerous or impassable areas and also to gain the greatest enjoyment
from his hike. But the reply of his learned friend turned out to be an
explanation of the geological origin of the mountain range in question.
This was no doubt quite scientific and well worth knowing, but it
failed to answer the hiker's question, and it may well be that he never
did find the beauty which he would never have forgotten if he had
had the opportunity to find and enjoy it.

During the past century scholars have devoted much time and energy
to showing in what great measure every literary work is flesh of the
flesh and blood of the blood of its creator, and to demonstrating how
the life of the author and his emotional and intellectual experiences are
reflected in his works. Other scholars were concerned with establishing
models and sources, and quite often were content to do no more than
to trace the subject matter of a literary work to its origins. And yet the
goal of such an investigation as this must be more than that: it must
show how this raw material was *transformed* into a work of art.

The classical example of how an author and his writings mutually
elucidate each other is to be found in the life and works of Johann
Wolfgang von Goethe. In very few artists do we find such a close
affinity between the man and his work. In *Dichtung und Wahrheit* he

views his life and his work as one. And it is truly remarkable to see how his *Faust* grows out of his own spiritual struggles.

Scholarly investigations of the genesis of works of art, which are often excellent, have come to be taken for granted in the field of literary history. But Goethe's *Faust* could not fully be accounted for even if it were possible to give an exhaustive account of its genesis—and this, by the very nature of things, is not possible. *Don Quixote* possesses enduring validity, and we are far from a complete comprehension of it even though we do know something about the life of Cervantes. The story of the knight, the hero of the novel, is much more remarkable than the biography of the author and casts more light upon the author's life than his biography does on his literary work. And it is obvious that the less we know about an author and about his sources and models, the less value the genetic method has for our understanding of his work.

Expressed somewhat differently: the work of art assumes an independent existence as soon as it has been completed, just as a child does in regard to its father. If it cannot live on the basis of its inherent qualities of excellence, it is dead. It is only its artistic merit which can preserve it from oblivion. In other words, we must ask what the work of art *is*, and not from what roots it has sprung. And it goes without saying that the first task of all literary criticism is to try to arrive at an understanding of the intrinsic merit of the work. And as far as that is concerned, this is also its final task, for a study of the sources and an analysis of the genesis of the work do not render a full account of the matter unless we explain what has become of the raw material in the work of art itself.

I tried in the previous chapter to state my views regarding the background and the genesis of *Njála*, in anticipation of any questions the reader might have had about them. Now I shall turn to the saga itself and ask what it has to offer and what it is that gives it life. I shall discuss the art of the saga, its character portraits and pictures of human life, and the life views and ideals which are revealed in it. I shall inquire into the question of its truth—not historical truth, but rather the truth about human life to which I have previously alluded. I have already given a brief account of my views concerning the historical reliability of *Njála*, and I see no reason for further discussion of this matter since for the most part it has no bearing on the artistic merit of the saga. Of a work of art we demand a certain realness (which must not be equated with realism or historical veracity), a certain verisimilitude or semblance of truth. Anachronisms or other historical inaccuracies are actual artistic flaws only to the extent that they impair this illusion of truth, for example, by clashing with the notions or the knowledge of the reader through obvious incongruities in regard either to known facts or to the spirit of the times in which the story takes place.[1]

It need scarcely be emphasized that the critic who attempts to interpret a work of art as it exists should avail himself of the knowledge which investigations of its sources and genesis can give him, whether it be for the purpose of explaining distinctive features of the work or to get a better understanding of this or that description by comparing it with its model in respect to points of difference or similarity. But research into the origins of a work can be no more than a means of assistance. The highest judge of a literary work is the reader or listener, and in the final analysis, every single feature of the work will stand or fall according to whether or not it pleases him.

To attempt to investigate the genesis of a work like *Njála*, where so much is and will always remain obscure, is not unlike trying to explore the vastness of space with a flashlight on a dark and cloudy autumn night. Such attempts can be intriguing and exciting, but because of the inescapable uncertainty of the results they can never be intellectually satisfying. One "perhaps" is piled upon another, and even the most ingeniously contrived hypothesis, in which everything appears to be in

---

1. This applies, of course, only to those works whose authors endeavor to create an atmosphere of historical reliability. In certain types of fiction, to be sure, the artistic design may call for a deliberate departure from historical fact or the spirit of the times, but that is scarcely the case with our ancient literature.

perfect harmony, can be farther from the truth than the seemingly most improbable possibilities. But when we turn away from all this and turn our attention to a consideration of the saga itself, as it actually exists, it is like coming out into the warm sunlight. And what is more beautiful in the North than the light of the sun?

Here we are no longer delighted at the success of our clever theorizing, but at what the eye sees and the ear hears. And the eye delights both the mind, which demands knowledge and certainty, and the heart, which desires art and beauty. From the open pages of this ancient work there arises a whole world, which the reader can see and hear and judge for himself. For he no longer walks by faith, but by sight.

II

It is not my intention to expatiate on the subject of the complexities of literary criticism, and I shall limit myself to a few brief observations. The beginning and the end of literary criticism is this: as a reader the critic must to a certain degree possess the perception and the imagination of a child, his unconditional belief in what he sees, hears, or reads, and his wonder at it all. It is not far-fetched to compare literary creation to the gift of clairvoyance, and the reader is in the position of the man in the fairy tale who got to peek under the arm of the clairvoyant man and thus came to share in his supernatural gift. And then it is best for him not to impair this gift through eccentricity or intransigence.

This is the basis of criticism, its beginning and its conclusion, but its essence is something quite different. That which, as a reader, he experienced emotionally or intuitively, he must now, as a critic, attempt to express logically, in terms of opinions and ideas. He compares, summarizes, states reasons, and draws conclusions.

Here many things must be taken into consideration. First of all, the critic must base his judgments exclusively on the work of art itself. He must abide by the unconditional rule: *Quod non est in actis, non est in mundo*—what is not in the text, does not exist. At the same time, the critic must put forth every effort to comprehend as much as possible of what actually *is* in the literary masterpiece, even though this can never be more than endeavor. Furthermore, he must be able somehow to resist the influence of other works, and—what is still more difficult—to avoid projecting his own ideas into the work, ideas which do not exist there. Here there is great need of care to strike a just balance: he must utilize to the utmost his imaginative powers to gain insights into the work while at the same time employing his critical judgment to avoid being misled by bias or favoritism.

Every episode in the course of a saga evokes an attitude or a mood, which is often the beginning of artistic enjoyment and understanding; but this also involves the danger that irrelevant influences can easily come into play, since so much depends on the momentary disposition of the reader. On the other hand, the mood created by a single incident can lie like a cloud over the reader's interpretation of an entire character or event. This is where the reader's critical acumen comes into play: it must help him to reject irrelevant influences and at the same time weigh the validity of the impression which for the most part seems to have come from the work itself. Some incidents provide keys to the understanding of important episodes of a work; others prove upon closer consideration to be of less importance than the initial impression seemed to indicate. In such cases there is need of careful comparison, which must strive as far as reasonably possible to harmonize the discrepancies —as far as reasonably possible, but not farther, since allowances must be made for possible defects in the work itself.

Special consideration must be given to the peculiarities of the genre or "school" in question and to all attendant circumstances. Whoever undertakes a critical investigation of *Njála* must have a comprehensive knowledge of the *Íslendingasögur* as a whole, of their distinctive nature and artistic method. He must be well acquainted with their dramatic manner of presentation, which demands so much of the reader. He must be able to understand the temperament and the deeper motives of the characters from their words and deeds. He must familiarize himself with the austere style of the sagas; he must learn to appreciate

the significance of the slightest nuances in phraseology and to understand the art of the half-sung song. The saga authors observed such
restraint and remained so consistently behind the scene that many
readers overlook them. Many a reader is startled when he is shown for
the first time the numerous and varied ways in which the individual
scenes in *Njáls saga* are connected with each other and in which coming
events are anticipated: these reveal a far greater degree of planning and
deliberation than one would expect to find in our ancient literature.
On the whole it can be said that this saga will open up if the reader
patiently knocks on the door, and that he can gain an insight into and
an overview of the saga which did not at first seem possible—without
ever going beyond the limits of the work itself.

It is not certain that the author fully succeeded in his purpose, and it
is furthermore not absolutely certain that he had complete control over
or complete understanding of the events and the characters he portrayed.
Nevertheless it is extremely important to pay close attention to everything which reveals his attitude toward both characters and events,
whether in the form of obscure hints or clear judgments.

First of all there are the descriptions of the characters when they are
introduced into the saga. According to the practice of the *Íslendingasögur*, the author was permitted in this connection to express himself
freely. And the narrative, of course, often shows the author's attitude,
even though it is usually revealed only through fine nuances of his
language; not infrequently, however, we find unequivocal opinions
expressed by the author, as for example when he states (chapter 46) that
Mörður "had a vicious, cunning nature" and that he "bitterly envied
Gunnar of Hlíðarendi." The latter statement is essential for the reader's
interpretation of the subsequent relationship between Mörður and
Gunnar. The same is true of the account of Njál's words of comfort to
his household during the burning (chapter 129), where the author adds
his own opinion: "Such were the words of solace he spoke to them,
and others still more stirring"—obviously he does not want the reader
to fail to appreciate Njál's manliness. But there is further significance

in this comment on Njál's words: the author in this way underscores what Njáll says and at the same time calls the reader's attention to it. This is a characteristic feature of his style. One of the methods he employs is to precede the words of a character by a moment of silence. A good example of this is in the scene (chapter 1) in which Hrútur remains silent for quite a while before speaking the prophetic words about Hallgerð's thief's eyes. In various other ways small details in the saga are used as what we might call designators, and it is always necessary to pay close attention to them. And quite commonly, of course, the author's own views are revealed through the voice of the common people or through the words of intelligent individuals, as for instance, when he tells us (chapter 9) that people said that Þjóstólfur "did little to temper Hallgerð's character," or when he has Hrútur say of her (chapter 33) that her character is "rather a mixture" (*blandin mjök*). And finally there remains one very important feature to be mentioned, and that is the repetition of words or details; sometimes this occurs in the form of a direct reference to what has already happened (recapitulations, quotations, allusions); sometimes the connection is tacitly understood, and even if there is no causal relation, one incident is always clarified by another. This is such a remarkable and characteristic trait that it will be necessary to return to it later for a fuller discussion.

III

The great works of literature have had very diverse fates. There are those which have never been read except by the chosen few, and there are those which soon became best sellers, so to speak, and have maintained their popularity through the years.

Without doubt *Njála* belongs to the second group. We have five manuscripts of this saga which were made only fifteen to twenty years after it was written, and just as many more from that period may have been lost. We have fragments of a score of medieval manuscripts of *Njála*, and in this respect *Njála* far exceeds all other Sagas of Icelanders. *Egils saga* is second with thirteen manuscripts from the Middle Ages.

Most of the *Íslendingasögur* have been preserved in only two or three medieval manuscripts, and for quite a few sagas no such manuscripts survive. From the period following the Reformation there are thirty to forty manuscripts of *Njála;* there would be more were it not for the fact that the first edition was printed as early as 1772. The number of printed editions also is indicative of its great popularity. In Iceland it is the most popular of all the sagas: it is constantly being bought and read, and it is certain to attract a good audience whenever it is presented in serial form on the radio. Beyond the shores of Iceland too it seems to be one of the best-known sagas. Evidence of this is the large number of translations which have been made into many languages. The rare excellence of its style is a constant challenge to translators, even when older translations are available. It seems that each age demands a revised version of it. One has the impression that these translations are sold in rather large quantity.

Njála has all the good qualities and some of the not so good qualities of the best seller. It exhibits a sureness of style and a superiority of technique, but at the same time, here and there, a certain nonchalance. One is reminded of the lists of inconsistencies that scholars have culled from the works of Shakespeare. It happens in *Njála* that the same individual is formally introduced into the story more than once; conversely, the author tells us that a certain character is "out of the saga"— only to have him make his appearance again later on. The author has been faulted because his battle descriptions are monotonous, or because his accounts of voyages abroad are stereotyped after the manner of the *fornaldarsögur*—and yet one should not overlook the fact that in these accounts variation is present to a substantial degree. In addition the author has been censured for exaggerating now and then or for sometimes showing his sympathies and antipathies too clearly. The last-mentioned criticism is by far the most serious of all. And yet, when one considers this matter more closely, one would in most cases think twice before wishing it otherwise. There is no more doubt that the saga's villains are villains than there is about Iago or Edmund. Yet most of them are interesting and clearly drawn. And then there is Hallgerður, who is depicted with a kind of antipathetic perceptiveness—I am reminded of some of Saint-Simon's character descriptions; but in the final analysis the author's portrait of Hallgerður is, in spite of everything, grand and unforgettable. Hallgerður is seen from without, in a rather pitiless light, but if one looks closely, one sees that she has been given some good qualities. In this connection I should like to refer to the story of her second marriage, which was written with great consideration and tact. Hallgerður has not wanted for defenders—against the saga. (In Iceland this is an old story, which we shall consider further in a later chapter.) And yet the entire case of these defenders is based on what the saga endows her with; and if one gives further thought to this, one discovers that they are actually under the spell of the saga to a great degree.

In various passages in the saga strong light is focused on certain characters, Höskuldur Hvítanessgoði and Kári, for example, but here too one finds upon closer inspection that within the composition of the saga the pictures which the author has drawn of them have their significance and justification: they are precisely as they should be.

As already mentioned, anachronisms and historical inaccuracies such as we can find in *Njála* are of concern to the literary critic only to the extent that they are detrimental to artistic illusion, but in general that is not the case here. It is possible, of course, to detect disturbing details with the help of a magnifying glass, but that is something else again.

When one reads the saga, or better yet, when one hears it read (for it was written to be read aloud), one soon discovers that the list of sins committed by the author is of little significance. The saga's qualities of excellence are so great and the author's artistic mastery is so surpassing that a few little careless slips here and there cannot seriously impair his creation.

IV

If I had to characterize the art of *Njáls saga* in one sentence, I would do so with a quotation of Cardinal Nicholas of Cusa. It seemed to him that in a single moment he was able to view the world in its totality, and he tried afterward to describe this view with the words *coincidentia oppositorum*, the coincidence or harmonization of opposites. At first glance this definition may seem far-fetched or beside the point, but I think that a closer examination of the matter will bear it out.

These well-known words of Cardinal Nicholas are leading words in a whole system of theology or mysticism, which has no application to the question under discussion; but when they are isolated from their original context they possess a general validity that can be applied to art and artistic design, to the life view or outlook of a writer or poet, especially one who has lived his life amid opposing forces which in the end are harmonized one with the other.

Njáls saga takes place in Iceland, but this scene is too limited; it is expanded to include all of northwestern Europe, and even Rome and Constantinople. The saga shows that the author has a mental picture of the entire Christian world. He sets his goal so high that the substance of his work would crush any other saga; and he is so insatiable in his desire to understand human life and so enchanted by all of its manifestations that we can apply to him the well-known and often used words that no aspect of human life lacked concern to him. He delights in telling about cold, human intellect, but he is no less intrigued by prophetic powers and mysterious events. His mind is broad and comprehensive. And in addition to this, he possesses an uncompromising will to mold his material into artistic form and the capacity to resolve the diverse and heterogeneous parts into a cohesive, well-articulated whole. He can breathe the breath of life into it, give it vitality and movement, and imbue it with his own life views. He organizes and articulates his material without impairing its variety; he cannot portray human existence except by means of opposites which are brought into harmony, just like the individual instruments of an orchestra.

V

Andreas Heusler speaks of the *Stoffreude* of the author of *Njála*, by which he means the author's delight in the raw material of his saga, or, indeed, any kind of matter, regardless of whether it is necessary for his story. Heusler's feeling was shared by those who wanted to eliminate whole chapters from the saga because they regarded them as extraneous interpolations or additions. This hunger for material is most evident in four features of the saga.

In the first place there are the genealogies, which are much fuller and more detailed than necessary and which are sometimes repeated unnecessarily. On the other hand, however, there is no doubt that it was not hunger for matter or thirst for knowledge alone which prompted the author to include them. If they are read aloud and in context, it becomes clear that they serve not only to supply the reader with information, but also to endow the saga with an air of pomp and ceremony, and the attentive reader soon learns to distinguish between what is embellishment and what is necessary for an understanding of the saga.

In the second place, there are the legal formulas. The author of *Njála* is not content to report the results of the lawsuits in his story. He is not even content to limit himself to a description of the high points in the course of the cases. Instead, he copies whole series of legal formulas from his law book and fills page after page of his saga with them. This is especially true of his account of the litigation following the burning of Njáll.

In the third place, there is *Brjáns þáttur* (chapters 154–57). No one who reads *Njála* can fail to perceive that this rather long episode seems to be somewhat of a digression. Its chief connection with the saga is the fact that Þorsteinn Síðu-Hallsson and some of the incendiaries take part in the battle of Clontarf. And yet this *þáttur* has an artistic function: just at this point the saga is beginning to lose momentum, and it is fitting that it be reinforced momentarily through the description of these supernatural events before the final reconciliation and the cessation of hostilities. At the same time the battle of Clontarf is sufficiently remote from the chief concern of the saga and contrasts appropriately in tone and atmosphere with the main course of action, on which it has little influence.[2]

2. See *Um Njálu*, p. 76.

In the fourth place, there is *Kristni þáttur* (chapters 100–105), and this is the only episode which strikes the reader as being extraneous, chiefly because of the many small, irrelevant details. But the question of Christianity has great significance for the saga, and it may be that this point of view strengthened the author's desire and decision to include this material. Furthermore, we must consider the question of whether or not a retardation is desirable at this point in the saga, and this retardation is provided by the account of the acceptance of Christianity in Iceland.

Various other sections of the saga reveal how the author develops his material into detailed accounts even though he might have treated it more briefly. We can think, for example, of the story of Hrappur before he meets Þráinn. The author cannot avoid relating and showing Hrapp's escapades, but he by no means lets himself be carried away. It does not take long before the reader realizes what tremendous motive force these episodes have for what is to follow.

Everywhere in the saga we encounter the author's hunger for material and his desire to give a good account of it, but with a firm hand he gives this enormous quantity of material artistic form, contextual coherence, and unceasing movement.

The composition of *Njála* is unusually tightly knit. First there are two "preludes," the story of Hrútur and Unnur, and the story of Hallgerður before she meets Gunnar. They are connected through the fact that the brothers Höskuldur and Hrútur play important roles in both of them. Many persons have raised objections to these two episodes because they delay the introduction of the chief characters until chapters 19 and 20, but we must not forget that they are essential links in the story and that it would have been awkward to "squeeze" them into the saga anywhere else. The truth of the matter is that this arrangement of the material is unusual but excellent.

With chapter 19 the main saga begins, and it falls naturally into three parts. Guðbrandur Vigfússon has called it a trilogy. The first part deals chiefly with Gunnar and concludes with his death and the events connected therewith. The second part deals with Njáll and his sons after the death of Gunnar and ends with their deaths in the burning of Bergþórshvoll. The third part deals with the vengeance for their deaths and concludes with a complete reconciliation between Kári and Flosi. Each of these three parts, which are clearly separated from each other, again falls into distinct acts, which are again subdivided into scenes (to use somewhat loosely the terminology of the drama), and the division between the acts and sometimes also between the individual scenes of an act is likewise usually quite clear. Good examples of this from the first third of the trilogy are the scenes depicting the slayings of the menservants (including the slaying of Sigmundur), which are kept distinct from the act concerned with Gunnar's dealings with Otkell, and in turn there is a clear line of demarcation between this act and the one which treats of the conflict between Gunnar and the sons of Starkaður. The separation between individual scenes is most obvious and regular in the act devoted to the servant slayings, but is also found elsewhere. At the beginning of each of the two major parts of the story we find "preparatory scenes" in anticipation of the main events (corresponding in large degree to the exposition of a drama). This preparatory material includes, among other things, the initial descriptions at the beginning of each act (and sometimes at the beginning of individual scenes) of characters who are introduced into the story for the first time, or a sort of brief recapitulation of such characters who have not been presented immediately preceding the act in question. Only seldom are characters introduced into the narrative without having been previously identified and described. Thus the reader always has a list of the dramatis personae before him, so to speak, and is never at a loss regarding the identity of the characters involved.[3] All this demonstrates the author's great control over his material, and this is revealed even more clearly when we consider the relationship between the articulation of the saga and its narrative force. The skill of the author

3. See *Um Njálu*, section 44, and Björn M. Ólsen, *Um Íslendingasögur*, pp. 90 ff., in *Safn til sögu Íslands*, Vol. VI.

is revealed through the arrangement and articulation of his material, and his artistic genius is demonstrated through the resulting power of his narrative.

Among the *Íslendingasögur* we find examples of biographies of individuals, accounts of families, and histories of entire districts. It is obvious to everyone who has read it that *Njála* is not a family saga, and scholars have racked their brains in the attempt to identify it more precisely. It has sometimes been called a biography, and more frequently the saga of a district, or even a history of the entire country. But it is none of these. *Njála* is the saga of a complex chain or network of events, and despite the author's "hunger for matter" he is careful not to include too much inappropriate material. In a biography or family saga, the individual or the family always binds together unrelated events, and the thread of the story often tends to become tenuous; in *Njáls saga*, on the other hand, it is the complex connection of events which brings together unrelated individuals.

From beginning to end *Njála* is an articulated, unified complex of events, all of which precipitate others. The initial impulse is not a single event, but many individual and originally unrelated events which appear somehow to be harmless and insignificant. Each one draws its nourishment from its own roots and its own soil. It grows and develops, and soon sends out shoots which take root far from their point of origin, and then become entwined and entangled with other unrelated events. Through this a new course of events is initiated, which acquires a new content and a new direction through contact with other apparently unrelated and innocuous events, and thus the saga continues. Hrútur becomes engaged to a woman in Iceland, but at the same time a man dies in Norway who has made him his heir. Hrútur is compelled to postpone his marriage in order to sail to Norway to collect his inheritance, and there becomes the paramour of a woman with supernatural powers—otherwise he would not have been able to come into possession of his inheritance. Through her baleful influence his married life is so poisoned that it ends in divorce and quarrels. Now the story

turns east to the Rangá District. Here two friends, Gunnar of Hlíðarendi and Njáll of Bergþórshvoll, live in peace and quiet, as it seems.
Hrút's former wife, Unnur, appeals to her kinsman Gunnar to help
her regain her share of the property from Hrútur, and Gunnar seeks
advice in this matter from Njáll. The result of all this is that Unn's
financial circumstances are so improved that she becomes a very
desirable match, and she marries a man, Valgarður inn grái, without
the advice of her friends and kinsmen. Her son by this marriage is
Mörður, who hates Gunnar and Njáll with such hatred as only ingratitude can spawn. Mörður does not enter the story until Gunnar for
other reasons has become involved in quarrels and manslaughter, but
then he helps Gunnar's enemies and does not desist until Gunnar—and
much later Njáll—are dead.

It is strange how unrelated events collide in such a way as to bring
about other, unforeseen events, yet a close parallel to this can be found
in the inner life of the characters, as we shall see later.

Thus one event springs from the other, and the reader often has the
feeling that these events are tied together, one with the other. But if I
had to explain their connection with one word, I would hesitate to use
the formula "cause and effect." For this there are too many incidents
and circumstances which seem to be fortuitous. We would come closer
to the heart of the matter if we spoke of an organic growth, which
nonetheless has its own internal logic and laws. But often it seems to
the reader that he can see the spider's web carried by the winds to
another web which was predestined for it, and then it appears as though
there were a will behind the drama. But this is such a complicated
matter that it would require a longer digression than is possible here to
unravel it.

There are more than causal connections of events which bind together the individual sections of the story. In the first chapter of the saga
we read about a feast on the estate of Höskuldur Dala-Kollsson, at which
Höskuldur sits chatting with his brother Hrútur. Höskuldur calls his
daughter Hallgerður, who is playing on the floor with some other girls.

She was a tall, beautiful child, and had hair as fair as silk which was so long that it hung down to the waist.

Höskuldur called to her, "Come here to me."

She went over to him at once. Her father tilted her chin and kissed her, and then she walked away again.

Höskuldur asked Hrútur, "What do you think of this girl? Don't you think she is beautiful?"

Hrútur remained silent. Höskuldur repeated his question. Then Hrútur replied, "The girl is beautiful enough, and many men will suffer for her beauty, but I do not know how thief's eyes have come into our family."

Then Höskuldur grew angry, and for a while there was a coolness between the brothers.

The silence preceding Hrút's words intensifies his prophecy of disaster, and no one can fail to notice it. At the same time the prophecy anticipates events far in the future, of which Hrútur has a foreboding: Hallgerð's instigation of the theft at Kirkjubær by the slave Melkólfur (chapter 47) and all the other misfortune which results directly or indirectly from Hallgerður and her beauty. This is one example which shows that the author's memory and his view into the future are no less remarkable than those of his character Njáll. But this is not the author's only indication of coming events in his story; he employs a great profusion of them, which appear in the form of prophecies, forebodings, visions, dreams, and the devising of plans. When in chapter 2 of the saga he tells us of Hrút's foreboding, upon seeing Unnur for the first time, that their marriage would not be a happy one, he anticipates events that are not long in coming. During Hrút's sojourn in Norway, Queen Gunnhildur puts a spell on Hrútur which is both clear and awful. The premonition of misfortune is intensified by the fact that at the wedding Unnur is downcast. In a similar manner the author includes hints and forebodings in his account of Hallgerð's younger years. In the story of Gunnar the most important vehicles of anticipation are Njál's plans and prophecies, but dreams and forebodings also play an important role, and frequently the very tone of the account awakens a suspenseful anticipation of future events. The way in which plans are worded can sometimes give a rather too clear indication of the manner in which they will be executed, especially in the first section of the story. Generally, however, the words of Goethe are valid here: "*Die größte Wahrscheinlichkeit der Erfüllung läßt noch einen Zweifel zu; daher ist das Gehoffte, wenn es in die Wirklichkeit eintritt, jederzeit überraschend.*" ("The greatest probability of fulfillment still permits doubt; therefore that which is hoped for [in this case, one should rather say 'that which is expected'] is always surprising when it becomes reality.") Besides, the forebodings are nearly always veiled in some mystical haze, and therefore the events themselves retain their freshness and affective power when they finally come to pass. They exert their influence on the imagination and the emotions of the reader rather than on his mind by arousing feelings of foreboding, dread, and tension. They lend everything that happens a half-darkened background and are more akin to the world of sound than to the world of sight.[4]

Since I have already begun to speak of the realm of tones, I cannot refrain from referring to another feature of the author's art which can be explained most easily in musical terminology, namely with the words "theme" and "variation."

In the initial description of Hallgerður the author emphasizes her beauty, for which, Hrútur says, many men will have to suffer, and he especially emphasizes her beautiful hair. When she is fully grown, the author again speaks of her beauty, and especially of her hair, which is now so long that it can completely cover her. When Glúmur asks for her hand in marriage, the author describes her and her apparel, and he does not forget to mention her hair. When she and Gunnar meet at the General Assembly, the author describes her apparel more fully than before—and does not forget her hair. Indeed, there is no reason not to

---

4. A few examples of forebodings and other techniques of arousing interest and maintaining suspense through anticipation will suffice here, since the problem has been treated in detail by A. U. Bååth in his treatise *Studier öfver kompositionen i några isländska ättsagor*.

emphasize her beauty, for which many men must suffer, and especially her hair, which is her greatest adornment and which is to play such a decisive role in the scene in which Gunnar loses his life.

Another example of theme and variation: Hallgerð's first husband, Þorvaldur, slaps her face, and for this she has him killed. Her second husband, Glúmur, whom she loves dearly, also strikes her. For this he is slain—but against her wishes. Gunnar strikes her because of her theft, and this blow eventually leads to his death. These events perhaps do not seem credible when isolated from their context, but within the continuity of the narrative we accept them as natural. And it is as though an echo is carried from one event to the next, so that each succeeding one acquires an increasingly more deadly content from the preceding ones. This is not merely a matter of poetic ingenuity; there is a psychological profoundness in the circumstance that Gunnar is made to suffer for the blow of Þorvaldur.

It is easy to find examples of repeated motifs in the story, whether they be words or incidents. Sometimes they are in the form of identical quotations or verbatim repetitions. This is true of Skarphéðin's thinly veiled metaphor about going to look for sheep when he sets out to slay Sigmundur and again when he leaves the house to slay Þráinn; and in both cases the primary motive is vengeance for the killing of his foster father, Þórður leysingjason.—Or think of Gunnar's difficulties with Otkell: here there are many small details which are repeated as "reminders" in identical or slightly varied phraseology. When Otkell rides Gunnar down and wounds him with his spurs on his way east to Dalur (chapter 53), Gunnar expresses his indignation with these words: "All can see . . . that you have drawn blood. This is dishonorable: first you summon me, and now you trample on me and ride me down." Skammkell gives no one else a chance to reply. "You are taking it well, Gunnar, but you looked far more wrathful when you won self-judgment at the General Assembly with your halberd in your hand." This venomous sarcasm refers to the halberd about which there has already been a great deal of loose talk, both among Otkel's followers themselves as well as to Gunnar. "When we meet again," Gunnar replies, "you will see the halberd." Skammkell gives his horse the whip and shouts, "That's brisk riding, lads!"—Over in Dalur he boasts that they made Gunnar weep. While they are on their way home, Gunnar's halberd rings out on the wall, and it seems to his mother that she has never seen him look so wrathful as he does while riding out to meet Otkell and his followers. When they meet, Gunnar says, "Make ready to defend yourselves; the halberd is here now. And you can also find out whether you can make me weep." After the encounter Gunnar and his brother Kolskeggur swiftly ride up along the river bank, and Gunnar leaps from his horse and lands upright on his feet.

Kolskeggur says, "That's brisk riding, brother!"

Gunnar replies, "That's what Skammkell said to mock me when I said, 'You rode me down.'"

"You have avenged that now," says Kolskeggur.

"I wish I knew," says Gunnar, "whether I am so much less valiant than other men because I am so much more reluctant to kill than other men are."

Here Kolskegg's words, which are almost identical to those of Skammkell, recall for Gunnar the encounter on his grain field, and Gunnar in turn recalls and repeats the words he spoke on that occasion. This section of the saga is tightly woven together with all kinds of "reminders" (both words and incidents), which occur again and again in constantly varying forms and connections. This is characteristic and artistically consummate, for here there is a steady stream of address and response; each word evokes another, and every incident leads to another. The entire episode concludes with a sort of final reply to the most vexing questions posed in the preceding narrative, and we gain an insight into the hidden recesses of the mind of a valiant warrior which reveals a remarkable tenderness and moral sensibility.

Much more common than direct "quotations" is the repetition or reiteration of themes or characteristic features in the accounts of the same individuals or similar situations, such as the details in the description of Hallgerður just mentioned. Such "leitmotifs," which are frequently employed in this saga, are always of great importance, both for the unfolding of the story and for the reader's understanding of it.

And finally we find repeatedly throughout the saga motifs which have no causal connection with each other, but which bear a certain resemblance to each other in regard to content and function. Some of them are well known from elsewhere, such as certain details of dreams or portents: the attack of birds of prey, the rain of blood, and a thunderous crash of sound.[5] Others are of a more personal nature. There is always evil brewing when individuals converse for a long time in a subdued tone of voice. The display of intimate friendship is almost always a signal of impending evil. Many apparently trifling details are explained by other, similar ones, and the knowledge which can be derived from them is often of great importance, but the reader must be very perceptive in evaluating it. An analysis of the motifs of the saga must not detract from their subtle aesthetic effect, nor must it cause us to overlook the influence that comes from their interrelationship and harmonization.[6]

We could say that one incident heralds the other, and that each of them changes its appearance through the influence of the others. Each incident yields an altered mirror image of the other. It is just as though the mind of the reader were a vast space which responds to echoes from various directions, whether they be harmonious or discordant, clear or obscure.

When we consider all of this, I think we must agree with the statement of Bååth, already mentioned, that the author of *Njála* had such a

5. The rain of blood and the thunderous din are reluctantly explained by Óspakur (chapter 156): "The blood raining down upon you signifies that you will shed the blood of many men—your own and that of others. And the violent crash that you heard portends the bursting of the world—and you will all soon die."

6. Repetitions of words and descriptions are enumerated in *Um Njálu*, section 44.

firm mastery of his material that he had the last sentence of his story
in mind when he wrote the first one.

VI

As we have seen, *Njála* is characterized by a meticulous disposition
and closely knit composition of the vast amount of material which it
embraces. And now we come to a third characteristic, without which
the saga would be dead, and that is the force and swiftness of the course
of events. However inert and sluggish some of the matter itself might
be, the author has succeeded in galvanizing it into dynamic movement.
Even dry legal formulas are transformed into an exciting contest, a
suspenseful struggle affecting the fortunes and lives of many persons.
To appreciate this fully, compare the swift course of *Njála* with the
epic calm of *Laxdœla*—or even with the current of events in *Egils saga*,
which is sometimes strong, but never so rapid as in Njála. Only in
Kristni þáttur does it seem for a time as though the wind fails to swell the
sails. In the episodes dealing with voyages abroad, too, the narrative
is different from the account of events here in Iceland. These tales are
mostly adventure stories designed to entertain the reader, and individual details in them usually have little influence on the main course
of events. Only the outcome of such voyages is of importance. Even if
a saga character were to be killed on such viking expeditions, it would
be an unfortunate rather than a tragic occurrence—unless, of course it
had a bearing on the main events in Iceland.

As has already been mentioned, each part of the trilogy (and indeed,
each act and even each scene) begins with a sort of exposition in which
the "components" are indicated: characters are introduced or reintro-
duced into the story, previous events are recapitulated when necessary,
and details and particulars of coming events are alluded to. At first
glance this all seems purposeless, but before long the relationship of all
these details to each other and to past and future events becomes evident.
Tensions mount, conflict erupts between opposing parties, and this sets

in motion chains of events that continue far into the future. Some of these clashes are masterpieces of dramatic narration, such as the altercation between Hallgerður and Bergþóra, or Hildigunn's goading of Flosi. The author pays particular attention to the outcome of events which occur in distant places, and especially to the manner in which unrelated events unleash the latent force of old enmities. When this happens, it seems as though the results are unusually perilous, so that the consequences increase rather than decrease, involving more and more people and growing ever more ominous.

Yet on the other hand there are forces which try to check the onrush toward grave events, conflict, and killings. Peace-loving men of good will try to bring about reconciliation. Such efforts are successful to a certain extent. Most episodes end with the serenity of a clear evening sky; all evil seems to have ended. But the following episode shows that quite the opposite is the case: the accomplished reconciliation contains within itself seeds from which new misunderstandings and disagreements sprout. Or else some incident from an entirely unexpected source upsets the precarious balance. Gunnar's battles usually end in victory and bring him increased honor. Yet no matter how just and moderate the settlements are which Njáll arranges, people envy Gunnar's honor more and more. Sometimes the reader cannot escape the strange feeling that it is success and good repute per se which contain the seeds of misfortune which only exceeding good fortune and extreme precautions can prevent from growing to maturity.

Thus the battle rages, a battle between two formidable adversaries, a battle between the forces of peace and the forces of war. The outcome of this battle is not immediately apparent, for the advantage shifts back and forth from one contestant to the other, so that it is difficult to see who will finally win the victory. A good example of this fluctuation is the lawsuit following the burning of Njáll, during which alternately the prosecution and the defense gain the advantage. Thus the reader wavers for a long time in suspense between hope and fear.

Nevertheless we can see a definite plan in the story. The first two movements of the trilogy are marked *crescendo*. Gunnar's quarrels and killings increase constantly in magnitude, and misfortune turns more and more unequivocally in the direction of Njáll and his sons. And yet for a long time it seems possible that all will turn out well—if Gunnar goes abroad and keeps the terms of the settlement, and if a reconciliation can be brought about following the death of Höskuldur. But then two incidents occur which can be called the crises or turning points, which result from the failure to take advantage of the final opportunities to avert disaster: when Gunnar returns home instead of going abroad, and when Skarphéðinn and Flosi transform reconciliation into enmity. Now nothing more can be done, and within a short time those events occur which drag the chief heroes to their destruction.

The pattern of the final part of the trilogy is quite different from that of the first two. At first it seems as though matters will turn out the same as before, but here enmity and hostility soon reach their climax: in the battle at the General Assembly. Immediately afterward the final turning point occurs, when Flosi chooses full and complete peace. With this decision the enmity begins to abate and everything tends to move—not, to be sure, without zigzags and obstacles—toward a final reconciliation.

Nolens volens the characters are swept along irresistibly by the swift course of events. Does this mean that man is nothing in this blind vortex? On the contrary. In man himself, in his individuality, his achievements, his personality, and his character is the latent force which through the exigencies of life is galvanized into action. Human character plays such a great role in the events of the story that one might almost say that those events are nothing but the revelation of character. The peculiar characteristics of individuals thus are of paramount importance in this saga, and none of the Sagas of Icelanders contain such a large variety of complex character portraits as *Njála*. This is an important aspect of the saga, which can only be mentioned here in passing, but which will be discussed in later chapters of this book.

VII

Let us now look at the saga from another point of view. Let us consider the account of the quarrel between Hallgerður and Bergþóra, in the course of which they have each other's menservants killed. Or Skarphéðin's quest for support at the General Assembly, or that of Flosi in the East Fjords, or the lawsuit following the burning of Njáll, in which Þórhallur Ásgrímsson and Eyjólfur Bölverksson try to outdo each other in legal adroitness and chicanery. All of these episodes share two characteristic features: carefully planned structure and order. All of them are characterized by a series of events, each of which leads to the next one in an orderly, planned sequence. Now, order is chiefly the work of the human mind, and many chapters and events reveal a large measure of planning and design, such as the other lawsuits and all the many well-laid schemes. An example of another kind is the use of ambiguous language or veiled metaphors, such as Skarphéðin's pretending to go out to look for sheep when he really intends to wreak blood vengeance against his enemies.

Perhaps the reader (or listener) might feel that in many passages the saga writer adheres too rigidly or mechanically to his outline. I do not think, however, that this is the case except possibly in the first counsel given by Njáll and in some of the lawsuits. For the saga abounds in a variety of motivating forces, which fill every bit of the story with teeming life and activity. This animation stems from the author's love of human life in all its manifestations and his fascination for the diversity of reality. A leaf of vellum is inscribed with the names of the chieftains at the General Assembly, and suddenly those names have been transformed into a series of living portraits, each different from the others, and some of them unforgettable. The battle descriptions of the saga have been adversely criticized because of the author's ignorance of warfare, yet on closer inspection they reveal great imaginative power on his part. Even the legal formulas in the litigation following the burning conjure up pictures of the people and life of the times, and the clever moves and countermoves of the legal experts transform the sea of spectators into stormy tumult.

In order to get a clearer picture of all this it might be well to consider several examples, especially from outside the mainstream of events.

At the beginning of chapter 39 Þórður leysingjason is introduced into the story: "There was a man named Þórður, who was called leysingjason. His father was named Sigtryggur, and had been given his freedom by Ásgerður. Sigtryggur drowned in the river Markarfljót. It was for this reason that Þórður, who was a tall, powerful man, afterward lived with Njáll and fostered all of Njál's sons. Þórður grew fond of a kinswoman of Njál's named Guðfinna Þórólfsdóttir, who was the housekeeper there and was pregnant at that time." (Their son Þórður was burned to death with Njáll.) In this episode one incident leads directly to the next, until they form a unified, unique little biography. Another freed man, Bjálfi, who had belonged to Ásgerður, is introduced into the story in a similar manner. Bjálfi was the grandfather of Björn of Mörk. No other thralls are mentioned by name except Melkólfur. Then there are menservants, shepherds, the old woman Sæunn, each with his unique individual characteristics, and some of whom, like Þórður, have a little biography of their own in the saga. Kaupa-Héðinn (chapters 22–23) is the embodiment of the traveling huckster, wandering about the countryside peddling his wares. And then there are the bands of vagrants, nameless and faceless, yet the tales about them are teeming with life and activity. One of the best illustrations of this is the episode of the beggar women in Hallgerð's quarters (chapter 44).

Nor do these individuals sit around doing nothing. Svartur is killed as he is cutting wood in Rauðaskriður. Kolur meets his fate while transporting supplies from his mountain dairy and after having been up all night. Atli is slain while making charcoal in the woods, and Sigmundur and Skjöldur, while they are going to look after their horses. Þjóstólfur kills Þorvaldur as he is laying in a supply of dried fish in the islands called Bjarneyjar, and Glúmur while he is out looking for his sheep. According to the report of the beggar women just referred to, the activity in Njál's household was as follows: Skarphéðinn was whetting his ax, Grímur was shafting a spear, Helgi was riveting the hilt of his sword, Höskuldur was reinforcing the handle of his shield, one of the thralls was carting manure out on the hummocks in the field, while Njáll kept busy sitting still!

It would be possible to add many more examples, but this brief selection will suffice to illustrate the point. What is of the greatest significance is the fact that all of these characters are living, breathing people. In the episode about Þórður and his father, Sigtryggur, it does not take long to find a warm human heart. The pictures of the life of the people in *Njála* are in harmony with the rest of the material—the same variety and comprehensiveness, the same sympathetic understanding of human life, with its joys and sorrows, its hopes and fears, whether it be revealed in major conflicts or in the hustle and bustle of everyday life. Was this not what Goethe meant when he said, "*Greift nur hinein ins volle Menschenleben!*"

Thus everything is interwoven with this luxuriant growth of minor incidents of human life and reality. But the reader does not merely hear about these events, he actually envisions them before his very eyes. It is well known that some writers have such a vivid imagination that the things they write about seem to come to life as they write. In fact, Dickens declared that he first saw his stories and then later wrote them. Ibsen said, "To write creatively is to see." Much the same can be said about the author of *Njála*. He frequently writes as vividly as though he were an eyewitness reporting the events as they occurred.

To illustrate this let us compare several passages in *Njála* which have close parallels in other works. In *Ólafs saga Tryggvasonar hin mesta* we read the following about Þangbrand's journey over Mýrdalssandur: "But on the day on which Hallur and his company rode from Kirkjubær, the earth opened beneath Þangbrandur and his horse sank down into it, but he managed to get off its back and save himself with the help of God and his companions." *Kristnisaga* says about Þangbrandur that "he sprang from his horse and stood unharmed on the brink (of the cleft)." There is nothing wrong with these descriptions, and the one in *Kristnisaga* evokes a picture, albeit a somewhat sketchy one.

But let us now see what the author of *Njála* does with the same material:

> After this they rode from Skógahverfi to Höfðabrekka. By then all the news of their journey had become known. A man named Galdra-Héðinn was living at Kerlingardalur. The heathens hired him there to kill Þangbrandur and his companions. He went up on the mountain called Arnarstakksheiði and there held a great sacrifice. While Þangbrandur was riding westward (probably from Kirkjubær), the earth beneath his horse burst asunder. He leaped from his horse and got up on the brink (of the chasm), but the horse was swallowed, gear and all, and was never seen again. Then Þangbrandur praised God. Guðleifur went in search of the sorcerer Héðinn, and found him up on the mountain. Guðleifur chased him down to Kerlingardalur, and when he got within range, he hurled his spear, and it went through Héðinn.

The news which precedes the arrival of Þangbrandur sets everything in motion and creates an appropriate eerie atmosphere around him. The entire account of Galdra-Héðinn is very brisk and lively, but the chief incident is the story of Þangbrand's horse. It far exceeds all other descriptions of the same incident in swiftness, power, and vividness: then the earth *burst asunder*, Þangbrandur *leaped* from his horse, and the earth *swallowed* the horse with all its gear. Here the reader actually sees the horse disappear into the voracious jaws of the earth, and it all happens so quickly that he just catches a glimpse of the saddle before it disappears from view.

Many other passages in the saga are equally good. Throughout the work we can observe how vividly the author portrays the action, so that we feel as though we actually see the events occurring before our very eyes.

Sometimes we can detect a delight and pleasure on the part of the author in depicting and describing. In the midst of the swift course of the action he suddenly seems to hold up a picture before us, large and clear—and often colorful and splendid. As an example let us consider for a moment the account of the defense of the Njálssons and the merchants against the vikings in the fjords off the coast of Scotland. They

have been forced into a precarious position, but are determined not to
yield or surrender.

> At this moment they happened to look out to sea. There they saw ships
> sailing around the headland from the south, and there were no fewer than
> ten, rowing swiftly and making straight for them. The gunwales were com-
> pletely lined with shields. At the mast of the foremost ship stood a man with
> a fine head of hair. He wore a silk tunic and a gilded helmet, and held in his
> hand a spear inlaid with gold.

Thus Kári Sigmundsson makes his entry into the story, like a romantic
hero coming from far away.

Or let us think of the description of how Gunnar and Hallgerður
meet at the General Assembly, or the picture of the Njálssons and Kári
when they set out to slay Þráinn, fully armed and carrying shields, two
of them even decorated with coats of arms, yet each person distinguished by his own individual characteristics. This is one of many
examples of the same kind of delight in describing beautiful objects
which plays such a prominent role in *Laxdæla*. But the author is not
content to limit himself to the description of beauty. He describes all
sorts of things, some of which are of an unrelieved, starkly realistic
nature. During the winter following the burning of Njáll (chapter 135),
Þórhallur Ásgrímsson "developed an infection of the leg so severe that
above the ankle his leg was swollen as thick as a woman's thigh, and
he could not walk without the help of a staff. Þórhallur was a tall,
powerful man with dark hair and a dark complexion. He was quiet
spoken and yet quick-tempered." He was deeply concerned that fitting
vengeance be meted out to the slayers of his foster father, Njáll. When
his father left the booth to return to the court proceedings against the
incendiaries, "his face was as red as blood, and (tears like) large hail-
stones fell from his eyes. He asked that his spear be brought to him."
And when he heard that the lawsuit against Flosi had been lost, "he
was so stunned that he could not utter a word. Then he sprang from
his bed, seized the spear given him by Skarphéðinn, and drove it

through his foot. There was flesh and the core of the boil on the blade as he cut it out of his foot, and blood and pus gushed across the floor like a stream. Then he left the booth without a limp," walked to where his adversaries were, and thrust his spear through the first man he met.

This passage well demonstrates how strongly the author was entranced by reality, reality in all its varied aspects, beautiful as well as ugly and ominous. Thus this writer, who had grown up in the tradition of the moderation which characterizes the classical Sagas of Icelanders, could not refrain from making that which was already starkly realistic even more so by supplementing and augmenting it. As a consequence, the events are made to appear even more true to life and assume an even greater semblance of wonderful reality, refined as well as unrefined.

Several times the appearance of people is described when they are introduced into the story. Such descriptions are naturally static, but they can well be memorable. More often, however, such descriptions are given in the course of the narrative. They do not disturb or retard the story. They usually occur in passages in which the action of the story is swift and strong. The picture which is given appears suddenly, and the story continues immediately. The picture is drawn with a few strokes, which suffice to stimulate the reader's imagination: in this work, as in other Sagas of Icelanders, it is assumed that the reader is endowed with a vivid, unspoiled receptivity.

The description of Þórhallur and his malady is really nothing but a revelation of the deep grief and bitter hatred which he bore in his breast after the burning: they become a physical sore which cannot heal until vengeance has been taken. In other passages the scene seems to be illuminated by small details in such a way that men and events assume a special significance. Let us recall, for example, the scene in which Flosi and Glúmur Hildisson and several other men go up onto the gable end of the burning farmhouse at Bergþórshvoll.

Then Glúmur said, "Do you think Skarphéðinn is dead yet?"
The others said that he must have been dead long since.

Now and then the fire flared up, and then it died down again. Then in the flames down before them they heard a verse being uttered. . . .

Grani Gunnarsson said, "Was Skarphéðinn alive or dead when he recited that verse?"

"I won't venture any guesses about that," replied Flosi.

Then Grani wanted to look for Skarphéðinn and the others, but Flosi absolutely forbade that and ordered them to leave as quickly as possible.

The dialogue is in itself excellent and quite noteworthy; the nucleus of the passage is the verse and the doubt as to whether Skarphéðinn spoke it dead or alive. But what completes and rounds out the scene are small, seemingly unessential details: the fire which now blazes up and then sinks down again. The eerie flickering of the fire, alternately flaming up and dying down, casts an ominous, uncanny hue over the entire scene.

This portion of the saga half opens the door to a world of mystery. In other passages in *Njála* there are accounts of strange events, sorcery, or dreams, and most of these accounts are, to state it briefly, excellent. Some are of modest scope, but are strangely reminiscent of personal experience; for example, Njál's uneasiness upon sensing the menacing wraiths of Gunnar's enemies at Þórólfsfell (chapter 69), or the clairvoyance of Earl Hákon Sigurðarson (chapter 88). Others are of grand dimensions and powerful, and among the most skillfully written passages in the saga. One need only think of the weaving witnessed by Dörruður and of various other apparitions in *Brjáns þáttur* (chapters 154–57), or of the giant from the mountain Lómagnúpur, or Gunnar of Hlíðarendi in his burial mound, with exultant mien and four blazing lights illuminating the mound, and over the entire scene a mysterious hue: outside there is bright moonlight, but it wavers as it is darkened now and then by drifting clouds.

The account of Hildiglúm's vision at Reykir (chapter 125) is written with consummate craftsmanship. It is night. A man goes outside and hears a thunderous crash, so that both earth and sky seem to him to tremble. The apparition begins with a sound which seems to come from afar through the gloom of night. Then it comes into sight, and the vision is a mixture of brightness and darkness: a man carrying a flaming firebrand is seen within a fiery circle. He rides a gray horse, and he himself is pitch black, and all around is the dark of night. The man declaims in a powerful voice a verse which is filled with murky mystery:

> I ride a horse
> with frosty forelock
> and dripping mane,
> bringing evil.
> Fire at both ends,
> Venom in the middle;
> Thus are Flosi's plans,
> like this flying firebrand—
> Thus are Flosi's plans,
> like this flying firebrand.

Then the man hurls the firebrand eastward toward the mountains, and a sea of flame erupts there, but the man rides to the fire and disappears. Hildiglúmur enters the house and falls down senseless.

All of this happens with furious swiftness. The vision appears, enveloped in flames, out of deep darkness. It is preceded by a thunderous crash. Its essence is the song of the pitch-black rider, if it can be called a song. Visually the scene is as sharp as others in the saga, but modified to suit the situation, so that it is transformed into clairvoyance. What predominates here is the sensation of sound, united with vividly imaginative and powerful emotion. The crash which rends the silence of night and fills it with gloomy mystery fills the heart of the man with dread. *Hljóð* (which means both "silence" and "sound") always portends something ominous in the saga, whether it be the silence which conceals the hatching of schemes or the crash which ruptures the peace and quiet of night.[7]

7. Cf. the violent din in Flosi's dream (p. 13), the three thunderous crashes in the portent which appeared to Bróðir (chapter 156 of the saga and p. 60 and note 5 above), and the singing in Gunnar's halberd.

VIII

No one will deny that the author's manner of writing is often very effective, yet this style is achieved neither by verbosity nor by bombast. The narrative is for the most part extremely natural and simple. Andreas Heusler refers to the saga's light, elastic pace ("*leichten, elastischen Schritt*"). The style of the saga is in some respects similar to that of colloquial speech: it has its lightness as well as its vigor. But it is more strongly accentuated, more tightly compressed, and especially more refined. This becomes immediately evident when the saga is read aloud. The spoken language was not the model for the author; whatever influence may have come from that source was involuntary, a natural inclination of the author in that direction. His real model, the school in which he learned, were the classical Sagas of Icelanders, in which we find a balance between strong passions and their disciplined expression; their authors have attained such complete mastery over their language that they can achieve very rich, varied nuances with the simplest means. Nature and art meet halfway.

But in the style of *Njála* we can also distinguish influences from other genres. Elements from the chivalric sagas (*riddarasögur*) and clerical writings have already been discussed. The chivalric sagas left little imprint on the style of *Njála;* their influence is found rather in the subject matter, which occasionally reflects the ideals of chivalry. On the other hand, the subtly nuanced phraseology is somewhat enriched through the influence of clerical language. In regard to sentence structure, for example, we find long, well-articulated periods, and here and there the use of antithesis. Even more important, however, is the fact that people's words take on a special warmth and even sentimentality. In other passages, on the other hand, the author's thirst for reality draws into the saga some of the abusive and vulgar language current in his own day such as the following: they are full of baseness; there are thieves and wicked people there; you are either an outcast hag or a harlot; dungbeardlings, scoundrel, pervert, bitch, etc. But when we gain an overview of the language of the saga in its entirety, we realize that this element must not be exaggerated: the classical saga style predominates.

We noted above that the language of the saga differs from colloquial speech through its greater refinement, its richer nuances, and its stronger accentuation. Among those who appreciated these stylistic qualities was Finnur Jónsson, who commented on the word order within the sentence and the varying rhythm it lent to the sentence as a whole and the emphasis it placed upon individual words. As an example he cites Hallgerð's suggestion to Þráinn Sigfússon (chapter 41): *"'Mágr þætti mér nú vera,' segir hon, 'ef þu dræpir Þórð leysingjason.'"* ("'I would regard you as a *real* son-in-law,' she said, 'if you were to slay Þórður leysingjason.'") His comment on this strongly accentuated utterance is: "*Welch ein einschmeichelnder tonfall wird dadurch vorausgesetzt!*" ("What an ingratiating modulation of the voice is provided by this word arrangement.") By contrast let us consider the gentle words of Bergþóra: "*Ek var ung gefin Njáli,*" in which the sentence stress does not occur before the word *ung*. In the narrative the alternation between the preterite, the normal tense of narration, and the more dramatic present (*præsens historicum*) is quite evident. Less evident, but far more important artistically, is the variety in the sentence rhythm referred to above. On the one hand we find clauses and sentences connected with conjunctions such as *ok, nú, þá,* through which the narration gains a certain fluency and evenness, whether the pace is slow or rapid. On the other hand, we find sentences which are not connected in this manner, many of which begin with the most emphatic word, making the style brisk, dramatic, and vigorous. This technique is sometimes employed in battle descriptions, but especially in the dialogues.

No other saga can distinguish so clearly the "voice" of one individual from that of another. The words of each person possess their own distinct tone, and they retain it through thick and thin. Let us consider, for example, the deep earnestness in the words of Njáll, tinged with good-natured humor; as time goes on, the sorrow of life transforms this earnestness into melancholy, and the smile fades away. Or think of the words of Gunnar, with their moral consideration and sensitivity, which can sometimes border on sentimentality; the flattering

sliminess which characterizes the falseness of Skammkell; the un-
blushing impudence of Hrappur; the seering sarcasm in the taunts of
Skarphéðinn; the solemnity which accompanies the ostentation of
Björn of Mörk. . . .

It is in the dialogues that the author especially excels, and they are
justly famous far and wide. It does not matter whether the tone of the
dialogue is mild or wild, concordant or discordant. In them we find
in turn words as gentle as a soft breeze, grief and sorrow, sentimentality,
malevolence, jesting, discontent, mockery, anger, and expressions of
abusive slander. There are conversations which contain words that are
like a kiss or caress, such as Hallgerð's response to Sigmund's malicious
verses about Njáll and his sons (chapter 44): "What a treasure you are,
to comply with my every request." There are assertions of warm
friendship, as when Njáll replies to Gunnar's first request for advice
(chapter 21): "I have many friends who deserve that I give them good
counsel, but for you I think I will take the greatest pains to do so."
More often the exchange of words is like an exchange of blows, as in
the encounter between Hrútur and the viking Atli (chapter 5): "Your
Norwegian kings have never had any love for my father and me," said
Atli. "That's your hard luck, not theirs," was Hrút's retort. Often the
words seem to rear up against each other. After the slaying of Höskuldur Hvítanessgoði (chapter 118) Njáll asks his sons and Kári what plans
they have in mind, and receives this reply from Skarphéðinn: "We
don't usually follow our dreams in most matters!" Often it seems as
though the dialogue flashes in many colors. When the news that
Þórður leysingjason has slain Brynjólfur reaches the General Assembly,
Njáll has the messenger tell him this astonishing report three times,
whereupon he remarks, "More men have now become killers than I
would have expected." To this Skarphéðinn adds, "The man who died
at the hands of our foster father, who had never seen human blood
shed, must have been doubly doomed." These are just a few examples
from many to illustrate how varied, how rich in nuances, how swift
and lively the verbal exchanges are. There are certain features they all

have in common: they are concise, terse, and emphatic, and at the same time light and rhythmical. Here we find the finest from living language, from colloquial conversation, but refined, intensified, and perfected.

Phrases and sentences from this saga become apothegms which go flying out through town and countryside to become proverbs quoted by all Icelanders. It has been said of Horace that scarcely any event occurred on which he could not be quoted. For Icelanders *Njála* has become a similar storehouse of quotations.

IX

Let us now return to a matter already referred to: the variety of the subject matter and the firm rule with which it is treated: no two lines of the vellum are filled in the same manner. This is a path which we have previously passed by, but now the time has come to follow it. The farther we pursue it, the more rewarding is the view which opens up before us.

This diversity is one of the many qualities which make *Njála* such a fascinating saga to read. The tone and mood are constantly changing. Accounts of voyages abroad have a poor reputation among saga critics, since they are regarded as having so few individual characteristics that they could be made to fit into almost any saga whatsoever. And yet Hrút's voyage abroad is quite unlike that of Gunnar. Viking voyages to the Baltic are not the same as those to the North Sea—possibly the chief difference is that of names and small details, yet these suffice to distinguish the tone of one from that of the other; but the story of Hrappur in Norway is quite different from that of Þráinn (and much more entertaining), at least until the two stories merge. There is also a tremendous difference in the tone and character of Kári's swift expedition of revenge with Þorgeir to Kerlingadalur (chapter 146) and the more leisurely one with Björn of Mörk along the river Skaptá (chapters 150–52). There is no need here to discuss the battle in *Brjáns þáttur*, since that is quite distinct from all other voyages abroad.

Stories of expeditions, especially expeditions abroad, all border on the adventurous popular tales. But the chief events of *Njála*, which take place in Iceland, are equally varied in tone and character. For the most part they are bathed in daylight, but there are various shades of daylight, and among these events there are some which are enveloped in twilight or distorted by optical illusions, the marvelous magic-born lyric of portents and dreams.

Let us consider first of all the most serious scenes of the saga: the burning of Njáll and the battle at the General Assembly. Here the lives of many persons are at stake, persons who are very dear to the reader. And if we look closely at the basic ideas underlying these accounts, it is clear that the author is deeply moved by them. Nevertheless, right in the middle of the first of these scenes we find an incident which seems more fitting in a farce than in a tragedy: Grani Gunnarsson taunts Skarphéðinn by insinuating that he is weeping, whereupon Skarphéðinn throws one of Þráin's jaw teeth into one of Grani's eyes with such force that the eye falls out on his cheek.

In a similar manner the battle at the General Assembly is full of grim humor. Some poor wretch, who is cooking something in a kettle, taunts the men from the East Fjords for running away. They reply by dumping him headfirst into the kettle of boiling water. Skafti Þóroddsson, the Lawspeaker and one of the most distinguished men of his day, happens to be struck by a spear. He is unceremoniously dragged into the booth of some sword sharpener (according to the narrative) or into the booth of some juggler (according to a verse recited by Kári). And when the men begin to discuss the matter of peace and reconciliation following the tragic slaughter, everything at first breaks down into disgraceful quarreling and mutual reproaches. In other words, the greater the earnestness of a situation, the closer it is to becoming humorous; and when mirth and gaiety are at their height, death is often lurking nearby. Seriousness alone is an incomplete depiction of human life. The life of man is made up of tears as well as laughter, and the true nature of human life is best depicted when these two opposites are brought into close proximity. King Lear must have his jester beside him; otherwise his world is but half complete.

These examples reveal a grim and gross common humor, and it would be easy to add to them and thus make the picture more detailed. This humor is often rude and offensive in nature, sometimes with unsavory sexual implications. Sometimes there is a flood of shameful, abusive language; but just as often the humor tends toward sarcasm, cutting remarks, and vicious gossip. This is similar to the type of humor which we encounter in *Bandamanna saga*, but there it is accompanied by droll narration and bizarre character portrayal, whereas in *Njála* the tendency in this respect is toward the more refined, aristocratic irony found in the works of Snorri and in *Eyrbyggja*. The situation can be coarse and queer, and so can the words of various characters, but never the language of the author himself.

In such seemingly ingenuous portrayals, so rich in contrast, of comical subjects, another main aspect of the author's humor comes to light, and that is his subtlety and artfulness; the narrative reveals simultaneously matters as they seem to be and as they really are (*Schein und Sein*). A good example, in which there is an almost equal degree of coarse humor and subtle cunning, is the account of Þorkell hákur, the swaggering, puffed-up warrior who had had his valorous feats, performed abroad, carved on his bed-closet: here one could see the highwayman he had fought with, a flying dragon, and some other fabulous monster. When Ásgrimur Elliðagrímsson and his companions seek his support (chapters 119–20), he replies with malicious taunts, directed especially at Skarphéðinn. And the retort of Skarphéðinn is not slow in coming:

". . . you have no reason to try to dishonor me, for I have done you no harm. I have never bullied or browbeaten my father, as you have done to your father. You have seldom come to the General Assembly or taken part in litigation. You probably feel more comfortable milking cows at your farm on the Öxará River back in the hinterland. It would be more fitting for you to pick out of your teeth the mare's guts which you ate before coming here— your shepherd saw you doing it and was amazed at such disgusting behavior."

Then Þorkell sprang to his feet in great rage and seized his short-sword and said, "This is the sword I won in Sweden by killing a great warrior, and since then I have killed many a man with it. And when I get at you, I'll thrust it through you, and that's what you'll get for your foul language."

Skarphéðinn stood there with his ax poised and said with a grin, "This is the ax I carried in my hand when I sprang eighteen feet across the Markará River to kill Þráinn Sigfússon, while eight men stood nearby and none of them could lay a hand on me. I have never raised a weapon against anyone without hitting my mark."

Then he thrust his brothers and Kári aside and rushed up to Þorkell. "And now, Þorkell hákur, either put away your sword and sit down, or I will sink my ax into your head and split it down to your shoulders."

And the great warrior, who always boasted that he would never back down from anyone, promptly sheathed his sword and sat down—"and this was something which had never happened to him before or afterward." It is as though we hear the accompaniment of laughter resounding when this inflated windbag bursts—laughter both from the far ends of the bench as well as from the seat of honor.

It need scarcely be mentioned that such a tour de force as this hardly shows the author's artistic mastery of irony at its very best. But there are many examples which might be cited to show his subtle art on a higher level, mockery tempered and disciplined to the proper degree of moderation, in appropriately attuned harmony or disharmony with the context, sometimes mild and good-natured, much more often bitter, cold, and finely honed, and sometimes imbued with deep concern and anguish.

At the end of chapter 49, Otkell, who is being duped by Skammkell into taking legal action against Gunnar for the theft perpetrated by Hallgerður, makes the statement: "Now you are all wavering except Skammkell." And through his puerility we seem to hear the cold irony of fate. The Norwegian, who had climbed up on the roof of Gunnar's house to reconnoiter, when asked whether Gunnar was at home, replied: "You'll have to find that out for yourselves. But one thing I did discover: his halberd is at home." And he fell down dead. When Gunnar's mother, Rannveig, is asked whether she is willing to grant room on her land for the burial of two men who were slain in the attack on Gunnar, she retorts: "All the more so for two, since I would gladly grant enough room for all of you."

Frequently several such utterances are made to harmonize with each other. An excellent illustration of this are the comments of Njáll and Skarphéðinn when they learn that Þórður leysingjason has slain a man (see above, p. 74). "More men have now become killers than I would have imagined," says Njáll. "That man must have been doubly doomed to death," says Skarphéðinn, "to die at the hands of our foster father, who never before saw human blood spilled." Both retorts are tinged with irony, yet each in a different way. Njáll inclines toward mild mockery; his words are gentle and good-natured. Skarphéðin's retort is a cry both of exultation and of derision of the slain man. It is as though the narrative in such passages as this is resolved into a song for several voices, a song in which each voice harmonizes with another, defines and augments it. Each voice is related to another, and is understood from this relationship. It is the art of *punctum contra punctum*, as the musicians who long ago created this style of music named their innovation. In *Epic and Romance* (p. 220), Ker discusses the demeanor of Njáll and Skarphéðinn during the burning; he emphasizes "the irony in which the temper of Skarphéðinn is made to complement and illustrate" that of his father.

Another excellent example of this is the account of Sigmundur and Hallgerður slandering Njáll and his sons, and the reaction it causes at Bergþórshvoll. But here there is a still greater difference between Njál's good-natured teasing of his wife ("All in good time, woman, slow but sure—"), which is transformed into calm earnestness, and the bitterly indifferent words of Skarphéðinn: bitter because they turn the barb inward no less than outward. But the author is not content with the irony of father and son: the stage is filled with continuous comical incidents, such as Bergþóra's vehemence and the beggar women's shyness and impudence, which surround the serious matter that is being enacted there. Here it is the account itself which is twofold: despite the gravity of the scene as a whole, minor incidents can nevertheless be ridiculous or humorous. And even though the author holds Bergþóra in high esteem, he cannot refrain from poking a little fun at her now and then.

X

Unremitting irony and deep sympathy are intertwined in the account of Björn of Mörk. From every line the disparity between pretense and reality, between *Schein und Sein* grins out at the reader; and behind all this we catch a glimpse of something different: *das Werdende*, that which is momentarily becoming reality. Nowhere in the saga is the irony so subtle, so sophisticated, nowhere is the comedy more refined or purer: and indeed, this is one of the most masterful passages in this great artistic masterpiece.[8] It is interesting to note how carefully the author describes the relationship between Björn and his wife, Valgerð-ur, at the beginning of the episode (chapter 148). After tracing Björn's genealogy to his grandfather, a freed slave, and enumerating the illus-trious forebears and kinsmen of Valgerður, the author states: "She had been married to Björn for the sake of his money, and did not have much love for him. Yet they had some children together. They had plenty of everything at their farm. Björn was given to bragging about him-self, and his wife disliked this very much. He was keen-sighted and good at running." (And yet they had some children together!)

After taking leave of Þorgeir Skorargeir, Kári rides alone up to Mörk and asks farmer Björn for lodging for the night. The following morning they have a conversation.

Kári: "I would like you to let me stay here. I think that I have found a good place, here at your farm. I would also like to have you along with me on my travels, since you are keen-sighted and swift of foot. I also think that you will be a good companion if we are attacked."

8. Excellent treatments of Björn are found in Ker, *Epic and Romance*, pp. 262–63 and in Sigurður Nordal's paper "Björn úr Mörk," *Skírnir* XCIII (1919), 141–52.

Björn: "I do not deny my good eyesight nor my courage nor any other kind of manliness. You have probably come here since all other places of shelter are closed to you. And because of your request, Kári, I shall not treat you like just anyone. I shall certainly give you any kind of help you ask for."

Valgerður, who happens to overhear these words, cannot control herself. "The trolls take your boasting and bragging! Don't try to talk yourself and Kári into believing such nonsense! I will gladly supply Kári with food and with anything else that will be useful to him. But don't put any faith in Björn's hardihood, Kári, for I am afraid that things will not turn out for you the way he claims."

Björn: "You have often heaped abuse on me. But I have such confidence in myself that no one can make me take to my heels. And the proof is that nobody ever picks a quarrel with me because they are all afraid to."

As we have seen, the author states, when he introduces Björn into the story, that he is inclined to self-praise (this is a form of anticipation or foreshadowing, which the author employs in a variety of ways); but this would scarcely have been necessary. The reader senses immediately that not everything is as it should be. It is as though the words of Kári and Björn evoke echoes which more or less reverse their meanings. Each word is thus ambiguous or equivocal. The passage is so firmly and finely conceived that nothing can be changed or omitted.

Kári supports his request for Björn's assistance with praise of his keen vision and fleetness of foot. These are the qualities of a man who saves his head with his heels rather than with his sword. In regard to Björn's courage Kári ventures nothing more than a well-intentioned conjecture. He probably knows quite well what sort of warrior Björn is.

Björn lives completely in his own world of wishful thinking. In his reply to Kári he omits the reference to his unheroic fleetness, but he becomes quite excited when he thinks about his keen vision and his heroism and all kinds of manly virtues. And he also feels that he is a chieftain and a magnanimous host: he realizes that all other places of refuge are closed to Kári, and it never occurs to him to treat Kári as though he were just anybody. He is pleased at being able to help him, and he promises him his complete support. To the reader it is obvious that these are nothing but daydreams. But he also perceives that what Björn longs and strives for is in reality worth striving for.

The words of his wife are full of the disappointment and resentment of an entire lifetime: You'll soon discover, Kári, that what my husband says is nothing but foolishness and worthless boasting. Enough of all of this empty bombast. But I will see to it that you are provided with food.

We must take it for granted that Björn's wife knows her husband better than the reader does. He seems to be damned from the first to comic exposure and disgrace, to use Ker's expression, and his wife is certain that his immovable optimism will accomplish nothing except to hasten this disgraceful fate.

Kári asks Björn to accompany him eastward into Flosi's district. Björn has certainly accomplished similar feats in his imagination, and so he has no great concern about this undertaking. Danger is both uncertain and distant, as it usually is in his daydreams. "This is a very dangerous expedition, and very few people would have the courage to undertake it except you and me." He has rather quickly compared his courage with Kári's, and found that they are equally good. But then his wife intervenes with her ingrown mistrust: "If you fail Kári, you had better know that you will never share my bed again, and my kinsmen will bring about a division of our property between us." Björn replies with his customary optimism and mildness, and yet he is alarmed at his wife's threat: "It is more likely, housewife, that other grounds than that will be needed for our divorce, for I shall bear witness on my behalf to what a warrior and hero I am in fighting with weapons."

Almost before he is aware of it Björn is on a journey with Kári which *is* a dangerous venture, and from which it is not so easy to turn back. Bur Kári encourages him with constant good-natured teasing.

To be sure, at times Björn's fleetness, his rabbitlike nature, attempts to carry him away from the field of battle, but circumstances are merciful. They show him that the disadvantages of flight are so great that it is better to remain and be a hero. Let us follow his train of thought at Kringlumýri:

Kári has been asleep, and Björn wakes him. "You are certainly in great need of me. Anyone less brave than I am would already have deserted you, for your enemies are riding toward you—and you had better get ready." Kári lets Björn decide whether to stand behind him or to ride away. Björn: "I don't want to do that, and for several reasons. First of all, malicious tongues might say that I deserted you for lack of courage if I ride away. Secondly, I know what a fine catch they would regard me, and two or three of them would ride after me, and then I would be of no use or help to you. I prefer to stand by you and defend myself as long as it is granted me."

However we may judge his motives, Björn chooses to fight—under the protection of Kári, to be sure, but fight he does. He risks his life—not in his imagination, as he usually does, but really and truly. He transforms a part of his daydreams into reality, and to that extent he becomes greater.

No one could help knowing that Björn's ideas about his own heroism were false. But now the reader sees that the housemistress at Mörk had also had a false image of him. Fate offered Björn the opportunity to realize a tiny fragment of his dreams, to grow a little bit in the direction of his ideals.

It is not insignificant to note how refined and appropriate to its purpose the irony is in this episode. This is an indication of culture. No "barbarians" write like that. And there is here an additional element which is a true innovation. It is easy to find a Þorkell hákur in Greek and Roman comedy: his name is *miles gloriosus*. But a Björn of Mörk is not to be found there. The story of Þorkell hákur deals with a man who imagines he is something other than what he really is, and who thereby makes himself ludicrous. In the story of Björn the author's heart is on the side of the very person he ridicules. Björn too is a man who believes that he is something he is not; he too is a ridiculous figure at the beginning of the story—but he ends by attaining at least a part of what he imagines himself to be, and he deserves to do so. He grows. The mockery directed at him is imbued with deep sympathy.

Considerably older than *Njála* is *Hreiðars þáttur heimska* ("The Tale of Hreiður the Foolish"), and this story may well be the first in which such sympathetic irony is a basic element. But *Njála* is devoid of all the glibness of tongue, the grotesqueness, and the drollery which characterize the *þáttur*. The narrative is quite clear, the irony pure and transparent. But the sympathy is the same. We catch a glimpse of it also in other works, but with the decline of saga literature it disappears again. Later it again emerges elsewhere, and in *Don Quixote* it becomes predominant and has been regarded ever since as one of the most noteworthy innovations in the literary history of the Western World.

Anatole France once said: Sympathy is the true basis of genius. Perhaps so. At any rate it plays a very great role therein.

4. Character Portrayal

The Danish literary critic Paul V. Rubow has estimated that *Njáls saga* contains twenty-five carefully and skillfully executed character portraits.[1] That is a considerable number, and yet it is somewhat too low rather than too high. In addition to these full-length portraits, there are sketches of at least a dozen men and women which are as distinctive as the main characters of many another saga that does not approach the richness of *Njála* in this respect. And finally we meet a host of individuals who appear briefly, some of them only once or twice, but who leave a distinct image on the mind of the reader. Even more impressive than the number of characters, however, is the consummate skill and profound understanding with which they are portrayed. In some cases the author shows us a picture of the external appearance of his characters; in all cases he affords us a description of their internal nature, of their mental disposition and temperament. To be sure, we may sometimes have questions regarding the true motives of the characters when under strong emotional stress. As examples we might mention Gunnar's fatal decision to defy the law and return home instead of going into exile (chapter 75), or Flosi's sudden change of heart following the slaying of Höskuldur Hvítanessgoði (chapter 123). It is also difficult to understand Skarphéðinn completely. But in all these cases we will arrive at a satisfactory understanding if we read the saga thoughtfully and with an open mind. In so doing we must be careful not to jump to conclusions regarding any of the characters on

1. *Smaa kritiske Breve*, Copenhagen, 1936, p. 30.

the basis of the first impression or of a single episode. It is necessary to keep in mind everything a character says and does, without subtracting anything from or adding anything to the author's account. And it goes without saying that we must not indulge in speculation regarding the historical reliability of this or that scene or character.

Not a few scholars have been so led astray by their search for historical truth in the saga that they quite failed to see the characters as the author depicted them. Some critics have been unable to resist the evidence and influence of other sources, which cast a false and confusing light on the characters of *Njáls saga*, with the result that the account in *Njála* was often not fully understood and appreciated. Others have tried to fill in what they felt to be missing features of some of the character portraits. Still others became so impressed with or engrossed in this or that incident that they arrived at distorted, fragmentary views of certain characters which are substantially different from the composite pictures that are revealed by a careful consideration of their total role in the saga. In *Njáls saga* especially it is essential to see the characters in their totality. All of the widely scattered and seemingly contradictory words and deeds of a given character must be brought together; each must be examined in the light of the others in order, if possible, to find the common denominator. Only when the critic has exhausted every effort in this direction is he justified in trying to assess the degree of success achieved by the author in his character portrayals. We must not forget that what sometimes seem to the casual reader to be artistic flaws and inconsistencies in the character portraits can well be the author's intentional revelation of disharmonies and incongruities in the complex natures of the characters themselves.

And finally, we must constantly remind ourselves that all attempts to "rehabilitate" or plead the cause of a particular character in the saga are futile. All we can (and must) do is to make an honest effort to see and understand the author's characters as he portrayed them. The only question we are permitted to ask is: Are the character portraits artistically good or faulty? If the characters are well drawn, we must accept them as they are, whether or not we are pleased with these pictures of our saga heroes.

II

The first question which arises when we begin the review of the host of characters in *Njála* is this: Which characters emerge from this "shadow army" sufficiently to assume distinct individuality and the appearance of real living beings? To be sure, it is not difficult to find certain types among them or to divide them into groups on the basis of common characteristics; and yet, when compared with each other, each one is found to have his own individual stamp.

Although a spiritual affinity exists between an author and his characters, he has to maintain a certain degree of artistic objectivity and impartiality toward them. Thus in a sense he exists both inside and outside of his characters. This affinity tends to bring the character closer, and if it is very strong and personal, there is a danger that the characters may get out of focus and become blurred. On the other hand, if the author's objectivity and impartiality predominate, his characters recede into the distance and his sympathy may be transformed into cold, heartless comprehension or at best into uncertainty or ambivalence. In some authors, both sympathy and comprehension yield to feelings of aversion and animosity, and under the undue influence of such feelings they may create characters not unlike the stock villains in modern detective thrillers.

The author of *Njála* is not entirely free of such bias; his sympathies are rather unevenly distributed among his many children. But we must not blame him for this until we have considered the possible causes or reasons for his partiality. The division of characters in *King Lear* into "good guys" and "bad guys" is no less striking; there too we find men of the most noble qualities beside monsters in human form.

Actually, the author of *Njála* has been seriously criticized for his one-sided character depiction in connection with only four persons in the saga: on the one hand there is Hallgerður, who is treated rather harshly, and on the other hand, there are the three shining heroes,

Gunnar of Hlíðarendi, Kári Sölmundarson, and Höskuldur Hvítaness-goði. Hallgerður will be discussed at some length in the next chapter; the other three characters will be reviewed briefly here.

As early as 1700, or perhaps even earlier, we find Icelandic poets expressing mixed feelings toward Hallgerður and Gunnar. Aside from this, the Norwegian novelist and critic Hans E. Kinck was probably the first to assail the portrait of Gunnar as we find it in *Njáls saga*. It seems clear that this picture of Gunnar got under his skin. And Sigurður Guðmundsson, who sought in his thoughtful, penetrating treatise in *Skírnir* to trace the history of this saga hero and the development of the Gunnar legend, goes so far as to say that the author's fondness for his warrior-hero vitiated the saga. At the same time, Sigurður is able to appreciate the ethical refinement of the character portrait and the high esteem it has enjoyed for this reason. And I suspect that the view is quite generally held that the strong romantic radiance which has fallen on Gunnar has distorted the human dimensions of his image to a greater or lesser degree.[2]

I am afraid that such views have been strengthened by the suspicion that not everything which is related about Gunnar is historically correct, and that his portrait and personality bear the stamp of a later age. But as we have already noted, historical inaccuracies are of importance

2. Gunnar has been the subject of such a vast amount of critical and speculative writing that it would not be feasible to attempt an exhaustive listing of titles here. A treatise on Gunnar was written by Friðrik Bergmann (*Vafurlogar*, Winnipeg, 1906). A. Ritterhouse discusses him briefly in *Altnordische Frauen*, 1917, p. 176. Especially important are Hans E. Kinck, "Et par ting om ættesagaen," *Festskrift til Gerhard Gran*, 1916, pp. 32 ff. (reprinted in *Mange slags kunst*, 1921, pp. 1 ff.); and Sigurður Guðmundsson, "Gunnar á Hlíðarenda," *Skírnir* XCII (1918), 63–88, 221–51. These two papers are critically discussed in *Um Njálu*, section 37. A new interpretation of Gunnar's reason for returning home in defiance of the sentence of banishment is advanced by Hallvard Lie, *Studier i Heimskringlas stil*, 1937, p. 15, and a quite different explanation is set forth by Rolf Pipping in "Et dubbeltydigt omen," *Budkavlen* XV (1936), 80–82. Both Lie and Pipping attempt to go beyond the saga, but I think the account of the saga is sufficient. See also Sven B. F. Jansson, *Sagorna om Vinland*, Vol. I, 1944, p. 130, and Dag Strömbäck, *Tidrande och diserna*, 1949, p. 40.

only if they are detrimental to the verisimilitude of the literary work. And such suspicions regarding historical inaccuracies in the portrayal of a character have nothing to do with the aesthetic enjoyment of a work of literature. Even if the anachronisms or the transgressions against the spirit of the times are obvious, narrative and character depiction can be so excellent that the historical inaccuracies fade into the background. Who would dream of making a fuss about the fact that *Antony and Cleopatra* bears little resemblance to the Egypt of the Ptolemys? All that matters is the excellence of the character portraits themselves. Of course the portrait of Gunnar is not realistic, but realism is not the only form of art. It is also artistic to be able to expand the dimensions of a man in a poetic manner. This character portrait is enveloped by an idealistic, romantic radiance—but let us not forget that this contributes to the poetic beauty of the picture. Gunnar is endowed with those characteristics which, because of the nature of his role in the story, he must not lack; and what is even more important, his portrait still bears the stamp of a real human being, the appearance of a living man, despite the romantic radiance surrounding it. And above all, Gunnar's portrait possesses a unique and unmistakable individuality. The more I study this portrait, the more deeply impressed I become with its gentleness, as it emerges from the narrative, and with the author's interpretation of Gunnar's sensitivity and self-control, of his competitive spirit and conscientiousness, and of the fine nuances of these traits of character. Gunnar of Hlíðarendi is the most modern of all the characters of the saga. He is what we might call a man of the nineteenth century. Is it not strange that so many people today find it difficult to recognize and accept him for what he is?

The depiction of Kári, on the other hand, seems to me to have suffered much more from romantic influence. This character portrait lacks richness. And yet even here we are sometimes surprised to discover unsuspected traits, such as his ironic sense of humor. But if we read the story in its entirety, we can see that the author had good reasons for depicting Kári as he did. We shall return to this problem later on.

Höskuldur Hvítanessgoði is a character I should not like to have
missing from the saga. Many persons object to this character portrayal
because, they maintain, no one like that could have lived in Iceland
during the eleventh century. In this they are probably correct, although
it is difficult to measure the remarkably strong influence of new currents
such as Christianity on certain individuals, especially when these spiritual currents are just beginning to become effective. But men like
Höskuldur certainly did exist in Iceland during the thirteenth century—
not many, to be sure, but some. From the point of view of our own
day this character portrait seems unrealistic and unnatural; indeed, it
seems almost incredible. But all of this tells us nothing about its authen-
ticity. Truth is often stranger than fiction, and real events sometimes
impress us as improbable when utilized in fiction. For the thread of the
story the figure of Höskuldur is essential. Without it, the tragedy in
the life of Njáll and Skarphéðinn would not be nearly so profound and
dreadful as it is. And finally, there is great poetic beauty in this character
portrait.

III

Because they contrast so markedly with the remaining twenty-two
major characters, these three portraits add to the broad diversity of the
saga. Character portrayals in which the colors are more blended, and
in which the author's curiosity and his sympathy with his characters are
in balance, are less strongly molded and colored by his idealism. "Paint
me as I am," said Cromwell, "wart and all." These words must not,
of course, be taken at face value, for the photograph is scarcely the
highest form of art. But properly understood, they possess a certain
validity: a picture should reveal and not conceal the characteristic
features of the subject. Even the wart is worth including insofar as it
can be given some artistic significance and if it does not conflict with
the nature and purpose of the work. A good example of this is the
beardlessness of Njáll—an apparently trifling detail, which nevertheless
plays an important role in the story. Another example is the paleness

of Skarphéðin's face. Similarly, small incidents can be filled with great meaning, as for instance the description of Þórhallur Ásgrímsson when he learned of the burning of Njáll: His body became swollen; a stream of blood gushed from both ears and could not be checked. He fell down unconscious, and then the bleeding stopped. His deep grief and desire for revenge are revealed (and find momentary release) in this manner, and these feelings also, it seems, later on cause his foot ailment, which cannot be cured until he is on the field of battle.

In *Njáls saga* Verðandi prevails.[3] Events approach, pass by, and continue on their swift, unrelenting course. Willingly or unwillingly men become involved and are swept along. Sometimes the stream of events lifts them up toward the light and the sun, and sometimes it drags them down into the depths. It brings them happiness which is never completely exhausted, and inflicts wounds which never heal. Most of the people in the saga are consistent within themselves; their basic character does not change under the stress and strain of life, but merely responds to challenge. But sometimes the onslaughts of life have a permanent affect on the mental and emotional life of individuals; their basic character is not altered, but the course of their inner life is changed. The most remarkable examples of such character development are Hallgerð- ur and Njáll.

This process of genesis and evolution is not simple; it is not merely a matter of stimulus and response. Events are brought about by many causes. The provocations and motives which impel a man to perform a single deed are usually many and varied. Events are brought forth through the combined force of a whole complex of external and internal causes. And it must not be forgotten that frequently these motives and stimuli occurred over a considerable span of time. Often new irritations aggravate old, encapsulated, half-forgotten wounds. And no form of hatred is more certain to erupt into violence than when old, repressed, smoldering resentments are inflamed by new provocations.

3. On the concept of *Verðandi* see chapter 8, footnote 5.

In the story of Gunnar we see a great warrior and hero who is more reluctant than others to kill, a man who is not easily provoked to fight, but who is most formidable when he cannot escape doing so. The heart of such a man is moved by many feelings and emotions which no one else is aware of. Finally all these precipitate the critical decision of his life: contrary to all expectations and driven by a powerful impulse, he defies the sentence of banishment imposed upon him by the General Assembly. He refuses to depart from his beautiful farm even though this should cost him his life. The reason may be that he has grown weary of living, but another passage in the story suggests that he is unwilling to capitulate to his enemies.[4]

In the story of Flosi following the slaying of Höskuldur Hvítanessgoði we can discern a mind in conflict with itself. We can sense the storm which rages there as Flosi rides away from his farm, Vorsabær, to attend the Assembly; later all signs seem to point toward a peaceful reconciliation. But then mere trifles suffice to rekindle the smoldering anger so that it gains the upper hand.[5] At still another place in the saga we see a Norwegian who knows that death awaits him if he settles in Iceland; yet he does so, even though he certainly does not want to die. We see Eyjólfur Bölverksson, who becomes Flosi's chief advocate at the trial following the burning of Njáll. He well knows that it will seal his own doom, and yet Flosi's golden arm ring and harsh demands are more persuasive than this certain knowledge. These men act as though under a spell which has deprived them of their normal manner of behavior. The author of *Njáls saga* doubtless knew stories of spells and enchantments which robbed men of their will power or drove them into actions which were contrary to their nature. But he no doubt had also seen and experienced such inconsistencies and incongruities in human thought and behavior. *Njáls saga* is very much concerned with the role of the will in human life.

4. See *Um Njálu*, pp. 209 ff.
5. See *Um Njálu*, pp. 133 ff. Somewhat similar is the story of Ingjaldur of Keldur (chapters 124 and 130), but in his case the inner struggle is less evident.

As in *Njáls saga*, psychological struggle and emotional conflict are very much in evidence in the dramas of Racine and Corneille. But here everything is out in the open. The audience sees and hears everything on the stage; the characters do not hesitate to express themselves freely. In *Njála*, too, many individual incidents and utterances bear unmistakable and memorable witness to the inner struggle of the characters. But the reader is not given a constant insight into their minds and hearts; rather, he is given brief views or glimpses of what is going on there. And what he perceives is not a logical debate, but a blind storm of passion. It sometimes seems to the reader as if he were gazing into the twilight, where half or fully concealed forces and unknown motives are at work no less than those which are fully apparent. Sometimes he may doubt that this or that person really understands himself. Modern psychology has helped us to gain a deeper comprehension of such matters through a better understanding of the subconscious and of other related factors. And writers today have learned much from psychology. But the author of *Njála* had to depend entirely on his own observations and insights and on his artistic instinct.

All of this tends to make it more difficult for the reader to understand many of the saga characters. To be sure, all of the characters are drawn with clear and distinct lines, and each portrait possesses an inner consistency. But a relatively large number of these men and women are of a complex and puzzling nature, and a great deal is said about them in the saga. It is quite obvious that the author was strongly attracted to them, and that he put forth every effort to portray them. His people are not like the characters of Sophocles or Menander, but Hallgerður and Lady Macbeth would have had a great deal to talk about, even though their fates and passions were not the same. But that is a long story, and I cannot attempt to tell it here.[6]

6. On this see Einar Ól. Sveinsson, "Tvær kvenlýsingar," *Helgafell* II (1943), 16–31, reprinted under the title "Klýtæmestra og Hallgerður" in *Við uppspretturnar*, Reykjavík, 1956, pp. 91–114.

IV

It may be that people who are used to the psychological analyses of modern literature will find some of the preceding statements strange or surprising. They may regard the comments in the saga about the motives, feelings, and thoughts of the characters somewhat meager. And at first they may think that what has already been said here about the character portraits in *Njála* is overstated or exaggerated.

It is true enough that the psychological analyses in *Njála* are few and modest in extent. The thoughts and feelings of the characters are not dissected before the reader. To be sure, the reader is now and then given a glimpse into the mind and heart of a character, but this is something quite different from the modern stream of consciousness technique. The statements about the characters of *Njáls saga* constitute portraits in the literal sense of the word. The author wishes to portray his people as they are, as living entities in all the struggles and vicissitudes of life. The inner character, the internal nature of the people, is the nucleus, of course, for it is from this internal nature of a man that the forces derive which exert an influence on the outer world, on other individuals and events.

As is customary in the Icelandic sagas of national heroes, the author gives us a preliminary description of his characters when he introduces them into his story. Farther along in the saga, at the most suitable places, he lets us know something about their thoughts and feelings. But these revelations never turn into psychological analyses. For the most part, the people are depicted from the outside. We know what they are from the way they appear, from what they do and say, and from what others say about them. Frequently the basic characteristics of an individual are revealed through his dealings with others. In this method of relative or indirect character delineation the author of *Njáls saga* has achieved a degree of skill that may be called consummate. One minor incident can suffice to characterize many persons. This is a narrative technique which the author of *Njála* learned from earlier masters of the art of saga writing. It is a technique which reminds us somewhat of modern stage plays, especially those in which the characters are not permitted to indulge in lyric effusion and introspective monologues. The techniques of the saga writer are narrowly circumscribed by convention. But once a writer has mastered these techniques, he can achieve considerable success in depicting the inner motives of even the most complex and puzzling characters. Psychological analysis tends to encroach upon artistic convention, and artistic convention threatens to dull analysis. When the artist succeeds in reconciling the demands of both, he may be destined to create a literary work of exceptional merit.

V

I tried to indicate in the preceding chapter the magnitude of *Njála*, which is revealed in the diversity of its subject matter and its profusion of events, and to show how all of this is given life and movement and visible form by the author. The same qualities are to be found in the saga's galaxy of character portraits.

Let us first look at the wide range of people portrayed. We see here men and women from all walks of life and from all social classes. We find a host of aristocrats with the rank of *goði*, and yet each one is different from the rest: Höskuldur Dala-Kollson, Mörður gígja, Mörður Valgarðsson, Gizur hvíti, Hjalti Skeggjason, Skafti Þórodds-son, Snorri goði, Flosi, Hallur of Síða, Guðmundur ríki, and many more. There is no sharp line of demarcation drawn between these *goðar* on the one hand and chieftains without authority and farmers on the other hand, and this includes both prosperous landowners and farmers of more modest means. In addition there are household servants, sheepherders and farmhands, freedmen and thralls. With this last group, the character depictions tend to be somewhat sketchier, drawn with a few, but usually clear, strokes; and Þórður leysingjason (the agnomen means "son of a freed thrall") and the farmhand Atli stand out clearly as individuals. There are also a number of Norwegians, most of them rather indifferent. Of the landlopers, the most memorable is Kaupa-Héðinn, whose coarse picture the author drew with genuine relish. And finally, there are bands of vagrants and beggars, a nameless mass, from which no individuals emerge. But even so, these masses are teeming with life and activity. The spread in age among the characters is equally large. At Bergþórshvoll lives the ancient crone Sæunn, half senile and yet prescient; her intriguing portrait is drawn with sadness blended with humor. At the other extreme is the boy Þórður, the son of Kári, who refuses to leave his grandmother in the burning house. As in the Icelandic sagas generally, however, the majority of the characters are adults, neither very young nor very old.

I shall not attempt to give a survey here of the traits of character of all the distinctive persons in the saga, but I cannot refrain from pointing out that to a certain degree these persons can be divided into groups according to their attitudes toward life and other qualities without in any way detracting from their unique individuality. I have already alluded to the fact that artistically portrayed characters of earlier poetic works can become models for later writers, and that large numbers of individuals are thus created who bear a certain family resemblance to each other. Thus Njáll has certain features in common with Óðinn, while Skarphéðinn belongs to the group I called the dark-haired heroes, and Gunnar and Helgi and several others can be classified among the blond champions. Gunnar and Kári are colored by a certain romantic light, and thus they have much in common with some of the splendid warriors of *Laxdæla*, although the colors in *Njála* are more subdued. But there are other attributes too which differentiate the characters and character portraits in *Njála*. First of all there is a striking difference between the men of thought and the men of action (and there is an exceptionally large number of sages and wise men: Hrútur, Mörður gígja, Skafti Þóroddsson, Mörður Valgarðsson, Snorri goði, Hallur of Síða, Þórhallur Ásgrímsson, Eyjólfur Bölverksson, and above all Njáll himself). Equally obvious is another division: that between men and women who possess will power and who discipline themselves in accordance with their ethical views, and those who lack moral scruples and restraints. All of the evil-doers belong to the latter group. It must be clear to all who have given the matter serious thought that to the author of *Njáls saga* this distinction is of the utmost importance in the life of man.

I shall mention two additional groups or types of characters, of lesser importance, and yet not unworthy of note. Several persons are endowed with the faculty of self-criticism and the ability to express this criticism in a mocking or ironic manner. Skarphéðinn possesses this ability, as do Atli and Hrappur also—both of whom quite candidly characterize themselves as rascals.[7] Njáll too is able to scoff at himself: when he lies down to await death in his flaming house, it is with the comment that he has long had the reputation of being fond of ease.

And finally, at two points in the story the conflict between wishful thinking and reality is the focal point of character portrayal. In the case of Björn of Mörk this is quite obvious, but the conflict also provides the key for an understanding of Skammkell. Regarded from this point of view, his thoughts and desires are clearly revealed to us. It is interesting to note that men who are basically so unlike each other as Skammkell and Björn share the qualities of self-adulation and braggadocio. Their similarity in this respect is underscored by their use of similar words in similar situations. On one occasion Skammkell says to his friend Otkell (chapter 49): "I shall go out with you, for we have to be clever about this. I want to be nearest to you when your need is greatest." The conversation between Kári and Björn runs as follows (chapter 151): "What plan shall we adopt now? I want to see how clever you are," said Kári. Björn replied, "Do you think it important for us to be clever?" "Yes, indeed," said Kári. "Then you will discover," said Björn, "that I am not lacking in cleverness any more than in hardihood." These words of Björn shed light on the character of Skammkell.

VI

With such a large number of character portraits in a single work, an author runs the risk of having them turn into a sort of chaotic picture

7. Their striking self-characterizations are found in chapters 37, 59, and 87 of the saga.

gallery. But the author of *Njáls saga* avoids this danger through his skill in arrangement and composition. A clear distinction is made between leading and secondary characters, and the saga naturally tells us more about the former than the latter. The figure of Njáll towers above all other people in the saga, but he shares the stage with Gunnar in the first part and with Skarphéðinn, Hallgerður, Bergþóra, and Mörður in the second part of the trilogy. In the final part of the story Kári and Flosi share the interest of the reader between them. The other characters come and go depending on the role they have to play in a given scene. We might say that the spotlight is constantly focused on the main characters, but only occasionally and momentarily on the minor ones. Quite often two characters are seen side by side, such as Hrútur and Höskuldur, or Njáll and Gunnar, and then one of them is usually a man of wisdom while the other is a man of action. Or else we find two warriors together, such as Gunnar and Kolskeggur, or Skarphéðinn and his brothers (both of whom together have the role of one man, in accordance with Olrik's "law of twins"). In such cases one of the two warriors has the center of the stage while the other serves as a sort of foil by means of which the dominant member of the pair is more fully characterized. From time to time, however, the spotlight also falls on the lesser character, so that we likewise get a good idea of his character. An example of this is Helgi Njálsson, who stands in the shadow of his brother Skarphéðinn during the greater part of the story. But when Helgi makes his voyage abroad, he occupies the center of the stage, and the reader almost has the feeling that he sees in him a rejuvenated Njáll. The portrait of Helgi which we are shown in this episode is both pleasing and fascinating.

Often little is required to delineate the secondary characters. One person wakes the other by arousing his sympathy or antipathy, and from this interplay both come to life. Thus dead names momentarily assume the features of living beings, and in turn quicken others, until the entire shadow host of *Njáls saga* has come to life. Each time they return to the stage, the supporting characters are made to reveal more about themselves until their portraits are complete.

From what has been said, it might seem that these characters are like pampered children, who simply accept everything which is given to them, and that the author can do with them as he pleases. But this, strangely enough, is not the case. Every significant work of art maintains a mysterious independence in relationship to its creator. It develops from its nucleus in accordance with laws which are difficult for the artist to master or to change. And so it happens that the author of *Njáls saga* becomes entranced and enchanted by his children, and they run away with him. We see in *Njála* how some of the secondary characters acquire intriguing peculiarities or become involved in striking incidents which arouse our interest in them and increase their power of attraction over us. Svanur of Svanshóll is not merely wicked; he also possesses magic powers, which cast a strange supernatural aura over him. In the picture of Earl Hákon we find the gift of second sight added to the sympathy and antipathy of the kings' sagas, and this added feature renews and retouches the entire portrait. Almost everything that is said about Þórhallur Ásgrímsson is intended to make him memorable and unique; no one reacts so strangely to the death of Njáll as he does.

Some of the minor characters are even more demanding of the author and the reader than these. Hrappur was intended, of course, to become an outlaw in Norway, and the composition and economy of the story require that this incident be related rather briefly. But the author soon becomes so intrigued with this villainous creature of his that he devotes two precious chapters to him. Björn of Mörk was supposed to add a light touch to the saga, which needs comedy at that point. At first the author is a bit hard on Björn, but he soon takes a fancy to him; by the time he finishes this episode, he has created a masterpiece of character portrayal. It is not at all unusual for great artists to lose control over their creations; a good example is Shylock the Jew, who strives with might and main and overwhelms the comedy about the merchant of Venice.

VII

The author of *Njála* is a great idealist. Like Boileau, he would call a cat a cat and Rollet a villain. But the phenomena of human life can have a strong attraction for him, the repulsive ones no less than the pleasing ones. Some of the most remarkable character portraits in the saga show this balance. If the author's sympathy for his characters is sometimes not very strong, his curiosity and desire to see and understand are so much the stronger.

Good examples of this are the four chief villains of the saga: Þjóstólfur, Hrappur, Skammkell, and Mörður. All are branded with the same mark: they lack moral checks and restraints, and live according to the view that they have a right to do as they please. Idealists around the turn of the century had a distrust of these character portraits, but nowadays at least we know that such people do exist. Except for this one common characteristic, however, these villains are quite unique.

Hrappur and Þjóstólfur are both homeless, unruly fellows who never hesitate to resort to violence if they feel that someone has stepped on their toes. Hrappur is an adventurous fellow, ingratiating or impudent as the situation demands, mealy-mouthed or loudmouthed, eager to seize every opportunity for pleasure—a ladies' man who thinks only of the passing moment. He does not hesitate to indulge every sensual desire, and for this reason he is constantly on the run, trying to escape the consequences. There is nothing to indicate that he is not content with this sort of life, and he is shrewd and slippery as an eel when it comes to wriggling out of just punishment. He is shameless, impious (he is the only atheist in the whole story), and malicious, and he dies with words of scorn about himself on his lips.

Whereas Hrappur can be smooth and polished, Þjóstólfur is always coarse and bristling. He is a turbulent fellow who can't avoid clashing with people wherever he happens to be. He is endowed with a certain primitive loyalty, and this loyalty together with a fear of several men are the only things which keep him somewhat in check. He does not hesitate to swing his huge, heavy-shafted ax, and he too is in the habit

of indulging every impulse. But there is one desire that cannot be fulfilled. As the poet Grímur Thomsen expressed it:

> Hallgerðar hann engum unni,
> og eigi mátti hann sjálfur njóta;
> þeir, sem ástir hennar hljóta,
> hans fá koss af öxarmunni.

("Hallgerð's love he granted no one, and he himself could not win her favor;
those who did gain her love received the kiss of his ax.")[8]

This deed of jealousy, his killing of Glúmur, does not bring him the
fulfillment of his wishes. His slaying of Hallgerð's two husbands does
not gain him her favor. The deeds of this man of action are the useless
and worthless outlets for his desires, and their very senselessness destroys
him inwardly. Hrút's sword stroke comes none too soon.

Skammkell is not the most imposing rascal in the story, but his
description is certainly not the least remarkable. He is somewhat harder
to understand than the first two. Skammkell is dishonest and malicious,
and constantly tries to harm others even though he himself does not
gain anything (or even hope to gain anything) by it. And yet he has
little in common with the conventional villains of popular mystery
novels or romantic tales who bear little resemblance to living human
beings and who do evil for no apparent reason. Skammkel's evil deeds
have valid motives. Let us take a look at the saga.

In chapter 49 Gunnar comes to the farm Kirkjubær to offer Otkell
compensation for Hallgerð's theft. Skammkell is already there, and
when Otkell and his men go out, Skammkell says the following words,
which have already been quoted in part: "I shall go out with you, for
we have to be clever about this. I want to be nearest to you when your
need is greatest as it now is. I advise you to act important." First of
all, we must consider the sliminess in these words of Skammkell about
his trustworthiness and his desire to help. His words are those of a
hypocrite, and here, as so often is the case with hypocrites, we find truth

8. Grímur Thomsen, *Ljóðmæli*, 1906, p. 91.

blended with falsehood. Skammkell wants Gunnar's visit to Kirkjubær
to turn out badly; indeed, he wishes him every possible kind of disgrace—if for no other reason·than that Gunnar enjoys great fame and
popularity. At first blush this may seem to be a strange explanation,
and yet envy is reason enough for ill will—at any rate in real life, if not
in fiction. Skammkell pretends to be Otkel's friend, and in the end they
are actually both killed together; yet he never is concerned about
protecting Otkell from danger as a friend would do—at least once in
a while. And this fact is significant, for it suggests that there are other
concerns which are of greater importance to Skammkell than the good
fortune and happiness of Otkell.

The similarity which we have already observed between the words
of Skammkell and those of Björn of Mörk afford us a glimpse into the
hidden recesses of Skammkel's mind. As strange as it may seem at first
glance, his manner of thinking is not completely unrelated to that of
Björn. He is a sullen daydreamer. He dresses up reality with lies and
wishful thinking, but he lacks Björn's kindness and nobleness of heart
and harmless boasting. He jumps at every opportunity to attempt to
make his desires come true; in so doing he confuses reality with his
own lies, and this makes him a most dangerous man.

Skammkell dreams of men who are independent and defiant, men
from whom the most famous warriors seek help but receive nothing
but haughty repudiation, men who make a litigant offer them every
possible redress and then subject him to humiliation and send him away
with nothing accomplished. The men Skammkell identifies himself
with in his daydreams are hard-bitten and proud. They thunder out a
scornful summons to their enemies to appear at the General Assembly
for trial, ride them down and bloody them with their spurs, and laugh
at them as they go racing off. These men are killers, proud, unrelenting,
and cruel—chieftains with great authority who terrorize people through
their overwhelming power.[9]

9. One is reminded of the line in *Midsummer Night's Dream* (I.ii): "My chief
humour is for a tyrant."

Skammkell himself is only an average man, if that. He has no out-standing qualities of excellence. He is despised and disdained—and that is the source of his cruelty and vengefulness. Far from being a warrior, he is actually a coward, as one can see best from the fact that he takes to his bed ill at the General Assembly at the very time Otkel's suit for theft against Gunnar is on the agenda. By contrast, he is quite cocky during the journey to summon Gunnar, and when Otkell rides Gunnar down and wounds him with his spurs, he is transported with delight, for his daydreams are being fulfilled. He is so beside himself that the thought of danger does not cross his mind.

Skammkell himself is neither a champion nor a chieftain. But he has Otkell, and through his friendship for Otkell he can experience vicari-ously the pleasure of being a hero and a chieftain. To be sure, this has its drawbacks. It is possible for Otkell to flex his muscles because of his relationship to the people of Mosfell, but in reality he often has to be prodded into action. Otkell is not averse to peace and reconciliation, and at such times Skammkell has to intervene as best he can. He mus-ters all of his shrewdness and shamelessness to convince Otkell of the defects of Gunnar's offers of redress, and in the end he succeeds in bringing Gunnar's attempted settlement to naught. Through his visit to Mosfell, Skammkell is able to compel matters to go as he wishes. Upon returning he lies unblushingly and with great enthusiasm: "There is no need to speak softly about this case. . . . They also thought it of the greatest importance that you behaved so boldly. . . ."

Skammkell is terribly eager for something big and exciting to happen —quarrels, summonses to appear in court, killings. He is quite en-chanted by such matters. And when reality threatens to grow dull, Skammkell is prepared to brighten it up with his untruths. Mörður Valgardsson, the other liar in the story, can always distinguish between truth and fiction, but I am not sure that this is the case with Skammkell. Dishonesty has penetrated to the very heart of this perverse daydreamer.

Unlike Skammkell, Mörður generally does not meddle in other people's affairs, but he too sometimes has to be prodded into action.

He is a clever man, skillful at maneuvering on the chessboard of life. For him the end justifies the means, and he has no compunctions about cold-bloodedly destroying his enemies, the innocent as well as the guilty. He can take swift action or bide his time as the occasion demands. He is endowed with a certain magnetic force; everyone is favorably impressed by what he says, and few can resist believing him. He is pleasant to get along with socially. He loves his wife as dearly as his own eyes, and shows concern for her kinsmen. This certainly does not make him a psychological puzzle. The only thing that is difficult to understand about him is the motives for some of his actions, especially for the evil he sows between the sons of Njáll and Höskuldur Hvítanessgoði.

Jóhann Sigurjónsson in his play *Løgneren (The Liar)* explained the slander which Mörður carries back and forth between Höskuldur and the Njálssons on the basis of two motives: the struggle for power and jealousy. But it is like carrying coals to Newcastle to employ two of the strongest passions of the human heart at one and the same time. A double motive tends to have a weakening effect when either one of the two would be quite sufficient. The author of *Njála* employs a different method: he has the past intensify the present. Mörður has harbored a grudge against Njáll ever since he unsuccessfully supported Gunnar's enemies, and he has harbored rancor toward Skarphéðinn ever since Skarphéðinn humiliated him by compelling him to grant self-judgment to Gunnar's son Högni (chapter 79). Additional hatred is engendered through the fact that Höskuldur has begun to draw some of his thingmen away from him to his newly-created *goðorð*.

When his father, Valgarður inn grái, incites Mörður to destroy Höskuldur and the sons of Njáll, he reminds him of the money Skarphéðinn forced him to pay after Gunnar's death (chapter 107). Mörður had twice accepted money in return for his support of Gunnar's enemies, and he freely admitted his avariciousness to Þorgeir Otkelsson (chapter 67: "It is well known that I never refuse money . . ."). And yet it would be absurd to regard his love of money as the basic cause of his enmity toward Gunnar or to assume that he joined Gunnar's enemies out of greed (and that his hatred for Gunnar was secondary to it). The opposite is the truth. Money helped to influence him to take part in these cases, but the underlying motive was his animosity toward Gunnar. This may seem strange at first, but it can easily be shown to be true.

Gunnar had done his kinswoman Unnur, the mother of Mörður, a great favor at the risk of his own life: he had reclaimed from her former husband, Hrútur, her share of their property—a large amount of money, which had made her a very desirable match (chapter 24). When Unnur offered Gunnar a share of the money in payment, he refused to accept it; "but he asserted that he felt he had a greater claim for future support on her and her kinsmen than on anyone else. And Unnur agreed with him." The cruel irony of this is soon revealed.

Now Valgarður grái (chapter 25) makes a proposal of marriage to Unnur, and she marries him "without consulting any of her kinsmen. But Gunnar and Njáll and many others disapproved of this, for he was a malicious and unpopular man." A coolness develops between Unnur and her kinsmen. A feeling of ingratitude turns this coolness into secret animosity. This is a strange and noteworthy situation. No one hates Skarphéðinn with more unrelenting fury than Grani Gunnarsson, the very person whose life he once spared and whose father's slaying he had avenged. Good deeds can lead to ingratitude as well as to gratitude, to hatred as well as to love. And it is not at all certain that the hatred of ingratitude is any quicker to die out than the love of gratitude.

From Valgarður nothing else was to be expected than animosity and resentment toward Gunnar. Gunnar had affronted him by disapproving of his marriage. And Mörður could hardly escape being poisoned by the venomous atmosphere which prevailed in his home as he was growing up. Thus it is scarcely a matter of chance that when he was fully grown, "he treated his kinsmen badly, but Gunnar worst of all." Later (chapter 46) we read that "he bitterly envied Gunnar of Hlíðarendi." Envy is a common emotion, which all human beings know and understand. Although some writers might hesitate to call it by its right name, that is not the case with the author of *Njála*.

VIII

Finnur Jónsson somewhere comments that in *Njáls saga* all human passions have a free rein except the love of man and woman. No one would ever suggest that *Njála* is a love story such as *Laxdæla* or *Gunnlaugs saga* or *Kormaks saga*.[10] And yet it does have something to say about this human relationship.

In *Kormaks saga* the author depicts the development of the love of Kormakur and Steingerður—at first as delicate as the dust on the wings of a butterfly, not unmixed with playful teasing, and then, quite suddenly, powerful and ardent. At one place in *Njála* the author would have had an excellent opportunity to do something similar: during the courtship of Njál's foster son, Höskuldur Þráinsson, when Flosi asks his niece Hildigunnur whether she wishes to accept him as her husband.

> She said she was a proud woman—"and I am not certain that this proposal is advisable for me, since such men are involved—and that all the more so, since this man does not have a *goðorð*. You promised me that you would not marry me to anyone who was not a chieftain."
>
> "That is sufficient reason," said Flosi, "for me to reject the proposal, if you do not wish to marry Höskuldur."
>
> "I didn't say," she replied, "that I don't want to marry Höskuldur if they provide him with a *goðorð*. But otherwise I won't consider it."

Hildigunn's pride is described extremely well, but the affection which is obviously already beginning to awaken between her and Höskuldur does not cast its faint warming light over the scene, nor is there any hint of encouragement or good-natured teasing in her expression as she makes her stipulations. But what could this great narrative artist not have made of this scene if he had been in the mood to do so! I must confess that I do not know whether the resulting portrait of Hildigunnur would have been any better than the cold, aristocratic picture he has created, but it would have been more humanly appealing.

10. For an explanation of the spelling Kormakur instead of Kormákur see Einar Ól. Sveinsson, "Kormakr the Poet and His Verses," *Saga-Book* XVII (1966), p. 19, note 1.

Nor does this saga show the glorious beauty of passion, as we find it revealed in some of the Eddic poems, in *Tristrams saga*, or in *Laxdæla*. The author of *Njála* had the story of Guðrún Ósvífursdóttir, the heroine of *Laxdæla saga*, in mind when he created the portrait of Hallgerður— but what a difference there is between them.

Passion can blaze with pure, clear flames. We see something of this in the grief of Hildigunnur over the death of Höskuldur. But usually it seems to smolder down deep and flash out through the`dross and slag, a searing fire that consumes and destroys more than it warms and illuminates. One need only think of the affair between Hrútur and Queen Gunnhildur, of the hurtful relationship between Hrútur and Unnur, or of the misfortune which resulted from the three marriages of Hallgerður, to cite but a few examples. At first blush we might feel inclined to attribute this to the ascetic spirit of the Middle Ages, which had such a deep-rooted aversion to the "lusts of the flesh." A closer view of the matter, however, shows that this explanation is not satisfactory. Something quite different is involved here, something that goes back to the life experience of the author rather than to the spirit of an age. It is just as though everything were enveloped in the grayness of pessimism, so that this great passion is revealed in its vehemence but not in its colorful beauty and splendor. In this connection I cannot help thinking of another writer who during a certain period of his life seems to have been seized by a similar kind of pessimism. The author of *Hamlet* seems to have been strangely obsessed with the idea of the corruption of the flesh, of defilement and incest, when he wrote about problems of human existence in that work.[11] And I doubt whether more is known about the reasons for his pessimism than for that of the author of *Njála*.

This grayness, which often darkens the colors in *Njáls saga*, is in no way prejudicial to the breadth and diversity of the subject matter.

11. See Caroline F. E. Spurgeon, "Leading Motives in the Imagery of Shakespeare's Tragedies," in G. F. Bradby, *Shakespeare Criticism, 1919–35*, selected with an introduction by Anne Ridler, London: Oxford University Press, 1936, pp. 18–61.

Indeed, matters are discussed here which occur seldom or never in other sagas. A story such as that of the married life of Hallgerður, for example, is not frequently encountered in saga literature. Most saga writers would have made a wide circle around such a problem, which is far more difficult to cope with successfully than, for instance, the story of Helga in fagra in *Gunnlaugs saga*. Episodes such as the affair between Hrútur and Queen Gunnhildur are very infrequent in the *Íslendingasögur* (even though they might not seem so strange to people today), and yet this episode is so essential to the story that the author endows it with sorcery. Scarcely any other saga author would have attempted a story such as that which Unnur tells her father about her experiences with Hrútur, and many a writer of later times would have hesitated to do so.

Njáls saga is a story for men. This is not to suggest that the author did not expect to have women among his audience, but he wrote from a man's point of view, with a man's understanding—and lack of under-standing—of women. It is difficult to say what is gained and what is lost thereby without weighing off one against the other. *Njáls saga* lacks the leniency and sensitivity of *Laxdæla* in regard to women. Although the author of *Njála* was a peace-loving and conciliatory man, the saga mentions only one woman who tries to prevent hostility: that is Hróðný, who dissuades her brother Ingjaldur from joining the attack against Njáll (chapter 124). But there were special reasons for this, and Hróðný made no attempt to dissuade her brother from fighting against the enemies of Njáll. On the contrary, she was actually exposing him to danger by persuading him to withdraw from the plot against Njáll. One of the most effective scenes in the entire story is the one in which Hildigunnur incites her uncle Flosi to avenge the death of her husband. It must be borne in mind that the author himself embraces the concept of honor which gives rise to her taunting words, as do almost all the characters in his story. Thus there is no cause for censuring Hildigunnur on this score.

Here, then, we have an example of how women incite men to vengeance and thus stir up active hostility. We have already pointed out instances in which love for a woman lead to distress and misfortune. Sometimes it seems as though an idea like that of Pandora crossed the author's mind when he wrote about women such as Gunnhildur, Hallgerður, Guðrún náttsól, and Kormlöð. It is strange, therefore, that, with the exception of the two killings by Hallgerð's foster father, Þjóstólfur (chapters 11 and 17), there is no violence in *Njála* caused by the jealousy of two men in love with the same woman.[12]

During the lifetime of Hallgerður there is one period which contrasts markedly with the rest, and that is her marriage to Glúmur. This period is characterized by a warmth and a remarkable candor and a tender congeniality such as occurs only rarely in the story. Something of this feeling is found in the words spoken by Gizur hvíti about the love of Mörður Valgarðsson for his wife (chapter 135), and especially in the union between Njáll and Bergþóra. So powerful can this harmony between husband and wife become that Hallgerður, during her marriage with Glúmur, is able to keep herself under control, and Bergþóra never transgresses a certain limit in her behavior. The most magnificent scene in the saga which is inspired by the love of man and woman and which glorifies their unity of heart and mind is the one in which Bergþóra refuses to leave Njáll in their burning house (chapter 129).

IX

Although some women might feel that the author of *Njáls saga* has treated their sex unfairly, most would probably be pleased at the large number of magnificent and splendid and memorable female characters he has included among his store of character portraits.

Many women are mentioned in the saga, and some of them, of course, are little more than names. This is true of Njál's daughters

12. To be sure, Queen Kormlöð comes to hate her divorced husband, King Brjánn, so fiercely that she urges her son Sigtryggur to kill him, but that is quite different from the violence resulting from the rivalry of two men for the love of the same woman such as we find in *Laxdæla*, to cite just one example.

Helga. and Þorgerður, and of his daughters-in-law Þórhildur and Ástríður of Djúpárbakki, as well as of Bergljót, the kinswoman of Earl Hákon. Somewhat more distinct are the pictures which emerge of the chieftain's daughter, Þórhalla Ásgrímsdóttir; Hildigunnur læknir (the Healer); and Þórhildur skáldkona (the Poetess); and Þorgerður, the daughter of Glúmur and Hallgerður. There are several examples of kindhearted women who were easily beguiled by men, such as Ormhildur, the kinswoman of Gunnar (chapter 71); Guðrún, the daughter of Guðbrandur í Dölum in Norway (chapter 87); and Guðrún náttsól, who had a fondness for foreigners (chapters 61 and 64). Two excellent chapters are devoted to Hróðný, the friend of Njáll and mother of his son Höskuldur; and Valgerður, the mistress of the house at Mörk, is also described vividly and in considerable detail.

Then there are the full-length portraits of the main women characters: Unnur, the daughter of Mörður gígja; Queen Gunnhildur of Norway; Hallgerður; Bergþóra; Hildigunnur; and Kormlöð, the mother of King Sigtryggur of Ireland. All of them are proud and passionate except Unnur, who seems broken in spirit because of her ill-starred marriage to Hrútur. The two queens are mature women, eager to enjoy life and wield power; both of them could have belonged to the life of the Renaissance. There is a certain grandeur about Gunnhildur. In her character we find voluptuousness and love of comfort strangely blended with harshness and cruelty, but the dominant trait in her personality is her insatiable sensual desire. She keeps Hrútur in her castle much as Tannhäuser was kept in the Mountain of Venus. But in time he grows more and more quiet and takes to thinking about returning home, and she begins to suspect that there is another woman in the game. She accuses him of having a sweetheart in Iceland, but he denies it. The thought rankles in her mind, and when they take leave of each other, she puts her arms about his neck and kisses him. Then she puts a curse on Hrút's union with her unknown rival and concludes with these words: "Neither of us has conducted himself well. You did not trust me . . . and I have laid a spell on you." Hrútur laughs and goes away.

Kormlöð is in many ways the opposite of Gunnhildur. She permits her son Sigtryggur to use her as a decoy both for Sigurður, Earl of Orkney, and for the viking Bróðir. She seems to be quite unconcerned about the possible outcome of this crafty scheming, and would quite likely not have been displeased if the two had come to blows on her account. She herself seems to be motivated by no other desires except for power and above all for revenge against her divorced husband, King Brjánn. She was good, the saga says, in all those qualities which were not subject to her will, but utterly wicked in everything which was subject to it.

Let us turn from these two women to two others, who resemble them in certain respects, but who are much more appealing: Hildigunnur and Bergþóra. The initial descriptions of these women are similar. The author tells us that Bergþóra was "a spirited and high-minded woman, but somewhat harsh-natured," and he says that Hildigunnur was "a spirited and very beautiful woman. She was more skillful at needlework than most women. She was very cruel and harsh-natured, but noble when that was called for." The two women have the qualities of spirit, loyalty, and harshness of nature in common, although the harsh nature of Hildigunnur is somewhat more strongly emphasized, and in addition she is called cruel. There is no doubt what the author had in mind here: her desire for revenge for the slaying of Höskuldur, which is not satisfied with the most honorable settlement short of blood vengeance.

Because of her beauty and skill in handicraft, Hildigunnur is a desirable match, just as Unnur was because of her beauty and courteous behavior, and this is scarcely surprising. In the description of Bergþóra, however, there is no mention of beauty, and Hallgerður can tell her to her face without contradiction that she has turtle-back nails on every finger. But everything about Hildigunnur is lovely.

The word "harsh-natured" can have various meanings, but the events of the saga define Hildigunn's character more precisely. When Höskuldur with his companions comes to ask for her hand in marriage, we get to see the pride of a woman who was descended from one of the greatest aristocratic families of Iceland and who was reared in one of the most majestic regions of that beautiful country, remote from the more densely settled areas. She hears a faint murmur from those far-distant places; but her spirit is molded by the magnitude and solitude of nature, and she demands of her suitor that distinction with which only a chieftaincy can endow him. A strange coolness lies over the beginning of their courtship; the loveliness of youth and the awakening fondness for each other are enveloped in a cold veil.

The saga does not deprive Hildigunnur of her loveliness, but reveals her finest qualities. She gets along splendidly with Bergþóra, despite the fact that both of them are strong personalities. The saga shows how her love for Höskuldur somewhat mellows her pride: she wants her husband to move to another district when an estrangement develops between him and the Njálssons in order to prevent more serious trouble, but Höskuldur refuses to do so despite his gentle nature. Later the saga shows her grief for her dead husband, and here her harshness comes to the fore, and her fierceness, which demands vengeance. The author judges this cruelty severely, as though it had gone somewhat too far, but the account of these events is remarkably good, and Hildigunn's emotions are revealed in all their beauty and glory. And even when her passions are most intense, as she taunts her uncle Flosi, she does not lose her aristocratic bearing.[13]

Hildigunnur is mentioned only once more in the story: at the very end she is married to Kári Sölmundarson. Doubtless this was a historical fact, which the author felt he could not dispute or avoid mentioning. But this marriage is not so romantic as other things which the saga relates about her, and the author quite neglects to explain how this proud woman could bring herself to marry one of the slayers of her first husband. It is almost as though the hand that holds the pen has grown weary. And yet it should be pointed out that this event is in no way at variance with the main theme of this part of the story; on the contrary, it is the very focus of it. It was not possible to find more

13. See *Um Njálu*, section 19.

cogent proof of complete reconciliation than the fact that Kári was able to win the hand of Hildigunnur in marriage.

Actually the author undertook a larger and much more difficult task in his portrayal of Bergþóra. From the Christian point of view, to be sure, Hildigunn's desire for revenge is blameworthy; but it is fully in accord with the pagan concept of honor and thus a fitting theme for heroic poetry and prose of all times. Within this frame of reference it does not offend our aesthetic sensibilities. Quite the opposite, however, is the case with Bergþóra, whose portrait reveals blemishes from both the aesthetic and ethical points of view. And yet the author succeeds in convincing the reader that she is the greatest woman character in his story.

He does not endow her with physical beauty, nor with proud lineage or the manifestly noble bearing of Hildigunnur. Rather, she is described as impetuous and revengeful, and she even brings about the death of several persons without regard for possibly dangerous consequences. She can easily be irritated, and "rages," as the saga puts it, when she grows angry. These incidents are generally described with a touch of good-natured irony, and this contributes greatly to the clarity with which her portrait is developed.

There is nothing crafty or cunning about Bergþóra. She is simple and straightforward. Her revengefulness is completely natural and fully in harmony with the pagan mode of thought. She is sensitive to everything that concerns the honor of herself, her husband, her sons, and her household. She does not bear a grudge long, nor is she cruel, judged by the standards of her own day. She is the personification of fidelity, a good mistress of the house, and radiates a vital warmth, so that the servants declare that they would rather perish (if that should be necessary) in the home of Bergþóra and Njáll than anywhere else.

Bergþóra commits a potentially dangerous offense by being harshly discourteous to Hallgerður while the latter is a guest in her home. This does not arise from common surliness, but from a lack of self-control. (Bergþóra has borne a feeling of antipathy toward Hallgerður from the first moment she saw her, if not earlier, and now this feeling finds the opportunity to express itself.) And yet Bergþóra does have a certain self-control and a feeling of propriety. This is demonstrated by the fact that under sufficiently grave circumstances she refuses to permit herself to be provoked. When Hallgerður boasts of the slaying of Bergþóra's menservants, Bergþóra makes no attempt to conceal her anger; but when Hallgerður causes the death of Þórður leysingjason and sends a messenger to inform her of this, the saga states that "Bergþóra declared that she would not use abusive language against Hallgerður, since that would not be suitable vengeance for such a terrible act." Here we see the difference between the two women. In a similar situation Hallgerður would have "raged." Bergþóra can distinguish the significant from the insignificant; she seems to know instinctively when it is out of place to rant and rave. The response must be suitable to the provocation. Her loftiness of feeling helps her to achieve moderation.

Bergþóra's magnanimity is also demonstrated in other ways. When Njáll learns about Otkel's refusal to sell hay and food to Gunnar (chapter 47), he gives vent to his indignation and displeasure. But Bergþóra immediately says, "What's the use of talking so much about such things? It would be much more manly to give him both hay and food, since you are short of neither." To which Njáll replies, "You are quite right." And when her rival, Hróðný, brings the body of Höskuldur, her son and Njál's, to Bergþórshvoll and asks for help, it is far from Bergþóra's nature to treat her cruelly because of jealousy. The situation demands something quite different from resentment over the paternity of Höskuldur. Instead, she immediately goads her sons to avenge the slaying of their half brother: "You men amaze me. You kill people for little reason, but now you stew about it and chew it over until nothing will come of it."

A casual reading of the saga can well evoke the feeling that Bergþóra dominates her husband. Njáll sometimes "strives mightily at sitting still," while Bergþóra not infrequently "storms" or "rages," as the author puts it. But the more closely we study the saga, the more obvious it becomes that this is far from the truth. To be sure, Bergþóra is highly regarded by her family and her servants, and she enjoys considerable authority within the household. This can best be seen, perhaps, in her curt comment to Atli (chapter 36): "I am Njál's wife, and I have as much authority in hiring servants as he does." But when the stakes are high, she is always sensitive to the will of her husband and never goes further on her own volition than he would forgive her for doing.

In the final event of her life Bergþóra attains her moment of perfection. Whatever was offensive or detrimental disappears, and the noblest qualities in her character come forth. Now that so much is at stake, she can afford to put them to good account. She and her husband and their sons are inside the flaming house at Bergþórshvoll. The women and children and servants are permitted to go outside, and their daughters-in-law and their daughter Helga take leave of their husbands. Flosi has Njáll and Bergþóra called to the door.

> "I want to offer to permit you to come out," said Flosi, "for you do not deserve to burn."
> Njáll replied, "I have no wish to go outside, for I am an old man now, and poorly fitted to avenge the death of my sons, and I do not want to live in shame."
> Flosi then said to Bergþóra, "You come out, Bergþóra, for I do not want you to burn under any circumstances."
> Bergþóra replied, "I was given to Njáll in marriage when young, and I promised him then that we would share the same fate."
> Then they both went back in.
> Bergþóra said, "What shall we do now?"
> "Let us go to bed," replied Njáll, "and lie down. I have long been fond of my ease."
> Then they lay down in the bed and placed the little boy, Kári's son Þórður, who did not want to be parted from his grandmother, between them. Then they made the sign of the cross over themselves and the boy and commended their souls to God, and that was the last they were heard to speak.

Where are now the turtle-back fingernails, the silly anger at trifles, the vehemence and raging? There is no trace of them left. All that remains is dignity, greatness, and beauty.

Thus the author takes leave of Bergþóra. With the exception of Kormlöð—and she seems to have been taken over almost unchanged from another work (*Brjáns saga*)—Hildigunnur and Valgerður, the housemistress at Mörk, are the last women characters to be described in the saga. I have already pointed out with what understanding the author depicted Hildigunnur at the end of the story. Valgerður is certainly not lenient with her husband, Björn; and yet, when he returns home from his expedition with Kári after having dispatched three men and having been wounded himself, the stern features of her face soften into a smile. We are left with the impression that the author's attitude toward women mellows as time passes. His own spirit is purified through the writing of the saga.[14]

14. Two of the women characters of *Njála*, Hallgerður and Bergþóra, are discussed by A. Rittershaus in her book *Altnordische Frauen* and by Einar Hjörleifs-son (Kvaran) in his article "Skapstórar konur," *Skírnir* LXXXIII (1909).

5. Hallgerður

I

Sand—gray, blue, black, but mostly gray—indistinct, faintly glimmering and constantly shifting in shade and hue. It is akin to rock, reliable and firm, but sand itself is the dissolution of all that is firm. In the mirage of the summer sun it blots out and dissolves the boundary between sky and earth. All is jumbled together. Hills and mountains loom up high; the world becomes a fata morgana, an optical illusion. Barren, and yet not infertile. Grass would grow there if it were not a storm world, where gales rage and sweep everything before them, living and dead.

A vast panorama of sand and seashore opens up before her eyes when the mistress at Hlíðarendi, the wife of Gunnar Hámundarson, gazes down over the land. There is something of the substance of sand in her soul; it possesses the splendor and the unreliability of the fata morgana. It is difficult to grasp—unstable, changeable, yet always self-consistent; barren, but mostly because storms seldom give seeds time to take root. Here tranquillity never prevails: when the winds abate, the mirage makes its tremulous appearance; and while the gales rage, clouds of dust perform their eerie troll dance.

II

I doubt if more has been composed and written and argued about all other characters in *Njáls saga* than about Hallgerður—so distinctive is she. In the saga we find considerable animosity toward her; it seems as though her description stems from Gunnar's circle of friends. For a

long time people's opinion of her was in accord with this hostile attitude, and Hallgerður was one of the most notorious examples of a
wicked woman in Icelandic literature. But in the saga there is much
that explains and extenuates her faults, and it may well be that long
ago there were persons who were eager to regard the question from
this point of view. The first notable example of this is found in a poem
by Sigurður Breiðfjörð entitled "Hallgerður langbrók," which was
published in *Ljóðasmámunir* in 1839. This roustabout with the soul of
an artist was well aware of the extenuating circumstances in Hallgerð's
life. In his poem he briefly recapitulates her story and pleads her case
with delicate tact. Almost all of this we can agree with for the most
part. The one event in the saga with which he cannot reconcile himself
is the episode about Gunnar's bowstring and Hallgerð's hair: his
benevolence toward Hallgerður sharpens his criticism, and he attempts
to show that the account cannot stand up under close scrutiny. He concludes that the episode is an emendation, added to the saga by a scribe
who had a strong dislike for her.

It is important to consider two unrelated circumstances which are
combined in Sigurð's poem. The first is this: it is possible to read
Hallgerð's story to her advantage—by emphasizing everything which
explains and exculpates her—and thus to arrive at an interpretation
which is more favorable to her than the one which seems most obvious
from a reading of the saga as a whole. The second is to find historical
errors in the account—and if this search for historical inaccuracies is
examined carefully, it is clear that the reason for such an attempt is
always to ameliorate the guilt of Hallgerður, to ennoble her.

The second notable defense of Hallgerður was made by the Norwegian novelist Hans E. Kinck in the well-known treatise which was first
published in 1916 in the *Festschrift* for Gerhard Gran. This article is
written with such poetic empathy and literary brilliance that its influence, directly or indirectly, can be detected in almost everything that
has been written since then about the characters in *Njála*.[1]

1. See Appendix B.

Kinck does not make it a point to dispute individual incidents in the story, even though he does do so occasionally. He clearly believes that the events in the saga actually occurred much as they are depicted there. But his artistic temperament is not content with the description of Hallgerður, with the author's concept of her character. The animosity of the saga toward her stimulates him. In his mind's eye there arises another picture of her, a picture which does not occur in the saga but which he fondly believes existed behind the written work: Hallgerður becomes one of those characters which "the saga" did not understand. From the very beginning her nature was difficult to fathom. She committed deeds which brought misfortune to her husband, Gunnar, the idol of the people. When the saga was related, the audience took a dislike to her and were unable to understand her. Her portrait grew shallow and became simplified. The saga tellers and the saga author were at the mercy of popular opinion, which was unable to comprehend profound and subtle psychology.

This is Kinck's viewpoint when he undertakes to explain and defend Hallgerður. He admits that everything which is needed to exculpate her was in the account of the saga itself, but that it was not utilized there. Important circumstances which clarify her behavior were either disregarded or pushed aside by the saga.

All around Kinck were people who were eager to listen to such a defense and such a vindication. Kinck's views spread like a grass fire from country to country—partly because of the brilliance of his style, but also because they found fertile soil among his contemporaries. I am not prepared to surmise to what extent the spirit of the times was identical to that of Kinck, for he was no ordinary person, but a poet who was wont to think for himself. But since the *Zeitgeist* of his day contributed so much to the dissemination of his ideas, I cannot refrain from commenting briefly on this matter.

In the course of the past century and down to the time of World War I, especially among intelligent and well-intentioned people, a mode of thought gradually developed and circulated which is expressed in the universally known French saying: *Tout comprendre c'est tout pardonner*, to understand all is to forgive all. Obviously it would be far-fetched to suggest that everyone subscribed to this view, yet it seemed to be the modern, prevailing manner of thinking. People grew eager to understand, to forgive, and to vindicate. The guilt of the individual was minimized through the process of analyzing him into his components: heredity, upbringing, environment, and the exigencies of life—these were the causes of his behavior, and therein lay the guilt. They are all impersonal forces or circumstances, but the individual himself is freed of guilt since his is nothing but an empty name according to this philosophy of life, which is the basic *Weltanschauung* of the literary movement known as naturalism. Now this or that ill-starred, unlucky individual attracted the sympathetic attention of poets, novelists, and dramatists, and they became the constantly recurring subject of literature, all aimed at transferring the guilt and responsibility of these individuals to mitigating external circumstances. In Iceland, for example, one endeavored especially to interpret, to elucidate, and to exculpate the sort of person one might call a vagabond or drifter, the unlucky fellow who fails where others succeed and who eventually becomes an outcast of society. Abroad it is the "painted lady," the noble or at least forgivable prostitute, and the honorable criminal who are favorite subjects for prose and poetry. This peculiar phenomenon, which has such deep roots in the culture of the past century, is mentioned here without praise or censure and without further comment. But hand in hand with this tendency to take the part of those who have experienced the condemnation of public opinion goes the widespread and clear inclination to reduce the dimensions of the national heroes and paragons of the past to those of ordinary people. A clear example of this sort of leveling is Sigurður Guðmundsson's treatise on Gunnar of Hlíðarendi, in which this is one of his two chief aims.

The spirit of the times strongly supported such men who held the same view of Hallgerður as did the poets Sigurður Breiðfjörð and Hans E. Kinck. The line of argument runs somewhat like this: It begins with the desire to cleanse and vindicate her. From this point of view the saga is read in such a way as to show her in the best possible light, by searching for all extenuating circumstances which can be found, including her heredity and upbringing, her environment, etc., in accordance with the usual naturalistic approach. Now all this is well and good. But whenever the saga presents a contradictory understanding of any incident, a strong effort is made to interpret that incident in conformity with preconceived desires rather than according to the statement of the saga. If this is unsuccessful, the saga is promptly accused of a shallow and distorted presentation. The progress of modern times and the doctrines of evolution inspired people with the notion that they obviously had a keener understanding of the human psyche than those fellows of long ago. If the saga described facts which could not be harmonized with the wishful thinking of the critic, he tried to defend his point of view by a subterfuge: the discrepancies were explained as fictitious emendations of later times, and the incidents themselves were branded as historically incorrect.

Let me mention just a few examples. The saga states that Hallgerður sent a thrall to steal meat at Kirkjubær. This, of course, would be an ugly blemish on her character if it were true. Few critics deny that the incident itself is true, but they insist that Hallgerður herself regarded this act as seizing booty and not as committing theft and therefore not particularly shameful. Yet this is diametrically opposed to all that is said in the saga. Then we would have to eliminate Hrút's prophetic words about the thief's eyes—but this incident, after all, is unrealistic by its very nature: history has no faith in the gift of prophecy! And then there is the account of the bowstring and Hallgerð's hair. Everyone regards Hallgerð's act as a most atrocious crime, and her defenders try especially to acquit her of it. Now it so happens that the psychology of the saga at this point is both distinct and acceptable, and no one has undertaken to improve upon it. But now the critics turn to history for help: it is incredible, they say, to regard it as possible that a bowstring could be made from human hair, and thus the episode becomes nonsense. But actually the crux of the matter is this: the episode would be valid and credible if Gunnar and Hallgerður thought it possible to make a bowstring from her hair, and this alone is decisive, whether it is really possible or not.

As I have shown elsewhere, the use of a woman's hair does not impair the verisimilitude of the story.[2] On the other hand, I cannot deny the unlikelihood that, as Sigurður Breiðfjörð has pointed out, the onslaught would have been delayed while the bowstring was being fashioned. Such a situation would have required a more advantageous kind of defense—on the battlements of a fortress or on the parapets of a stone castle or a fortified city. Indeed, there are numerous reports dealing with such situations. It is well known from Roman history that at times the inhabitants of a besieged city were reduced to such straits that as a last resort they used women's hair to braid ropes or cords for their catapults. Caesar refers to this in connection with the siege of Salona (49 B.C.), and in such a way as to suggest that this was a commonly known expedient. There are many such examples to be found in the writings of ancient historians or military leaders, the most widely known of which concerns the women of Carthage—and also the most reliable, since it probably goes back to an eyewitness, Polybius. In this case, to be sure, it is not a matter of bowstrings, but of cords or ropes in devices for hurling missiles, and it was perfectly natural that peoples unfamiliar with war machines of that kind would transform the cords into bowstrings when relating such events. As a matter of fact, there are actually ancient reports of the use of women's hair for making bowstrings, one of which is related by Julius Capitolinus in chapter 33 of his history of Emperor Maximinus, which tells of the siege of Aquileia. So great was the faith of the people of Aquileia in the Senate's opposition to Maximinus that they made cords out

2. "Hallgerður langbrók," *Lesbók Morgunblaðsins* XVI (1941), 65–68, 73–76, from which some of the following material is taken. For information on this motif in classical literature and history I am indebted to Dr. Jacob Benediktsson.

of women's hair when they ran out of thongs for shooting arrows. It is said that this also happened once in Rome. The truth of these accounts, of course, cannot be tested, but that is of little consequence.

Here we have the material for a nice little story. The enemy assaults a city so fiercely that almost all supplies are exhausted, but the defenders fight manfully and refuse to surrender. There is a shortage of materials for bowstrings, and bows are the most necessary weapons for their defense. But the women will not be outdone: they cut off their hair, if it may be of any use, so that the defense can be continued until the enemy is compelled to lift the siege or until help comes from elsewhere. Stories such as this may well have been the model for the episode about Hallgerð's hair. Some storyteller or writer who felt that he had been badly treated by the opposite sex turned the virtue of the women into a vice and thus created a story of the evil woman who refused to sacrifice her long, beautiful hair for her lover. This surmise cannot be proven, but it seems quite reasonable.

The discussion of these two examples from *Njála*—Hallgerð's instigation of theft and her refusal to braid a bowstring from her hair—show how two unrelated points of view, the psychological and the historical, are repeatedly blended in such a way as to confuse the issue beyond comprehension. The character depiction can be memorable and true even though the events themselves never took place; this is the truth of literature. And the portrait can be wrong, in both a historical and a poetical sense, even though the events are not tampered with. These two points of view are so incompatible that it is absolutely necessary to keep them separate: otherwise there is no hope of being able to give a meaningful interpretation of the story of this ancient work of art.

III

The historicity of the saga at this point is a matter which can quickly be disposed of: it is not on the agenda, and no more attention will be paid to it here than hitherto in our discussion of *Njála*. Nor do I doubt that this will be of advantage. Otherwise the author and the reader would become engaged in an almost endless debate and in fruitless speculations over matters about which extremely little can be ascertained. The truth of the matter is that above and beyond her genealogy we know practically nothing about the historical Hallgerður. It is impossible to arrive at any picture of her—if it can be called a picture— behind our saga.

People are fond of imagining that somewhere beyond the saga there must have existed another, more remarkable picture of this woman. But I am convinced that the picture of her in the saga was cast from fragments and that the portrait is much more remarkable than the raw material. And I wonder whether this view is not as good as any other.

IV

We will turn our backs on all historical deliberations, and now there remains nothing but the account of *Njáls saga*, the picture of human life, the work of art. It has the great advantage that it can be seen and grasped. But it also lacks shield and byrnie. It cannot flee behind anything or defend itself by means of magical mists. It will have to stand or fall on its own merits.

Many a person would accuse this saga of bias against Hallgerður. This is so well known that no examples need be cited. It was this antipathy above all else that impelled Kinck to protest. It is strange, and yet Hallgerður is not the only character who incurred the author's displeasure.

There is no need to expatiate on the fact that an author's bias often leads to a lack of understanding, distorted pictures of human life, and shallow and unimpressive character portraits. And yet there are exceptions to this general rule. There are instances that show that at the outermost limits of sympathy, or where inclination is in doubt and the winds blow hither and thither, or even beyond those limits, character portraits are created which scarcely have their equal. For antipathy can sometimes also possess keen discrimination. One would have to search long and hard to find a portrait of Louis XIV comparable to the one drawn by Saint-Simon, and yet this does not bear witness to a friendly disposition toward the king on the part of the author. Tacitus's work on the Roman emperors is anything but a bright and happy chronicle, and yet he has been called the greatest psychologist of all historians.

Naturally the critic must not let himself be swept away by the author's antipathy. He must constantly test the author's one-sided picture by comparing it with the testimony of the events themselves. Can the portrait be brought into harmony or not? With the character under discussion here he must proceed with the objectivity of the physician who seeks to make a correct decision from an examination of the symptoms without letting himself be led astray by his own wishes or desires. It is one of the highest values of great art that it affords us the opportunity of gaining a glimpse into the secrets of human existence: we are far enough away to remain independent of what is shown or related, yet sufficiently close to see and hear all and in a certain sense to live and experience it.

But what is the nature of this character portrait in *Njála* when we endeavor to see and understand, impartially, with no inclination toward exculpation, and with the firm determination completely to avoid pleading a case?

V

The reader sees Hallgerður for the first time briefly in her childhood. She is playing on the floor with some other girls: she is pretty and large for her age, and her hair is as fair as silk and so long that it reaches down to her waist. All around are kinsmen and friends, who are guests at a festive party given by her father. Then an incident occurs which was mentioned above and which must now be considered again. Höskuldur calls to his daughter: "Come here to me," he said. She went to him at once. He tilted her chin and kissed her; then she went back to her playmates. Then Höskuldur said to Hrútur: "What do you think of this girl? Don't you think she's beautiful?" Hrútur remained silent; he was clearly reluctant to answer. Höskuldur asked him a second time, and then he replied, "The girl is beautiful enough, and many will suffer for her beauty; but what I don't understand is how a thief's eyes have gotten into our family."

This episode has been a source of offense for many persons, and yet it contains an inner truth. Who has not experienced that strange feeling which can grip a person when he sees another individual, especially if it is for the first time? It is another matter that we usually do not mention such a thing to anyone, especially if the feeling is an unpleasant one—nor does Hrútur until he is pressed to do so.

Hrútur refers to Hallgerð's lineage, and if we look closely at this saga, we find that few works of this genre reveal a greater understanding of heredity—and, it might be added, of childhood experiences—than *Njáls saga* does in the characterization of Hallgerður. We cannot avoid looking into this matter carefully, not, to be sure, for the purpose of excusing Hallgerð's actions (as is usually the case), but rather for the purpose of seeing and understanding; and when this is done, it comes to light that there was a certain need, a necessity in her emotional life. To some persons it may perhaps seem that I am reading rather much between the lines, projecting contemporary knowledge of heredity and upbringing into this work of ancient times. But this is far from the case. Hallgerður herself speaks about the pride which she has inherited from her father's side of the family. She reveals her great disappointment at being married off to a man beneath her station and to the end of her good fortune entailed by this mésalliance (chapter 10). Great emphasis is placed on the spiritual affinity between her and her maternal kinsmen, the people of Strandir, as any reader can clearly see, and it is frankly stated that her foster father, Þjóstólfur, "did little to moderate" her character. Let us pursue the matter of her lineage and her upbringing a bit further.

On her father's side she is descended from the Dalamenn, the people of the Breiðafjarðardalir District. This is an old, aristocratic family, some branches of which can be traced back to royalty. These people drink in pride with their mother's milk, and are not inclined to tolerate dishonor without retaliation. But they possess a disciplined disposition and demeanor, know what is seemly and proper, and no misfortune attends them. On her mother's side, however, conditions are quite different. The saga describes her maternal uncle, Svanur of Svanshóll, as a man skilled in magic and devoted to heathen ways, primitive in his fidelity to his kinsmen by blood or by marriage, but primitive also in his ruthlessness to others: by temper and disposition he is unable to associate normally with people. Arrogance and willfulness, darkness and an inhuman awfulness are revealed in his countenance.

An illegitimate son of Svanur is Brynjólfur rósti, whose nickname means something like "the Brawler" and whom the author describes as "a great scoundrel" (chapter 38). Hallgerður is fond of both of them, and from this side of the family the saga derives (much as *Laxdæla* does in regard to her brother Þorleikur) all of the shadiness, the discord, and the deceitfulness in her behavior.

Hallgerður enjoys her father's indulgence, which nourishes her inborn pride. To this is added the influence of her foster father, who strongly arouses the strand of her character inherited from her mother's family. Þjóstólfur is a Hebridean malefactor who commits manslaughter but never pays indemnity for the slain. He encourages all the freakishness in her character and then heeds her every beck and call. As mentioned above, the saga states that "it was said that he did nothing to moderate Hallgerð's disposition." This unbridled indulgence spoils her. She grows accustomed to having every wish fulfilled and to abandoning herself to every desire. She observes that Þjóstólfur himself does exactly as he pleases, unbound by any moral bonds, and he thus becomes an evil example for her.

Þjóstólfur complies with every request of Hallgerður, and in time she discovers that his fidelity as a foster father is tinged with jealousy.

He begrudges anyone else the enjoyment of her love. Much can be said against Hallgerður, but she is neither frivolous nor flirtatious. And yet this dark power which she exerts over Þjóstólfur flatters her ego and his jealousy tickles her fancy.

Yet behind all of this felicity, like an undertone, discordant and pregnant with the inclination to misfortune, there are the premonitions of the wise man Hrútur. After the initial episode (chapter 1), time and time again, he reveals his opinion of his niece, speaks about her misfortune and her unreliability. All the while she is growing up she is surrounded by his prophecies of disaster, together with inordinate indulgence.

VI

Next we see Hallgerður as a marriageable young woman, exceptionally beautiful, tall, stately, with splendid hair so long that she could completely cover herself with it—but impetuous and willful. Now she is beset by the exigencies of life, which give her character its permanent stamp. Þorvaldur from Fell, a man of little significance, asks for her hand in marriage, and her father gives his consent. Hallgerður is reluctant to enter into this marriage; she regards the wooer as far beneath her and feels that her father has betrayed her trust in him: "Now I have learned for certain what I have long suspected: You do not love me so dearly as you have always maintained, since you did not even bother to discuss this matter with me. Nor do I think this marriage as desirable a one as you promised me." Höskuldur replies, "I do not take your pride so seriously that it should stand in the way of my arrangements. And if we disagree, it is I and not you who will make the decision." Hallgerður cannot but comply, but with these regal words: "Since you and your kinsmen are possessed of such great pride, it is no wonder that I have some too."

In her distress she turns to her foster father, Þjóstólfur, and he gives her the hope that her marriage will not be of long duration. During the wedding feast, at which Þjóstólfur and Svanur swagger about,

Hallgerður displays great gaiety, and she laughs at every word the bridegroom says to her. Her pride causes her to mask her feelings, but her laughter is discordant and ominous. When she and her husband have arrived at their new home, Hallgerður is demanding and imperious; she claims everything which belongs to others about her and soon has things in a mess through her extravagance. And now the provisions in the household run out, and she tells her husband to remedy matters: "You won't do any good just sitting about; we need both flour and dried fish for the household." In reply he reproaches her for her wastefulness, saying that the same amount of provisions has been provided for the winter as formerly, and now they are exhausted, whereas previously they lasted until summer. "It's no concern of mine," she says, "if you and your father have starved yourselves for money." Then her husband grows furious and strikes her in the face so that it bleeds. Now it seems to her that she has no one else to turn to but Þjóstólfur; she complains to him, and he kills Þorvaldur. But Hallgerður unlocks her chests and gives each member of the household a gift, and they all grieve for her. Thereupon she rides home to her father at Höskuldsstaðir.

Here nothing comes as a surprise. And *if* someone should raise the question of innocence or guilt, the judgment against this young and easily swayed young woman would not be severe. But here there are several factors which are worth studying, factors which have an influence on the future. The saga stresses Hallgerð's emotional instability. The psychology of a later period lays great emphasis on demonstrating how the prevailing ethical views of a society take up their abode, so to speak, in the mind of each individual and there form bonds and restraints which hold his inclinations within limits, so that they do not find an outlet in words and deeds until they are changed into such forms of expression as are morally and socially acceptable. But Hallgerður is obviously rather lacking in inhibitions of this kind. She is likely to do anything that happens to occur to her, no matter what its nature may be, and it is this which distinguishes her from other high-spirited women of ancient times, such as Bergþóra, Hildigunnur, or Guðrún Ósvífursdóttir in *Laxdæla*. This is a quality which she has in common with her foster father and Hrappur. To be sure, it does happen occasionally that she restrains herself—not because of moral considerations, but rather out of prudence, and this is an evil omen.

Still another factor is worthy of consideration. This woman at an early age undergoes the experience of having blood shed on her account, and it is quite likely that henceforth she will not shudder at such a deed. Would it be an exaggeration to suggest that there is something in her nature as a woman which takes delight in having men fight on her account—some primordial and deep-seated need in her breast which is whetted by this?

Time passes, and it is not long before another man comes to woo Hallgerður, a man whom she desires. She is permitted to make her own decision and declare her own betrothal, and she soon comes to love her husband Glúmur ardently. These are the most blissful years of her life. The old grief and distress fade into the past, her good fortune has a salutary effect on her, and her love for Glúmur teaches her to restrain herself, to gain control over her impulsive nature by her own will power.

But this is merely a lull in the storm. The evil spirit in her life, Þjóstólfur, again enters the scene. He manages to get permission to stay at their home, but is unable to keep himself under control very long. At first Hallgerður does not take his part, but finally matters come to the point where husband and wife get into a quarrel because of him, the end of which is that Glúmur slaps her face and then walks away. "She loved him so dearly that she could not constrain herself, and she wept bitterly." Þjóstólfur comes to her and says, "You have been harshly treated, but this will not happen often"—he recalls a similar incident from her first marriage and is terribly eager to play the same role again as he did before. "You are not to take revenge for this," she says, "nor meddle in our affairs, no matter how things go between us." But he pays no heed to her. Rather, he kills Glúmur when the two of them are alone searching for missing sheep up in the mountains, after which he comes to Hallgerður with his bloody ax. She asks what has happened, and he tells her. She bursts out laughing and says, "You are no mean rival when it comes to games." Thereupon she sends him to her uncle Hrútur, who perceives that the slaying was not of her doing and promptly dispatches the wretched killer.

Hallgerður wept when Glúmur slapped her. Now she laughs. There is a double significance in her laughter. To the attentive reader it reveals first of all that she is heartbroken. It is the laughter of despair. Secondly, her laughter conceals her decision that now Þjóstólfur must die. It is a dangerous omen when this impulsive woman masks her feelings, and an ominous one when she laughs.

Hallgerð's sick and disturbed mind never recovers from this calamity. The salutary influence of her few days of happiness quickly disappears. And now time slowly assuages the burning sore, and it is as though she becomes petrified in the condition which misfortune has brought about.

It is just as when a man suffers a broken bone, the pieces of which are twisted out of place and then grow together in a distorted shape. Her character is molded once and for all. The exigencies of life determine which particular trait of her nature is brought into play at any given moment and her life continues correspondingly. She herself changes little or not at all; she becomes neither better nor worse. It is furthermore worth noting that in the depths of her soul there is a certain force which has a tendency to cause the grievous experience of her past life to be repeated again and again.

VII

It is now safe to pass quickly over the account of the remaining years of Hallgerð's life, even though this is a long story. Her heredity from the maternal side of the family, the influence of Þjóstólfur, the great misfortune of her past life—all of these continue to dominate her disposition. Impulsiveness, vindictiveness, guilefulness—she does whatever comes into her head, feels justified in doing whatever she wishes

to, without regard for what is right or wrong. The pride of the Dalamenn, her paternal kinsmen, does not deter her in this, and she stoops
to being content with paltriness if there is no other possibility at the
moment: she is surrounded by vulgar and abusive language. She has a
weakness for violence, excitement, variety. She is eager for action, for
things to happen. And she does not shudder at the sight of blood.

Again time passes. Gunnar and Hallgerður meet at the General
Assembly (chapter 33). He has just returned to Iceland from a voyage
abroad—famous for his prodigious accomplishments and for the honor
bestowed upon him by royalty. He is wearing the stately apparel
presented to him by Haraldur Gormsson, King of the Danes, and a
gold bracelet, the gift of Hákon Sigurðarson, Earl of Norway. Gunnar
is on his way from the Law Rock when he sees down below the booth
of the Mosfell people a group of well-dressed women coming toward
him. In the lead is the most beautifully attired woman of all. She greets
him, he asks her her name, and she replies that her name is Hallgerður
and that she is the daughter of Höskuldur Dala-Kollsson. She speaks
to him boldly and asks him to tell her about his travels, and he says he
will not deny her this. They sit down and talk. "Hallgerður was
attired in a red, richly ornamented tunic. Over it she wore a cloak of
scarlet, which was trimmed all the way down with a lace border.
Her hair, which fell down over her bosom, was both thick and
beautiful."

They talk together for a long time—for the most part aloud. They
obviously feel attracted toward each other, and that very evening
Gunnar makes a proposal of marriage. When Hrútur fails to dampen
his ardor with words of warning, he declares that they are infatuated
with each other.

The marriage cannot be a happy one, for the personalities of husband
and wife are too different. Gunnar is calm and composed, peaceful, and
concerned about keeping his honor unblemished. He tolerates injustice
from others as long as possible, and there is no question as to how
foreign this is to Hallgerð's disposition.

From the very beginning Njáll is opposed to their marriage, and not much is required to make Hallgerður painfully aware of this. During a festive party at Bergþórshvoll, Bergþóra wounds her pride; she retorts as one might expect and receives an insult in return. She looks to Gunnar for the kind of protection a woman expects of her husband, but all she gets from him is reproach. Gunnar, however, does not break faith with Njáll, no matter what happens. He yields to Njáll more than Njáll does to him, and to Hallgerður it seems that he is behaving ignobly and that he is on the side of her enemies. This, of course, makes their life together more difficult. With the temperament Hallgerður has, her reaction in urging her menservants to kill some of Njál's men is but natural.

This storm comes to an end, and now we come to the quarrel between Gunnar and Otkell.

There is a great famine in Iceland (chapter 47). Gunnar has shared his hay and food with his neighbors, who lack everything, until finally his own provisions are exhausted. He rides to Kirkjubær to buy supplies from Otkell, but he is turned away in a humiliating manner. Nevertheless he buys a thrall from Otkell. Hallgerður takes great offense at the outcome of Gunnar's visit to Kirkjubær, and the following spring she has a thrall steal food from Otkell and burn down one of his storehouses. And the thrall she uses is the very one Gunnar bought from Otkell: she probably feels that this is the most appropriate way of settling the score. For I do not think there is any doubt concerning what is running through her mind. She intends in her own way to take revenge on Otkell for his humiliating Gunnar. She is, shall we say, trying to improve their marriage relationship, which has turned out much differently than it should have.

But this revenge and this amelioration are not without a flaw. Theft has always been regarded as disgraceful, and in olden times it was regarded as one of the most disgraceful of all crimes. Homicide could be excused, but theft was dishonorable. For those who have tried to plead the cause of Hallgerður this episode has been a heavy cross to

bear. They have tried in one way or another to acquit her; they have
asserted, for example, that she considered her act as plunder and not as
theft. But this is nothing but subterfuge. There is nothing in the saga
which indicates that she lacks intelligence.

But there is something else which she does lack—not only here, but
everywhere: control over her impulsiveness as well as critical judgment
of her desires before they are turned into deeds. And this one act of hers
demonstrates that her moral consciousness is badly out of joint.

It is obvious that Gunnar cannot endure being a thief's accomplice.
This self-disciplined man becomes so furious that he strikes his wife at
a festive party in the presence of many guests. It is not surprising that
she should also become angry. But her anger grows all the more
bitter because of the motives underlying the theft: her desire to avenge
Gunnar's humiliation and her hope to improve their marital relation.
She vows to avenge the blow, but otherwise keeps herself under
control, and we have already seen how ominous it is when she maintains her self-control while in a hostile mood. Her deadly hatred sinks
down into the depths of her mind and bides its time, but it does not
affect the tenor of everyday life. She does not defy her husband as she
previously did; indeed, she is afraid of him when he grows angry. She
enjoys his disputes and his manslaughters, she is delighted when he
meets force with force—that is the way her husband should act—but
she despises his hesitation to retaliate and his conscientiousness. She is
eager for something to happen, and continues to be attracted by
violence, without concern for the future.

Thus their life goes on, and the net encircling Gunnar grows tighter
and tighter. Finally he is sentenced to banishment from Iceland for a
period of three years. He has already set out from home, but he breaks
off the journey to the ship and turns back. "Hallgerður was delighted
that Gunnar returned home, but his mother had little to say," the saga
tells us. Who can say why Hallgerður welcomed his return? Did she
experience a sudden feeling of joy because she would not be deprived
of her husband? Or did she rejoice in Gunnar's bravery in not yielding

to his enemies? Or was she pleased that she could now look forward to exciting events again? Did she at this moment wish him ill? One thing is certain: her happiness is an evil omen.

And so it happens that one day in late summer a band of enemies comes to the farm at Hlíðarendi, and there is no question about their purpose. Gunnar is at home alone with his wife and his mother. But he defends himself skillfully with his bow and prevents them from getting close enough to take full advantage of their superior numbers. But then one of them succeeds in stealing up and cutting his bowstring in half. Now a swift decision and immediate action are necessary. He glances at Hallgerð's long, beautiful hair: "Give me two strands of your hair, and you and mother twist them together into a bowstring for me!" It may be that she was not overly eager to sacrifice her beauty for his sake, but the author makes no mention of this feeling; he does show, however, how an old memory awakens—she feels the sting of his slap on her face, and the disgrace of being revealed as a thief before all her guests again becomes vivid and bitter. "Does it mean anything to you?" she asks—and we feel the coldness and calculation of these words. "It means my life," he replies, "because they will never overcome me as long as I can use my bow." "Then," she says, "I shall remind you of the slap in the face you gave me, and I don't care one bit how long you hold out." The ambivalence of their love and the semireconciliation of their married life is now swept away; the only thing she is conscious of is the slap on the face. And beneath that blow is another one, which is intensely painful to think about, and beneath that one still another, and the resentment for the first one has still not died out. Hallgerður is now not merely repaying Gunnar's beating, but also Þorvald's blow. I wonder if this is not one of the deepest insights into this profoundly conceived portrayal of human character.

VIII

We meet Hallgerður once more in the saga (chapter 38), at the home of her daughter at Grjótá. We see that her disturbed mind is attracted to the adventurer Hrappur, who is not overscrupulous in his behavior. The saga has the following to say about this: "Some people said that Hrappur and Hallgerður were on very good terms and that he seduced her, but others denied it." Actually it is of little importance for an understanding of Hallgerður. It is quite natural that she should be pleased with Hrappur, considering their temperaments. But if anyone should wish to conclude from this statement that Hallgerður here reveals that she is flirtatious, that conclusion would be unjustified since it conflicts with all previous characterizations of her in the story. The only thing which seems to point in that direction are her flattering and fawning words to Gunnar's kinsman Sigmundur (chapter 41; see p. 73), and it is completely out of the question that Gunnar would have tolerated this if serious flirtation had been involved. Indeed, it is clear that Hallgerður had something quite different in mind, namely, to entice Sigmundur to insult Njál's family.

Thus it changes nothing in the portrait of Hallgerður. One can perhaps imagine, as Sigurður Breiðfjörð did, that in the autumn of her life Hallgerður fell in love with Hrappur, who had been quite attractive to the ladies (chapter 87). Or one may prefer to believe those who "contradicted this." The author lets the reader make his own decision. The saga takes leave of Hallgerður in this uncertain light, in the tremulous mirage of the shifting sand.

IX

Hallgerður is a very memorable personage. Throughout her story one detail after the other engraves itself indelibly upon the mind of the reader. But even though these pictures of her are so clear, people have nevertheless managed to arrive at contradictory opinions about her. Without doubt the antipathy of the author is partly to blame for this, but even more so the literary convention to which he adheres and which prescribed for him such a strict narrative method. If it had been customary to let the characters express themselves more freely, the task of the author would have been less difficult. And then this work of art would not have made such great demands of the reader.

But this is not the case, and so the reader has to have eyes on every finger, so to speak, when he sets about weighing and evaluating events which he trusted as completely as a new net as long as the story lasted. In this respect the saga is just like human life itself.

The events in Hallgerð's life reveal to us a character whose style remains the same throughout, but which nevertheless is changeable. We see her development and formation before she and Gunnar meet. Perhaps we can best understand her with the help of a comparison from the art of music. Her life is an organic unity, a continuous melody; in the beginning it is changeable in nature, free—but filled with the struggle of discordant forces which bring fortune as well as misfortune. In the second half all of the changeable elements are merely on the surface; underneath, compulsion and constraint seem to reign.

Every event in her life either heralds a coming one or is an echo of one from the past. The reader is constantly aware of distant and far-reaching relationships. No act is completely independent; nothing is completely without influence. Again and again we can perceive the same theme, in different variations and combinations. The reader feels as though there were a hidden inherent reason in all this. What brings it about that the same events pregnant with misfortune are repeated over and over? What is the nature of misfortune and what is its cause?

6. Skarphéðinn

"Skarphéðinn and the
Apostle Paul—these
are my men."—Ísleifur Einarsson

I

In the portrait of Hallgerður we saw a person who was rather difficult to fathom and who was portrayed very critically and with considerably more antipathy than sympathy. Now we shall consider a saga
hero, no less puzzling, who does many things which are far from
honorable, a noble-minded man who commits an almost incredibly
atrocious crime. Here too the author is very critical, but he is also more
understanding and conciliatory. The final picture we see of Hallgerður
is not a pleasant one, as she stands in the doorway at the farm Grjótá
furiously berating the Njálssons. But this character dies a hero's death,
and the author takes leave of him with these words: "Then all said
that it seemed less unpleasant to see Skarphéðinn dead than they had
expected, for no one felt afraid of him."

The author's description of Skarphéðinn resembles that of Hallgerður in two respects: his appearance is unusually clear and memorable,
and at the same time his behavior is frequently enigmatic. Even though
the reader accepts the account without reservation—"believes" the
story, so to speak—as he sees the events unfold before his mind's eye,
he would be momentarily tongue-tied if he later had to explain what
motivated each of Skarphéðin's acts. Nowhere else in the saga is it
more necessary to understand the art of the half-sung song—to supply
the missing parts correctly without introducing any extraneous material.

In preceding chapters we spoke of the emotions of a soul in semi-darkness, of a wavering mind, and of unrelated causes and motives which lead to the same course of action. Nowhere else is it more necessary to be fully aware of all of this than in the story of Skarphéð-inn.[1]

II

The saga relates that "Kári did not mention anyone as often as Njáll and Skarphéðinn." I doubt if any figure from the shadow army of the saga haunted the author as much as Skarphéðinn, especially as his story progressed. With his imaginative power he succeeded quite well in transforming his mental vision into a vivid picture. When Skarphéðinn is introduced into the saga he is described with unusual precision (chapter 25):

He was a tall, powerful man skilled in the use of weapons. He could swim like a seal and was exceedingly swift of foot. He was quick in making decisions and firm in adhering to them. He was ready with his words and spoke right to the point, but for the most part he maintained self-control. He had curly chestnut hair and fine eyes. His face was pale and his features were sharp. He had a crooked nose, prominent teeth, and a rather ugly mouth. He looked very much the warrior.

The ugly mouth and the paleness of his face—does not the first glimpse we catch of this remarkable man arouse the suspicion that some kind of misfortune awaits him?

Skarphéðin's portrait is brighter when he and his brothers and Kári set out to slay Þráinn Sigfússon (chapter 92): "Skarphéðinn was in the lead. He was wearing a blue jacket, carried a round shield, and had his

1. Skarphéðinn has been widely commented on in critical works, including the major histories of Old Icelandic literature. Among the most noteworthy treatments of this saga hero are the following: Hermann Jónasson, *Draumar*, Reykjavík, 1912; Hans E. Kinck, "Ett par ting om ættesagaen, skikkelser den ikke forstod" (Eloter follows Kinck in his literary history, Vol. I, p. 58); and Sigrún Ingólfsdóttir, "Skarphéðin," *Ársrit Nemendasambands Laugaskóla* I (1926), 50–66, a perceptive article which deserves serious study.

ax poised on his shoulder." There is a fresh, morning atmosphere and a spirit of combat in this description.

And finally there is the picture of Skarphéðinn at the General Assembly (chapters 118–20), as his friends and kinsmen seek support for their legal battle following the slaying of Höskuldur Hvítanesgoði. The chieftains harp incessantly on his chestnut-colored hair, his paleness and sharp, hard features, his formidability and swiftness, and his troll-like, ill-starred appearance. These two features, his paleness and his ill-starred expression, run like a leitmotif through their comments about him. But the author is not content with the one-sided description given by the chieftains. He himself seizes the opportunity to round out the picture by having Ásgrímur Elliðagrímsson caution Skarphéðinn to control himself and not to use strong language in speaking to Þorkell hákur.

> Skarphéðinn grinned in reply. He was wearing a blue tunic, blue-striped trousers, and black top boots. He had a silver belt around his waist, and was carrying a small, round shield and the ax with which he had killed Þráinn and which he called Rimmugýgur. His hair was combed back and held in place with a silk headband. He looked every bit the warrior, and everyone recognized him at first glance. He kept the position assigned to him, and neither crowded ahead nor fell back.

In these descriptions it is important to note that we are shown not only his outward appearance and behavior, but also, interwoven with this, traits of character, so that the pictures are always pulsing with life. In some episodes we get to see him in action. Let us first consider the scene in which the beggar women bring Bergþóra reports about the malicious slander of Sigmundur and others in Hallgerð's quarters (chapter 44). Bergþóra brings up the matter while they are sitting at the dinner table:

> "Gifts have been given to you, father and sons both, and you will scarcely be regarded as men if you do not repay them."
> "What kinds of gifts are they?" asked Skarphéðinn.

"You, my sons, share one gift among you. You have all been called 'Dungbeardlings,' and my husband has been named 'Old Beardless.'"

"We're not like women," said Skarphéðinn, "to fly into a rage about everything."

"But Gunnar flew into a rage on your account," she said, "and he is regarded as a good-natured man. If you don't exact vengeance for this, you will never avenge any insult."

"Our old mother is really enjoying herself," said Skarphéðinn with a grin. But sweat broke out on his forehead, and red spots appeared in his cheeks, and this did not happen often. Grímur remained silent, but bit his lips. Helgi did not change expression. Höskuldur left the room with Bergþóra, but she came storming back in.

Njáll said, "All in good time, woman. Make haste slowly. It so often happens, when people's tempers are tried, that there are two sides to the question once vengeance is taken."

Here all the participants in the scene are characterized by means of their outward reactions to the slander, and this is so skillfully done that the reader is in no doubt regarding their inner reactions. Skarphéðinn replies with indifferent, scoffing words and a grin, yet sweat breaks out on his forehead and red spots appear in his cheeks. His grin is a sort of leitmotif, like the "war tears" in *Víga-Glúms saga:* whenever Glúmur feels himself endangered or encroached upon, and falls into a fighting mood, he bursts out laughing and at the same time tears like hail stones fall from his eyes. Skarphéðin's scoffing and apparent indifference are his coat of mail, against both himself and others, his shell around the quick, so to speak. This sensitivity is the upper layer of a powerful, seething temperament which can best be compared to volcanic fire. But he has a will of steel. He walks neither too fast nor too slowly, and he strikes neither too soon nor too late. He disciplines his agitated feelings until he can transform them into positive action. Yet little of this suppressed agitation becomes apparent—except for the sweat on his forehead and the red spots on his cheeks. Skarphéðinn is one of the most manly figures in the saga, and although more will be said about his other qualities in this chapter, it is well to keep this in mind. The expression of manliness does not disappear from his face for a moment.

One of the most peculiar features of all the character portraits in *Njála* is the blending of heroic courage and sensitivity in this man. Nowadays the word "sensitivity" sometimes has the connotation of a lyrical, feminine sadness, but obviously nothing is further from the truth here. Nor is Skarphéðin's sensitivity akin to the refined sensitivity of Gunnar of Hlíðarendi; on one occasion Skarphéðinn actually refers to himself as a boisterous fellow. He enjoys trading blow for blow and matching word with word, not the least so when the fun gets coarse and crude. Neither Gunnar nor Kári engage in abuse or brawling, but Skarphéðinn always repays both in kind. His sensitivity is that of a lonely man who cannot bear to let others get too close to him.

Skarphéðinn both conceals and reveals his feelings through his scoffing. His words are as terse and pithy as epigrams, and never fail to hit their mark. Underneath the scoffing we can sometimes detect a feeling of sad sympathy, but more often we feel coldness or gloating. It embraces dissimulation, indifference, acrimony, scathing sarcasm, and unabashed abuse. He is also able to turn his criticism and his abuse against himself. Such an ability is evidence of a superior mentality, and many other things also point to a high degree of intelligence.

Yet despite this, Skarphéðinn lets Mörður trick him into killing Höskuldur Hvítanesgoði, who is completely innocent of any wrong. Furthermore, his conduct at the General Assembly following this slaying is anything but judicious. How is this possible? Many persons have been astonished and puzzled at this. In his *Draumar* Hermann Jónasson tried to mend matters by substantially revising the story. Hans E. Kinck dealt with Skarphéðinn in his well-known treatise and judged him to be mad. He regarded Skarphéðin's constant grinning as incontrovertible evidence that he was a bit addlebrained. If Kinck were correct in his judgment, we would be dealing here with a major flaw in character depiction. But let us look at the matter more closely.

III

Skarphéðinn inherited his mother's vigorous temperament and shared her philosophy of life. Their relationship to each other was always without friction. From his father he inherited a sense of humor, strength of will, self-control, and resourcefulness in accomplishing whatever had to be done. In his self-confidence and his alacrity in getting things done we can see how strands of character from both parents are woven together. His humor also contains a derisive strain inherited from the proud temperament of his mother. Skarphéðinn stands somewhat in awe of his father, and it is quite clear that he holds him in high esteem. During the burning he speaks several times of his father, but not of his mother.

And yet the differences between father and son are substantial. Whereas Njáll has a propensity to planning and pondering, Skarphéðinn is primarily a man of action. The time interval between thought and action is much shorter for Skarphéðinn than for his father. He is impatient of delays, waiting, and long-drawn-out struggles. His fiery temperament impels him to go forward. But now father and son have the same road to travel, and one of them must prevail. And of course it has to be Njáll, who is at one and the same time so gentle and yet so authoritarian.

Skarphéðinn is compelled to wait and bide his time. He has to proceed more slowly than is natural for him, and these heavy restraints press hard upon him. Sometimes we can detect a note of impatience in his voice. "How far will things have to go before we can set about doing something?" he asks after the slaying of his foster father, for whose death Njáll has accepted monetary compensation and made reconciliation with Gunnar (chapter 43). Yet he never displays displeasure or discontent with his father. When his brother Grímur, under somewhat similar circumstances (chapter 99), remonstrates with Njáll, Skarphéðinn terminates the conversation with the words "Let us not rebuke our father."

Far from reproving his father, Skarphéðinn always respects his wishes. Indeed, at a critical moment in the story Skarphéðinn upbraids a potential ally, Þorkell hákur, by berating him for having browbeaten and bullied his father: "I have never bullied or browbeaten my father as you once did." Yet so capricious is human life that even such respectful deportment is not free of danger. It is as though untapped forces are building up within Skarphéðinn, a powerful urge to assert himself according to the laws of his own nature—as when pockets of water, generated by subterranean heat, are trapped inside a glacier and build up until they suddenly gush forth in a violent flood. Because of Skarphéðin's love and respect for his father this process goes on in the mysterious depths of the soul without his conscious knowledge of it. How far will matters have to go before he intercedes on his own initiative and without the agreement of his father? It is precisely in men of such a temperament that the possibility of such an outburst is greatest. Sometimes it takes only a small flame to ignite the fire.

IV

From the very outset Skarphéðinn had an aversion to Þráinn Sigfússon. Þráinn was present when Þórður leysingjason, the foster father of the Njálssons, was slain. He was in Hallgerð's quarters when Sigmundur vilified Njáll and his sons. On these occasions he was present, but did not take an active part. But when Helgi and Grímur went abroad, they endured such great indignity and hardship because of their noble treatment of Þráinn that they came close to losing their lives. After their return to Iceland, Þráinn refused to pay them fitting indemnity, but he was cautious not to offend them directly and even reprimanded those of his household who did so. Through his passive intransigence he maneuvered the Njálssons into an intolerably awkward position. The outcome of all this was that Skarphéðinn slew Þráinn, but there is good reason to believe that he was uneasy about this killing since the enmity and offenses of Þráinn had not been made sufficiently known to the public.

Now Njáll takes Þráin's son Höskuldur as his foster son in an endeavor to bring about complete reconciliation. His own sons, who do not want to fail to do their part, try to forget what has happened; but the memory of the old enmity, the indignities suffered by them on Þráin's account, and their slaying of him persists under the surface. The Njálssons put forth every effort to demonstrate their warm affection for Höskuldur, and these demonstrations of friendship are all the stronger because of their treacherous foundation.

Höskuldur Hvítanesgoði forgives completely. He is absolutely impervious to the incitements and insinuations of his friends and kinsmen. But when they seek revenge by killing Höskuldur Njálsson, this act is a source of severe vexation to the brothers of the slain man. This time dissension between them is kept under control by both Njáll and Höskuldur, for they bring about a reconciliation following the slaying of Höskuldur Njálsson and the brothers of Lýtingur, and again after the vengeance wreaked on Lýtingur by Njál's blind grandson, Ámundi Höskuldsson (chapter 106). The protestation of friendship between Höskuldur and the sons of Njáll continues, but Skarphéðinn has been more than sufficiently reminded by these events of the injury he inflicted on Höskuldur by slaying his father. Would it not be the most difficult of all forms of forgiveness, especially for a man like Skarphéðinn, to forgive another for the wrongs he himself had inflicted upon him? At this point it is of the utmost importance that no mishap should occur which might upset Njál's plan.

This is the situation when Mörður enters the story. The saga does not cease telling about the warm friendship which exists between Höskuldur and the sons of Njáll. I doubt whether such strong protestations of affection occur in the saga unless evil of some kind is imminent. Thus they are a form of leitmotif which provides one of the principal aids in the interpretation of these events. The precarious nature of this friendship cannot remain hidden from anyone who reads the saga perceptively. In addition, we must keep in mind the relationship of Skarphéðinn to his father, as I have tried to explain it above. And now the slander of Mörður begins.

V

Why cannot the Ear be closed to its own destruction,
Or the glistning Eye to the Poison of a smile?

                                        WILLIAM BLAKE

As we have already seen, Mörður has long harbored a malignant
rancor against Njáll and his sons because of his unhappy dealings with
Gunnar (chapters 70–71) and because Skarphéðinn cowed him into
paying Högni Gunnarsson a large sum of money in atonement for the
killing of Gunnar (chapter 79). Now old injuries are aggravated as
droves of Mörð's thingmen desert him in favor of Höskuldur, whom
Njáll has had appointed Hvítanesgoði (chapter 97). Here the struggle is
for something which men have fought and risked their lives for
throughout the ages: power. It doesn't require much incitement from
Valgarður grái to prompt Mörður into slandering Höskuldur to the
Njálssons.

One day Mörður rides to Bergþórshvoll, where he finds Skarphéðinn and his brothers. "He struck up a conversation with them and
spoke to them with flattering words, and said he would like to see more
of them. Skarphéðinn took all of this well, but remarked that Mörður
had never sought their company before." This desire of Mörður to
associate with the Njálssons strikes Skarphéðinn as strange, coming as
it does so late and unexpectedly and without apparent reason. And yet
it turns out that Mörður "insinuated himself into their friendship to
such a degree that neither he nor they made any decision without consulting each other."

We do not need to find fault with this episode, in my opinion, in
regard to content. The previous dealings between Mörður and Skarphéðinn have not been such as to render a friendly relationship between
them altogether impossible. On the other hand, they have not had
anything to do with each other for such a long time that Mörð's visit
and proposal strike Skarphéðinn as a bit odd. But now Mörð's great
power of persuasion, which is displayed elsewhere in the saga, comes
into play. (We recall that he succeeded in persuading much more

experienced men than the Njálssons, such as Ketill in Mörk and Flosi, to believe his lies.) But although the content of the episode is credible enough, the presentation undeniably leaves something to be desired: the author neglects to let his audience hear the conversation between Mörður and the Njálssons, and thus to show how he succeeds in convincing them. This happens again when Mörður makes his final attack. Here too the author fails to develop the dialogue as carefully as he should, but in this case, of course, we are dealing with secret plotting, and the author of *Njála* usually doesn't reveal many details about such matters. But here of all places he should have made use of his fine art of expository dialogue. This would have stimulated the reader's imagination, and he would have been able to perceive what was happening, just as he is able to follow the slandering of Þórólfur by the sons of Hildiríður in *Egils saga* (chapters 12 and 15) or the scheming of crafty old Ófeigur in *Bandamanna saga*. Intrinsically these two instances are no more credible than Mörð's malicious behavior, but they are more convincingly motivated.

Mörður proceeds cautiously and quietly until he has wormed himself into the confidence of the Njálssons, but before long he has become their bosom friend. "Njáll always disliked Mörð's visits, and he always showed his vexation." His sons cannot help knowing how strongly he disapproves of this friendship, which has just a trace of the attraction of forbidden fruit. Skarphéðinn manages to keep each in its own compartment: his relationship with Mörður and his loyalty to his father. There is no estrangement between father and son, but they go their own separate ways. Njál's dismay and apprehension exert an influence on Skarphéðinn without his being consciously aware of it. This casts a shadow on his friendship with Mörður and imbues it with a peculiar inclination toward disaster. Njál's antipathy brings about an involuntary and subconscious resistance on the part of Skarphéðinn.

At a memorial feast in honor of his father, Valgarður, Mörður seals their friendship with costly gifts. When the Njálssons display these gifts at home and praise them, Njáll says that they have probably been bought at full price—"and beware that you do not reward him for them in the way he desires." A rift has now developed between father and sons, and his words of warning and prophecy of evil merely serve to widen that rift, so that they no longer consult him about their dealings with Mörður.

The illusory friendship with Höskuldur is at its height, but now Mörður boldly begins his calumniation. He soon has to give up on Höskuldur, who would rather endure an injustice than commit one— yet his false charges are crafty enough. He tells Höskuldur that the Njálssons merely wanted to mock him by giving him a young stallion unproven in fighting, just as he himself is young and untried. He reminds him of the slaying of Lýtingur, which is a delicate subject. He further tries to make Höskuldur believe that Skarphéðinn is plotting treachery against him because he envies him his *goðorð*, and Mörður backs up these false charges with specific trumped-up evidence. Nevertheless Höskuldur remains impervious to his malicious defamation.

At this point I must say a few words parenthetically concerning one of Mörð's accusations. It might seem natural to assume, as Jóhann Sigurjónsson does in his stage play *Løgneren* (*The Liar*) that Skarphéðinn has begun to look with envious eyes at Höskuld's popularity and power, and to imagine that his father has passed him over in favor of his foster brother. But a careful reading of the saga, in my opinion, yields no support for that point of view.

Skarphéðinn slays Höskuldur with the exclamation, "Don't bother to try to take to your heels, Hvítanesgoði!" In my opinion these words are very shaky support for that interpretation, and nothing else that Skarphéðinn says has any bearing on the matter. We must keep in mind that Mörður mentions the *goðorð* to Höskuldur and not to Skarphéðinn as he would have had to do if he had wished to arouse envy in him. This would then have been the essence of his calumniation. That he did not do so is, I believe, the crucial point.

In order to adduce sufficient evidence of Skarphéðin's alleged jealousy, Jóhann Sigurjónsson cites Njál's statement that he would rather have lost his own sons than Höskuldur. If these words had been spoken before the slaying, one could assume that they had some influence on Skarphéðin's behavior. But Njáll does not make that statement until after the slaying, and nothing is said by or about Skarphéðinn before the slaying which would indicate that he thought he was denied the full measure of his father's love.

Regarding Mörð's conversations with the Njálssons, the author says somewhat casually that he spoke "much" with them. He seems at first not to have had appreciably more success with them than with Höskuldur, but he has little difficulty in finding sensitive topics on which to center his false charges. He pretends that he has heard Höskuldur himself charge that Skarphéðinn broke the settlement with Lýtingur by instigating Ámundi's attack on him. This is a more sensitive matter for Skarphéðinn than one might believe at first, for Skarphéðinn did not voluntarily enter into that settlement. Furthermore, the mention of it aggravates old injuries that should have remained forgotten. Then Mörður tries to convince Skarphéðinn that Höskuldur suspects him of malice and treachery. He knows that if the brothers can be brought to half-believe this slander, the cordiality between them and Höskuldur will quickly dwindle away. He also tries to convince them that Höskuldur several times planned treachery against them. "And when he had said this, they at first rejected it, but finally they came to believe it."

There are many factors to be kept in mind here. The Njálsson's have no cause to doubt Höskuld's power as Hvítanesgoði or the fact that some of his many followers bear them no good will. But how can they believe such malicious slander about a man whom they have known since he was a child? Perhaps they are handicapped by lack of experience in human affairs, since Njáll has always led them by the hand and has made their decisions for them. And perhaps Skarphéðinn, as it were, sees himself in Höskuld's position. Would it not have been exceedingly difficult for him to "carry his father in his purse"—to forego blood vengeance and even treat his killers well? As we know from other sagas, the voice of blood relationship was wont to assert itself under such circumstances. Before it, the firmest friendship and fidelity toward foster relatives disappeared quickly, like fog before a gale.

Here then all streams come together: Skarphéðin's desire to make his own decisions and live his own life; a secret chafing from the bonds which his father's will has placed upon him; a lack of life experience which resulted from those bonds; the ambivalent feelings which underlie his cordiality toward the son of his former enemy Þráinn Sigfússon. His power of resistance to the venom of the slander bearer grows weaker than might be expected. It is as though the ear were straining to hear his words, the words of perdition.

As soon as the Njálssons begin to put faith in the slander of Mörður, the estrangement between them and Höskuldur sets in. This is natural and inevitable. They know well how distasteful it all is to Njáll, but they continue to go their own way. And Njál's dark forebodings cast an ever greater pall of impending misfortune over their actions. Thus the second chapter of Mörð's calumniation comes to an end (chapter 110).

VI

The estrangement between Höskuldur and his foster brothers has lasted for a whole year and has become firmly rooted. Mörður continues to mix poisonous draughts for them. He eggs them on to kill Höskuldur, declaring that Höskuldur will certainly get his blow in first if they do not attack him at once. Skarphéðinn believes Mörður, but shows caution. He matches Mörð's craftiness with a trick of his own. "You may have your way," he says, "if you are willing to go along and take some part in it yourself." Mörður is compelled to offer himself as a pawn for his words.

Now they ride to Vorsabær and kill Höskuldur Hvítanesgoði. Skarphéðinn strikes the first and hardest blow, but all of them inflict wounds upon him. It is important to consider the significance of this fact. When Sigmundur Lambason and his Swedish companion Skjöldur slay Þórður leysingjason (chapter 42), he challenges them to attack him one at a time in accordance with ancient rules of warriors, but Sigmundur declares that they will take advantage of their superior numbers: this is a practical but barbarous point of view. Skarphéðinn, who gives Sigmundur the opportunity of arming himself before he wreaks vengeance on him (chapter 45), would never have acted that way. But when they now all participate in the attack on Höskuldur, the situation is quite different: the purpose is to share the guilt among them. This killing is completely different from all the other homicides which Skarphéðinn has committed, for in all other cases he was willing to assume full responsibility himself. But this is a conspiracy into which he has entered with ambivalent feelings. To be sure, when the attack begins, he falls into a warlike mood: "Don't bother to try to take to your heels, Hvítanesgoði!" He deals Höskuldur a terrible blow with his ax, but Höskuld's counterblow is still more dreadful: "May God help me and forgive all of you!" This is the severest test which the noble-minded warrior has to endure: Höskuldur is guiltless, and his own deed is a contemptible crime.

Now they return home, and here another severe test awaits them—the confrontation with their father. They report to him what they have done. "This is sorrowful news," he says, "and terrible to hear, for I can honestly say that it grieves me so deeply that I would rather have lost two of my own sons to have Höskuldur alive." Njál's grief and displeasure cut Skarphéðinn to the quick, and the last words of his father are bitter to hear, but he masks his feelings as well as he can: "'You must be forgiven,' said Skarphéðinn, 'for you are an old man, and it is natural that you should take it so hard.'" This is the first but not the last time that he refers to Njál's age. Perhaps he realizes, as he gazes on this sorrowful man in front of the farmhouse at Bergþórshvoll, that his father is aging like withering grass.

VII

No longer content to follow the guidance of their father, the Njálssons had begun to go their own way. A rift had developed between them and their father, so wide that it was scarcely possible for the human voice to carry across it. Despite his superior wisdom and intelligence, they no longer sought his counsel, but instead went to Ásgrímur Elliðagrímsson for advice. The freedom which they had claimed for themselves had led them into heinous crime, into the misfortune of which Njáll had always warned them. For this reason it was all the more difficult for them to discuss the matter with him.

Misfortune and anguish filled the mind of Skarphéðinn; his crime was too infamous to allow him any hope for a tolerable settlement of the matter. If he had been permitted to live with the memory of his crime, he would have borne his burden in such a way that no one would have been aware of it. But this was not the case. His enemies taunted him incessantly about it; that alone would not have been unbearable, for he was quite able to match taunt with taunt. More trying was the fact that he and his brothers had to discuss the matter with their friends, Ásgrímur and Gizur—and with their father. They had to hear their father's and their friends' opinion of the terrible deed, counsel with them, and go about at the General Assembly begging for support for their lawsuit. Under these circumstances there was nothing left for Skarphéðinn but to grin. His grin was the shell which covered his feelings, an attempt to conceal his anguish. He had to hear from the lips of his own father the statement that he would rather have lost all of his sons to have Höskuldur alive. He could do nothing else but grit his teeth and grin.

Attempts to bring about a settlement by arbitration among the litigants were now initiated, and gifts from members of the Assembly began flowing in to help pay the huge compensation for Höskuld's slaying, which had to be paid immediately. The money was all gathered together into one place, and Njáll was happy at the good prospects of a solution: "I want to ask you, my sons, not to spoil this in any way." Skarphéðinn stroked his forehead and grinned. Was this not all a nightmare? Was this not too abhorrent to be real? How clean are weapons, how beautiful to fight, to risk one's life, to kill or be killed. But this!

For all that, Skarphéðinn did not intend to violate the settlement which his father was attempting to bring about, then or at any other time. It was not deliberate intent that prevented a reconciliation, but the vehemence of Flosi and himself. Njáll had added a gift of a pair of boots and a beautiful silk cloak to the required compensation, both as a matter of custom and as a sign of good will. But Flosi must have regarded the cloak, which could be worn by either a man or a woman, as an insinuation of unmanliness on his part, and at the same time he recalled Höskuld's bloody cloak, which he himself had given him, and Hildigunn's adamant demand for blood vengeance (chapter 116). He and Skarphéðinn exchanged taunting insults. Both of them knew full well what the consequences of their altercation could be, and yet both appeared to experience a feeling of relief at having given vent to seething, pent-up emotions. This could best be seen in Skarphéðin's grin, which had lost its former anguish.

VIII

Time passed, until one evening late in summer Flosi came with his band of men westward over the home field at Bergþórshvoll. Njáll and his sons and servants, thirty of them capable of bearing arms, were standing outside in front of the house. Father and sons discussed what they should do. Njáll asked, "How many men do you think there are?" "They are a tightly knit force," replied Skarphéðinn, "and large in numbers, too. But now they have halted because they suspect they will have a hard fight to overcome us." It was easy to see that Skarphéðinn was getting into a fighting mood. He weighed the odds, and decided it was best to fight, come what might. Njáll wanted to go inside, declaring that the attackers would find it difficult to overcome them, just as the men did who attacked Gunnar at Hlíðarendi.

> Njáll said, "Now you are going to override my advice, my sons, and show me disrespect, as you have done before. But when you were younger, you did not do so, and things went better for you then."
> Helgi said, "Let us do as our father wishes. That will be best for us."

"I'm not so sure about that," said Skarphéðinn, "for now he is a doomed man. But I am willing to please him by burning to death inside with him, for I am not afraid to die."

Although it may seem strange at first thought, these incomparable words of Skarphéðinn show that he is now a free man. He has attained the freedom which he had not gained by rebelling against his father. His actions are not governed by the submissiveness of a child, as is the case with Helgi. It is just as though life has become clear and transparent for him. He can see through it, weigh its values, and make a conscious, deliberate choice. He knows what his love for his father will cost, but he makes his choice nevertheless. The fear of the walls which hem him in loses its power before his seeing eyes.

Of course he does not sit by with idle hands; that is not his nature. He defends the door of the house bravely and kills those who venture too near. Like his brothers and Kári, he snatches up the blazing brands as they fall and hurls them with all his might at the attackers, and Skarphéðinn repays Gunnar Lambason's taunting by playing a grisly trick on him. Yet when Kári suggests that the two of them attempt to escape, he lets himself be persuaded, albeit with some hesitation, and he insists that Kári go out first. Because of Kári's entreaty, he is willing to surrender to his instinct to live; but life no longer holds any enchanting illusions for him. When he tries to follow Kári out of the house, the crossbeam breaks beneath him and the roofbeam crashes down on him. His only words are, "It is clear now what is to be."

As his father prepares to lie down to await his death, Skarphéðinn makes the comment, "Father is going to bed early, as is to be expected, for he is an old man." Skarphéðinn is completely himself, but now all the former bitterness is gone, and in these words we detect a remarkable peace and warmth. Later he says, "Now my father must be dead, and not a cough or groan was heard from him." With these admiring, valiant words he conceals his own emotions.

Finally his brother Grímur falls down dead beside him. Now he is alone. This is fitting and proper. Throughout the saga Skarphéðinn is usually seen together with other people, and yet there is a greater air of loneliness about him than about anyone else in *Njála*. Alone in the world, surrounded by flames. The author could not have provided a more appropriate framework than this for his final picture of him, for flaming fires have always burned within his breast. It may be that the author here has exceeded the bounds of what is called "realism," but he has thereby endowed his story with a higher form of reality. He gives Skarphéðinn the opportunity to do what remains to be done, regardless of how fiercely the fires rage and the smoke swirls around him.

We hear him speak a verse down in the flames, a troll-like verse which no one understands—it seems to be about a woman who cannot hold back her tears. . . .

A warrior loves his weapons. Roland addresses his sword Durendal and tries to destroy it so that it will not fall into unworthy hands. Skarphéðinn silently drives his ax into the gable wall of the house so that the steel will not lose its temper because of the heat.

There still remains one thing for him to do before he dies. He burns a cross on his back and another on his chest and then folds his arms in the form of a cross. Heathen warriors branded themselves with the point of a spear, thus dedicating themselves to Óðinn. It is just as if Skarphéðinn brands himself in a similar way, but with a Christian mark, thus dedicating himself to Christ. At the same time he expiates the heinous crime he committed against Höskuldur by burning it away. Now everything is complete.

When the fires die down, Skarphéðinn is found standing upright against the gable end of the house, between it and the fallen roof, his legs burned off almost up to the knees. He had turned away from the wall when the roof collapsed. He bit hard on his beard because of the intense pain from the fire, but his eyes were open and not swollen. He died with seeing eyes, undefeated, and free.

IX

Thus this great hero died. A man who constantly had to keep his powerful temperament under constraint—and not without danger to himself and others. A man of noble character whose conscience was tortured by the guilt of a heinous crime. A lonely soul who concealed his sensitive nature with mockery. One of the most memorable individuals in this magnificent collection of character portraits. The most fateful relationship he had with other people was his attachment to his father. Perhaps Skarphéðin's life story is not easy to understand, but if it is read carefully and perceptively, it will be seen that it is characterized by a consistency to its own inner logic. It is not necessary to rewrite the saga or to resort to other extreme measures. Admittedly this portrait was not created in accordance with the four computations of arithmetic, if I may resort to a mathematical simile, but in accordance with the dimensions of a higher geometry of human understanding and character portrayal, with the likes of which few poets are gifted. But even though we accept the story of Skarphéðinn as true—true in a poetic, artistic, psychological sense—we nevertheless do not completely lose our sense of awe and amazement at his prodigious personality and fate. It is the same sense of wonder that grips men when they stand face to face with human life itself.

7. Njáll

I

There was a man named Njáll, who was the son of Þorgeir gollnir, the son of Þórólfur. Njál's mother was Ásgerður, who was the daughter of the chieftain Áskell inn ómálgi ("the Silent"). She had come to Iceland and settled east of the river Markarfljót between Öldusteinn and Seljalandsmúli. One of her sons was Holta-Þórir, the father of Þorleifur krákur ("Crow"), from whom the men of Skógar are descended, and of Þorgrímur inn mikli ("the Tall") and Skorargeir. Njáll lived at Bergþórshvoll in the Landeyjar, and he owned another farm at Þórólfsfell. He was a man of means and of handsome appearance, but he had one blemish: he could never grow a beard. He was so skillful at law that he had no equal. He was wise, prescient, and benevolent. He gave sound counsel, and all the advice he gave people turned out well. He was gentle and generous. He saw far into the future and remembered far into the past. He solved the problems of all people who came to him for help.

Thus Njáll is introduced to the reader in chapter 20 of the saga.[1] We perceive immediately the two dominant traits of his character: on the one hand, his superior intellect, and on the other, his benevolence. We meet many other wise men in the saga, but in Njáll the distinctive features of his personality blend in such a unique manner that he cannot possibly be confused with any other individual.

1. Of the mass of scholarly writing on Njáll, the following are of especial importance in connection with this chapter: C. Hauch, "Inledning til Forelæsninger over Njals saga og flere med den beslægtede Sagaer," *Afhandlinger og æsthetiske Betragtninger* (1855), pp. 461 ff.; A. U. Bååth, *Studier* (1885), pp. 89 ff.; Helgi Pjeturss, "Úr trúarsögu Forn-Íslendinga," *Skírnir* LXXX (1906), pp. 55 ff. and *Vaka* II, pp. 288–91; and Einar Benediktsson's poem "Á Njálsbúð," *Hafblik* (1906), p. 19.

The description comprises in a few words the chief elements of his intellect, which embraces a wide area. He is endowed with an unusual degree of worldly wisdom. He remembers far into the past, sees far into the future, and possesses a keen calculating ability. He once makes use of the word "net" in outlining one of his complicated plans which lead eventually to the killing of Þráinn Sigfússon. He ends his counsel with the words "*ok er því langa nót at at draga,*" "and that is why we must cast a wide net" (chapter 91). His adversaries are like foolish fish which are caught in the net of the clever man. In his methods of procedure we often notice considerable craftiness. His skill in litigation is vastly superior to that of anyone else in the saga. His cleverness and practicality in handling individual lawsuits is matched only by his comprehensive knowledge of the law in its entirety. (This is not the place to discuss in detail the fact that many a lawyer from the time of the Commonwealth [930–1262] would not always have been impressed with some of his legal machinations, and the author of *Njála* would have devised them quite differently if he himself had been better versed in the law of Njál's day. But the more remote that day became, the more receptive readers were to the author's account of legal matters; and today both a careful reading of the saga and a sound knowledge of the ancient laws are necessary to detect the many anachronisms and discrepancies here. But this is a historical and not a literary problem, and so we shall pass over it since, as I have already indicated, the historical value of the saga lies beyond the bounds of this discussion.)

According to *Njála*, Snorri goði (the central figure in *Eyrbyggja saga* and a major figure in several other sagas) was the wisest man among those who were not prescient. The wisdom of Njáll, however, had more strands, for he was also prescient. He had forebodings of coming events, he had premonitions and dreams about them, he foresaw the approaching death of men in visions, and he perceived men's wraiths. Sometimes he made prophecies of future events, the sources of which the author did not reveal.

These two strands of Njál's intellectual powers—his worldly wisdom and his prescience—are intimately woven together, although to be sure from time to time one or the other is dominant, and they characterize his personality in a very unique manner. His active power of reasoning, which is directed toward achieving definite material aims and is fraught with egoism and the hope for the advancement of his own and his friend's interests, means that his personality seldom attains the remarkable dispassionate candidness peculiar to Hallur of Síða or Gestur Oddleifsson. But his prophetic powers transform the prudent man into a sage, so that the keen sight of the falcon is fused with or gives way to the gift of second sight. The battle of worldly wisdom develops into a profound ethical and spiritual struggle. And interwoven with all this, and beneath his profound earnestness, we can glimpse a good-natured sense of humor.

I have already referred to the different reactions of Bergþóra and Njáll at the news of Gunnar's shabby treatment at the farm Kirkjubær. Njáll gives vent to his indignation at Otkel's behavior, but Bergþóra curtly reminds him that it would be better for him to help Gunnar than to sit and waste words about it. She is always ready to act, while her husband needs more to be encouraged than discouraged. Does this mean that his habit of reflection has paralyzed his ability to act, as is the case with so many men of reflection? I do not know how that question would be answered on the basis of incidents like this one, but I am certain that a careful examination of the saga as a whole will reveal that it is not so.

Njáll is no warrior. He is never seen with a weapon in his hands except, so to speak, for the sake of convention, and even then he carries only a very small ax. Yet he does become involved in manslaughter now and then. He encourages rather than discourages the slaying of Sigmundur Lambason (chapter 44), and he seems to give his consent to the killing of Þráinn Sigfússon (chapter 91). But even though his honor was violated in both cases, the initial impulse to these deeds of vengeance does not come from him. Following the slaying of his friend Gunnar, however, it is Njáll himself who requests that Skarphéðinn help Högni Gunnarsson wreak vengeance on the slayers. Njáll has sometimes been accused of using others (and those others are, as a matter of fact, his own sons) as tools, but in reality there is no foundation for this accusation. The hand and not the head was made for striking, and it would never for one moment occur to Njáll to doubt this elementary fact. And with this we have arrived at one of the essential traits of his mode of thought: his patriarchal mentality. This can be explained most easily with a biblical metaphor: Njáll regards his family as one body, of which he, as a matter of course, is the head. The misfortune or death of any member of his family is comparable to a serious body wound or the loss of an arm or a leg—so close is the relationship among them. But there is no question in his mind as to whose will must prevail.

And when all is said and done, it is obvious that this is the case. As long as the slaying of the menservants is going on, Bergþóra is no less ruthless than Hallgerður in violating settlements made by Njáll and Gunnar—but only as long as the stakes are low and as long as she feels that Njáll will put up with it. But when he enters into a settlement after the slaying of Þórður leysingjason, Bergþóra does not violate it, and all of his sons' manslaughters (except one) are committed more or less with his consent. Njáll never doubts that they will honor any settlement he makes. His will is their command—until Mörður succeeds in duping them, and to a certain degree it is possible because they have not been given enough freedom by their father. Among the last words of Bergþóra in the saga is the statement that she was young when she was *given* to Njáll, and these words are to be interpreted literally.

Everyone submits to Njál's gentle but firm rule. Those who come into his household soon learn to respect the power of his personality. After the burning, Kári speaks of no one so often as of Njáll and Skarphéðinn, and Þórhallur Ásgrímsson comes to love him more dearly than his own father. Atli is deeply concerned about what Njáll will think about his slaying of Kolur, and declares that he would rather die in Njál's home than anywhere else.

Njáll is "the beardless man," and his enemies find this a convenient subject for ridicule. But he has had sons with his wife, sons who have not let their slain kinsmen lie unavenged before the door. When Kári enters the story, it is with the comment that father and sons bear a famous name. Gunnar is usually careful to follow Njál's counsels, Snorri goði recalls them with respect and gratitude, Ólafur pái is greatly impressed by them, and Mörður fears them. Thus he enjoys great respect both within and beyond the circle of kinsmen and friends. Among his friends and clients this respect is accompanied by love and veneration; among his enemies, it is strongly blended with fear and apprehension.

For everyone knows that Njál's plans are always effective. To be sure, he is slower to act than Bergþóra; he himself follows the advice he once gave her: "All in good time, slow but sure." (Yet when Þorgeir Starkaðarson and Þorgeir Otkelsson set out to attack his friend Gunnar, Njáll, to be sure, is anything but leisurely in both word and deed.) His counsels and planning are always appropriate to the situation, and the time interval between their conception and execution is not too long. As Einar Benediktsson so aptly says in his well-known poem about Njáll: "The steel of his will was tempered and tough and pure."

II

Early in the saga Helgi Njálsson says to his father, "I know that you are both wise and benevolent." Njáll possesses both intelligence and benevolence. It is well to keep in mind that these are two quite different qualities, and that they can easily come into conflict with each other. The author of *Njála* has a clear understanding of what might be called "intelligence viewed as a natural phenomenon." He well knows that great intelligence can eliminate all feelings other than the sheer pleasure of devising plans and of trying to reshape the world in accordance with these plans. The human beings who are involved or affected are simply figures on a chessboard or statistics on a chart. The planner concentrates only on the chart itself, and all human and personal considerations are disregarded in the sheer pleasure of scheming and the endeavor to turn the schemes into reality. Instances of this can be found on every page of human history, if we concentrate our attention on clever rulers, heads of state, church dignitaries, doctrinaire and domineering revolutionaries, etc. Many more men of this kind than is generally believed owe their success to the slogan that the end justifies the means. The historian Lord Acton once went so far as to contend that great men are nearly always evil. Even though this cannot be accepted at face value, it must be admitted that ambitious men in high position frequently are unscrupulous in their treatment of others—not because they are inherently evil, but because their intellectual powers outweigh all other considerations.

There is no doubt that Njáll thoroughly enjoyed the intellectual game of scheming to outwit his adversaries. But to arrive at a clearer understanding of the cooperation between heart and mind, it is necessary to consider both Njál's goals and the means he employed to achieve them. What did he endeavor to accomplish and what methods did he use?

In the society of which Njáll is a member most affairs are between or among individuals. Thus his endeavors are first and foremost related to individual human beings. I have already alluded to Njál's patriarchal mentality and indicated that his self-love embraces his entire family, but in such a way that he takes it for granted that his wishes will be respected: this is his only prerogative. He is always at hand with advice for his sons, especially with counsel designed to protect them from misfortune or disaster. On the other hand, he is always as moderate in avenging injuries as the prevailing code of honor permits. He does not use his superior intellect to gain wealth or power, either for himself or for his family, at the expense of others.

Next to his family, Njál's greatest concern is for the welfare of his friends. In the series of killings among his and Gunnar's servants, he takes pains not to break his friendship with Gunnar; yet it is clear that he regards his own servants more highly than those of Gunnar, and that it is Gunnar who must take the initiative and put forth every effort to please Njáll. But once these difficulties have been cleared up, Njáll is willing to do all he can for Gunnar, and he is a perfect friend to him. He is even prepared to endanger his own sons to help him, and he encourages Skarphéðinn to avenge his assassination at the risk of his life.

But Njál's helpful counsel extends beyond the circles of family and friends. In the description of him given above we read that he "solved the problems of all people who came to him for help," and this fact is repeated in various places in the saga. Here there is no longer any question of selfish motives whatsoever; not friendship or love of kinsmen, but benevolence alone prompts him to do this. It is as natural for him to give of his gifts of prescience and wisdom and to distribute them far and wide as it is for the sun to shine.

Sometimes Njáll champions causes without concern for the people involved. He supports as strongly as possible the Christian mission of Þangbrandur (chapters 100–105). Time after time he raises the banner of civilized society against brutality and unrestrained violence. His personal rule of conduct is based on the ancient proverb "With laws shall our land by built up, and not laid waste by lawlessness." [2] He endeavors to the best of his ability to replace the clash of arms with the persuasion of law, but most of all he strives for informal meetings of arbitration, for in such meetings the true facts of a dispute are ascertained and the highest possible degree of justice is attained. Such settlements are both most equitable and most durable, and above all Njáll is a fair and upright man.

Njáll is truthful. As Högni Gunnarsson says after the slaying of his father, Njáll has never been known to lie. He is concerned that the cause he supports be just. He is a friend to his friends (as the poem *Hávamál* requires), but his friendship makes high ethical demands. He

2. For a discussion of the origin and the variants of this proverb see *Íslenzk fornrit*, Vol. XII, p. lxxviii. The variant quoted here is from the law book *Járnsíða*. In the saga (chapter 70) Njáll says, "With laws shall our land be built up, but with lawlessness laid waste." But see also the variant MS readings in the edition cited, p. 172, note 6.

tolerates no baseness, importunity, or violence on the part of his friends. From the very outset Njál's personality is molded by this mode of thought. Although he mercilessly employs all of his legal cunning to defeat his opponents, he demands of the victors, his clients, that they be high-minded and moderate enough to accept a just settlement even though they might be, so to speak, in position to deliver a coup de grâce. And even though his friends' enemies sometimes feel the coldness of his counsels, I can find no indication anywhere of any special inclination on his part to inflict undue injury upon them. Coldness and superior intellect, after all, go together.

In several passages in the saga we can perceive this purely intellectual coldness in dealing with people, together with an unmistakable delight in devising plans. I shall not dwell at length on the first piece of advice proffered by Njáll concerning the manner in which Gunnar was to make good the dowry claim of his kinswoman Unnur against her divorced husband, Hrútur. As Gunnar himself said, Unn's claim was just and legal, yet the situation was delicate and unpleasant. Furthermore, according to Njál's plan a well-mannered man has to demean himself to play the role of a vulgar and disagreeable creature. There can be little doubt that Gunnar would have preferred to perform this unpleasant task in a more dignified manner. In this case the sheer delight in cunning and cleverness overrode Njál's better judgment and delicate sensitivity to what is appropriate for a man as well-mannered as Gunnar—a sensitivity which is more in accord with his uprightness.

And now one piece of advice follows the other, and it is difficult to determine whether Njáll is motivated more by his delight in devising plans or by his care and concern for his friend Gunnar. In the course of time the latter predominates, nor does it decrease when he realizes that misfortune is beginning to threaten his sons. But precisely under these circumstances he contrives two plans which are especially noteworthy.

The first of these is the advice mentioned above which he gives his sons upon their return from the voyage during which they have suf-

fered severe hardship and humiliation on Þráin's account without re-
ceiving the compensation they have a right to expect from him. Njáll
devises this plan only after there has been widespread derogatory
comment about the matter, and thus, in a sense, under duress. This is
the scheme which he himself describes as a wide net in which he intends
to ensnare his enemies. The aim of this scheme is to provide his sons
with moral and legal charges against Þráinn and his followers by luring
them into committing such acts as will lead to their destruction, that is,
such acts as will influence public opinion to accept them as legitimate
grounds for blood vengeance. Here it is necessary to give matters just
enough of a nudge to set them into motion, and then to let them run
their course, meanwhile biding one's time: to crouch like a beast of
prey ready to spring, or to sit back in peace and quiet like a spider giving
the flies time to enmesh themselves in its web. This is reminiscent of
Mörð's advice to Þorgeir Starkaðarson; it is the same game of sitting
back and waiting, and Mörður also talks about "hunting" (*veiða*) the
enemy.

The second of these plans is Njál's endeavor to obtain a *goðorð* for
his foster son, Höskuldur (chapter 97). When it becomes clear that
there is no *goðorð* available for purchase, Njáll resorts to a clever expedient: when people appeal to him for help at the General Assembly,
he gives them advice of such a nature as to make it impossible for their
litigation to be concluded. He is unconcerned about the possibility that
the unsettled lawsuits could lead to a chain of manslaughters without
end. People are amazed that this man, so highly esteemed for his sound
counsel, should be so devoid of all feeling of responsibility as to give
such advice. The following summer the men involved declare they will
settle their disputes with spear and sword rather than by due process of
law. And then Njáll proposes the establishment of a Fifth Court
(*fimtardómr*) as a solution for their difficulties, thereby securing a *goðorð*
for Höskuldur. Here we see combined in a very strange manner an
honorable, yet egoistic purpose (the acquisition of the *goðorð*), a crafty
and irresponsible method of procedure (the advice given at the General

Assembly), and finally a noteworthy social reform (the establishment
of the Fifth Court). So intricate are his dealings.

When Höskuldur obtains his chieftaincy, Njáll is unconcerned that
the new *goðorð* draws retainers away from the original chieftaincies,
and thus—without especially desiring to, of course—he treads on the
old serpent Mörður, who has not used his fangs for a long, long time.
And this does not escape revenge.

These examples show that Njáll, that benevolent and conciliatory
sage who gave counsel to all who wished it, also knew the temptations
of the intellect. He was well able to make use of cunning. The well-
known quotation from a poem about Ulrich von Hutten can truthfully
be applied to him: he was "*ein Mensch mit seinem Widerspruch*" ("a
human being with his own contradiction").

III

For a better understanding of what has gone before and what is to
follow, I must say a few words about Njál's moral and ethical views.

It is well known that the concept of honor was of fundamental
importance in the Icelandic code of ethics in ancient times. Almost every
page of the ancient literature reveals this fact. Honor consisted not only
in vanquishing an adversary, but in achieving excellence in every
respect. Closely related to the concept of honor was the ideal of noble-
mindedness (*drengskapur*), the highest virtue of all and the closest northern pagan parallel of the southern concept of *courtoisie*.

This concept of honor provides the basis for Njál's ethical views, and
he never quite abandons it. He several times gives his approval to the
wreaking of blood vengeance, and this too is closely connected to the
pagan concept of honor.[3] But he does not regard blood vengeance as
justified unless it is unavoidable. Njáll has an exceptionally high regard
for the code of ethics to the extent that it contributes to a more civilized
form of society and harmonizes with conciliation and benevolence. In

3. On this question see Ólafur Lárusson, "Hefndir," *Samtíd og saga* I (1941),
156–86.

his view the highest form of honor consists in being slow to retaliate for an injustice, and in being moderate, noble-minded, conscientious, and upright.

Njáll tries to bring the concept of honor as far as possible into harmony with peace and good will among men. The author describes him as a "gentle" man (*hógværr*), and Njáll refers to himself as being "fond of ease" (*værugjarn*). He knows that there is always a difference of opinion about an act of vengeance, once it has been committed, and indeed, that there is a difference of opinion about every action that is taken. He understands and loves all the many virtues which flourish under the protection of peace. In his hands the law is a powerful instrument of peace and reconciliation. Yet it cannot be denied that, although honor can exist side by side with peace and good will, the two concepts are so diverse that they can easily collide with each other. Consequently Njál's life is full of conflict.

Njál's benevolence is completely in conformity with the spirit of Christianity, and after the conversion of Iceland, is strengthened by the new religion. Yet according to the saga, Njál's benevolence is a gift with which he was endowed from the cradle; and in the author's mind, he is to be numbered among those pagan sages who realized the worth of peace and good will among men through their own intuitive powers. Such sages must have existed among all civilized peoples regardless of the religious faith to which they prescribed. Among theologians this phenomenon was known as *praeparatio evangelica*, the preparation for the proclaiming of the gospel. We hear about Njál's meditation in solitude; he often walked alone and spoke in a half whisper to himself. To be sure, the gift of prescience can exist independent of all moral endeavor, but in the case of Njáll and many other sages there is certainly a strong hidden connection between the two; and wisdom, which can be an amoral natural phenomenon, is here interwoven with the noblest ideals.

IV

After the slaying of Þráinn, to which Njáll contributed with great cunning, although not with equally great willingness, a new chapter in

his life begins: his desire to save himself and his sons from disaster
blended in a strange way with his benevolence; and when all is said and
done, his good will triumphs over his intellect. This happens when he
takes Þráin's son, Höskuldur, as his foster son.

Let us consider first of all the high odds against which Njáll wagered
here. One of man's most sacred duties according to the pagan code of
ethics·was to avenge the slaying of his father. And when a boy attained
manhood, public opinion as well as his kinsmen and friends demanded
of him that he exact vengeance. The voice of the blood called to him.
And then fostering and friendship and monetary compensation usually
availed little. Kálfur Árnason experienced this when Magnús góði came
to power in Norway; Geitir of Krossavík experienced this, even though
Bjarni Brodd-Helgason loved him; and Þorsteinn hvíti was unwilling
to take the risk of having Brodd-Helgi and Þorsteinn fagri, his father's
slayer, together once Brodd-Helgi had reached the age of eighteen,
since he expected him to seek blood vengeance. But Njáll, the wisest
of men, attempted to overcome nature itself. To this end he ventured
all that he had to lose—and he lost.

In order to get a better understanding of Njál's manner of thinking,
which is anything but simple, it is best to consider carefully the account
of what happened when his sons and Kári returned home and told him
about the slaying of Höskuldur (chapter 111):

> "This is sorrowful news," said Njáll, "and a terrible thing to hear, for I
> can truthfully say that it grieves me so deeply that I would rather have lost
> two of my own sons to have Höskuldur alive."
>
> "You must be forgiven for saying that," said Skarphéðinn. "You are now
> an old man, and it is natural for you to take it so to heart."
>
> "It is not old age," said Njáll, "so much as the fact that I know far better
> than you what this will lead to."
>
> "What will it lead to?" asked Skarphéðinn.
>
> "My death," replied Njáll, "and the death of my wife and all my sons."
>
> ... This was the only thing that grieved Njáll so sorely that he could never
> speak about it without being deeply moved.

Many things speed through the mind of the aging man in these few minutes. It is quite apparent that the author of the saga did not find the human soul so simple to fathom. It will be necessary to scrutinize this conversation more closely.

Njáll both grieves for Höskuldur and also anticipates evil consequences from the slaying. Some persons might be inclined to separate these two reactions as antithetical and to regard fear of coming disaster as the chief cause of his concern. But a more careful consideration of what the saga actually says refutes this view. According to the account the disaster which will result is *added to* the sorrow it has already caused. In the *Prose Edda* Snorri speaks about the slaying of Baldur in exactly the same way:

> But when the gods attempted to speak, they could not help bursting into tears, so that none could tell the others about his grief. But Óðinn endured this loss worst of all, for he understood best what great injury and detriment the death of Baldur would bring to the gods.

Even though this point of view is accepted, it is nevertheless true that Njál's knowledge of the consequences is involved in his distress of mind. Does this mean that he is apprehensive about his own death? In a certain sense the question can be answered in the affirmative. Njáll has advance knowledge of how he will die by virtue of his gift of prescience, as was stated long before in the saga. The gift of second sight is certainly as old as mankind (and possibly even older, for animals may have this gift to a certain degree), and is closely related to the most primitive impulse of man, the desire to live. This gift of prescience casts a shadow of gloom over everything that points toward disaster or death, regardless of ethical or religious belief. For this reason Njál's prescience is accompanied by gloom. Furthermore, although Njáll has a foreboding of how he will die, he does not know whether death will come in such a way that he can rest satisfied with it. Will he meet death bravely or badly? Under what circumstances will his sons die? It is therefore not surprising that the dreadful manner of dying, by being burned alive, should cause him to shudder. More men than he would have preferred that the cup from which they must drink might be taken from them.

I must emphasize here that this episode would be completely misinterpreted if one were to imagine that Njáll wanted to buy his own life with that of his sons. He, his wife, and his sons are one, as we have already noted, and this fact is revealed best of all in the words he speaks in this very passage. But he would rather have lost his own sons than Höskuldur, and here we come to the main cause of his grief and to the very heart of the matter in this part of the saga.

Two other passages can contribute somewhat to a better understanding of all this. When Flosi asked Runólfur of Dalur for the true story of Höskuld's death, he replied that there was no point in trying to conceal the fact that Höskuldur "was killed for less than no cause; all men mourn his death, but no one more than his foster father, Njáll." And at the General Assembly, when Njáll makes an appeal for reconciliation, he speaks as follows:

> "It seems to me that this case has come to an impasse, and that was to be expected, for it has sprung from evil roots (Mörður!). I want all of you to know that I loved Höskuldur more dearly than my own sons, and when I learned that he had been slain, I felt as though the sweetest light of my eyes had been blotted out. I would rather have lost all of my sons to have Höskuldur still alive...."

These are weighty words, and it must be evident to everyone that the story of Njáll is a closed book if they are not correctly interpreted and understood.

Njáll has reared Höskuldur as his foster son, and the two are therefore bound by bonds of unbreakable loyalty. Their life together is completely without friction. Höskuldur is such a kindly person that he is loved by everyone, and his kindliness plays a large part in the love of his foster father for him. But more than that—Njáll molds Höskuldur, endows him with his own ideals and ethical concepts, and Höskuldur is exceptionally eager to acquire these qualities. The ties between them become strong.

But the fostering of Höskuldur has a still greater significance in the mind of Njáll. Through it, and through the benefits he bestows upon Höskuldur, he makes atonement for the death of the boy's father. To attempt to efface that act is a prudent plan, but upon closer consideration it becomes obvious that Njál's heart was more deeply involved in the way it was done than was his mind. This endeavor of his is filled with a remarkably comprehensive good will and nobility, which deserves to be stronger than the danger with which it is threatened. It is as though the fostering of Höskuldur becomes the focus of all of Njál's most beautiful ideals, of his faith in the goodness of human life. And in Njál's mind Höskuldur becomes the symbol of all this.

Njáll declares that he loved Höskuldur more dearly than his own sons, and that he would have chosen their death rather than his. Njál's sons were flesh of his flesh in a literal sense; they were part of him, and their misfortune or death was the same as a wound or a loss of limb on his part (and in a sense irreparable). Thus he felt that somehow he had a right to lose them. Höskuldur had a more independent existence in relationship to him, and yet the ties between them were very close. I cannot explain them better than with these manly and profound words of the psalmist, which in a translation from Njál's time read thus: "*Drottinn mælti við mik: 'Sonr minn ert þú, í dag gat ek þik.'*" ("The Lord spoke to me, 'Thou art my son; this day I begot thee.'"[4] It is of no significance here whether the psalmist was referring to the Messiah or to the king at his annointment. The relationship of Höskuldur to Njáll is that of a son to his father—not of a physical, but of a spiritual nature, and very real. Njáll makes him his son. Höskuldur is his spiritual child and the embodiment of his conciliatoriness and benevolence and his most noble endeavors. He feels a deeper love for Höskuldur, who is his spiritual son and the symbol of his own soul, than he does for his

---

4. *Jacobs saga postula*, in *Postula sögur*, ed. C. R. Unger, Christiania, 1874, p. 533.

physical sons, who are parts of his natural being, and he chooses Höskuld's life over theirs.[5]

Njáll seems to be on the verge of winning a victory over human nature itself, which demands of a son that he avenge his father. His beneficence seems to have the power to heal all wounds completely. But then something incredible and dreadful happens: his sons permit themselves to be beguiled by Mörður into slaying Höskuldur, and thus into committing a most atrocious and infamous crime. No more profound grief could have been inflicted upon Njáll. It was as though a vital nerve had been severed.

Njáll had endeavored to make atonement for the slaying of Þráinn. But how was this act to be atoned for? How could his sons cleanse their hands, which had been defiled by this atrocity?

Njáll had made Höskuldur his foster son before the advent of Christianity in Iceland. Now he accepts the Christian faith, and this faith deepens all of the noble ideals which we have been discussing. It transforms the crime committed by his sons into sin. His sons have followed in the footsteps of the Jewish zealots who shed the innocent blood of the Redeemer, but Höskuldur has taken Him as his example: "May God help me and forgive all of you!" were his last words.

V

At the following General Assembly Njáll endeavors to bring about a reconciliation for his sons and thus to save them from disaster. For a while it seems as though he might succeed, but then mere trifles intercede to bring his efforts to naught. After this has happened, Njáll says, "Now that will come to pass which will bring disaster to us all." Now the summer passes until eight weeks before winter, and then Njáll is a

5. It is interesting to note two parallels in *Njála* in which the bonds between foster parent and foster child are declared to be stronger than those between natural parent and child. King Brján (chapter 154) loves his adopted son, Kerþjálfaður, the son of his enemy, King Kylfir, more dearly than his own sons; and Þórhallur Ásgrímsson (chapter 27) loves his foster father, Njáll, more than his own father, Ásgrímur Elliða-Grímsson.

changed man: he no longer seeks to prevent what he previously called disaster. On the contrary, he accepts it with ready willingness. How did this come about?

In the foregoing chapter on Skarphéðinn I mentioned the strange incident which occurred when Njáll and his sons were watching the approach of Flosi and his men, coming from the east across the home field at Bergþórshvoll. We recall that as soon as Njáll noticed that Skarphéðinn was eager to fight, he urged everyone to enter the house, and that he did not attempt to counter Skarphéðin's valid objections with rational argument, but merely complained that his sons were overriding his advice and showing him disrespect. What motivated this strange behavior on the part of the great sage? This is one of the weightiest and most perplexing questions which arise in the mind of the reader of *Njála*, and it is necessary to try to disentangle the matter as best we can. It would require a great deal of time to discuss all the many explanations of this question which have been advanced and so I shall omit doing so for the moment. Instead, I shall try to present the explanation which seems most probable to me.

It must have been obvious to Njáll that Skarphéðinn was right. But many years ago he had gained a mysterious insight into the manner of his death. (He stated this calmly but firmly to his friend Gunnar in chapter 55.) Now he expects that it will come to pass, and so it is not in the hope of saving his life and that of his sons that he leads them inside.

When Flosi offers to let Njáll leave the burning house, he refuses the offer with the oft-quoted words, "I do not wish to go outside, for I am an old man, and ill prepared to avenge my sons, and I am unwilling to live in shame." We must not overlook the important fact that Njáll is speaking to the chieftain Flosi, and he puts forth those arguments which he thinks Flosi is most likely to understand, just as he did when he spoke to Bergþóra about honor and dishonor in connection with blood vengeance, although at that time he certainly must have had something different in mind. In the same way I believe that the heart of the

matter is now something different from what seems to be the surface
meaning of his words, although it cannot be denied that he is not free of
the heroic concept of honor and that he is keenly aware of his old age.

Skarphéðinn says that his father is doomed to die (*feigr*), and Flosi
says the same thing when he sees them entering the house. That is
their interpretation, based on what they can see from the outside,
and it is a good one as far as it goes. But their interpretation is
something negative, whereas what Njáll has in mind is positive in the
best sense of the word.

Dante relates in *The Divine Comedy* that he went all the way down
the crater of hell until he came to the center of the earth. When he
continued onward, the directions were reversed, so that what formerly
was down was now up. The same thing takes place here. The directions
are reversed. Curse is transformed into blessing. That which was negative and fraught with disaster now becomes positive and replete with
blessing.

When the women in the blazing house begin to lament, Njáll says
to them: "'Take heart and speak no words of despair, for this will be
only a brief storm, and it will be long before another one like it comes.
Have faith in God's mercy, for he will not let us burn in this world
and the next.' Such were the words of comfort he had for them, and
others even more valiant." The last sentence serves to underscore the
words of Njáll; it is a sort of hint from the author that the reader
should pay particular attention to them. I think that this passage explains the entire episode, including Njál's insistence that they enter the
house.

Njáll himself is one of the main sources of the events of the saga, and
he tries to control their course by means of his wisdom. When they
rise up against him, he tries to reverse their course. He sees the streams
of fate rushing toward himself and his sons, and like a magician he causes
them to alter their direction, only to have them return to their former
beds again. Then his struggle to ward off disaster undergoes a change,
and it seems as though his good will were on the verge of stilling tem-

pest and sea. All the best qualities of his nature are joined in this endeavor to overcome the enmities of the past. But it is precisely this endeavor which brings him the deepest grief of all. At the General Assembly he finally comes to a full understanding of how uneven the game is, and how hopeless and useless his struggle is. But then he learns something great and glorious: he learns to accept and affirm what is destined for him. He long ago foresaw the manner of his death; now he recalls it and acknowledges it. But more than this, he comes to the realization that fate, blind and cruel, no longer exists; it has given way to benign providence, and to providence he commits himself and his family. Now there is no longer anything to fear. At last Njáll has found peace.

But as "fond of ease" as Njáll declares himself to be, and as weary as he may seem to be, this peace must not be confused with lack of strength. Njál's mind is as active as it has ever been, but it is no longer occupied with crafty scheming, and its goal is a different one. After the slaying of Þráinn he wanted to make amends for Þráin's death, and not merely in a legal sense: he wanted to heal the wounds and to eradicate the evil consequences of the killing by means of good works. The same desire awakened in him after the abhorrent crime committed by his sons in the slaying of Höskuldur; but this desire has a stronger religious significance than the other one: it is clearly a matter of penance: "God is merciful, and he will not let us burn in this world and the next." The torment which they willingly take upon themselves will efface their guilt and redeem them from punishment in the world to come.

Njáll is very insistent that his sons accompany him into the house. In this way he wants to spare them further grief and disaster, and he hopes that they will all travel the same path together as they have in the past. And when there is nothing else left for Skarphéðinn to do but to die, the thought of penance also arises within him. This is revealed especially in the fact that he burns crosses on his chest and back.

Njáll speaks about the mercy of God, but not about the justice of God. Everything he does before dying in the flaming house bears proof of his faith in God and his willing submission to divine providence, which he hopes will accept his penance and which he trusts will lead him through the dark valley of the shadow of death.

Njáll had formerly embraced the heroic concept of honor—to be sure, in its noblest form. Even now he seems not to renounce it completely. When Þórhalla Ásgrímsdóttir says, as she leaves the burning building, that she will urge her father to avenge the killings which are about to take place, Njáll does not try to dissuade her. He merely says, "You will do well, for you are a good woman." But these are the words of a man whose mind is occupied with other thoughts. To excite vengeance does not require first and foremost a good woman. Yet he does not protest, and the concept of honor is uppermost also in his words to Flosi. Either he does not feel that there is any unbridgeable gap between honor and the new attitude toward life he has attained, or else this is a perfectly natural incongruity of human beings: new concepts are accepted before old ones have completely been discarded.

As indicated above, this explanation of Njál's actions is far from being the only one which has been put forth. Various details in this episode have been seized upon and stressed. Various individuals have taken this or that statement of Njáll at face value and have insisted, for example, that he really believed his house to be strong enough to provide sufficient defense against the attackers. But those individuals have overlooked two important factors: first of all, the circumstance that the context shows his words to be an obvious pretext, and secondly, the fact that Njáll knew beforehand exactly how he would die. His revelation of this to Gunnar (chapter 55) is a characteristic proleptic structural and stylistic device employed with consummate skill by almost all saga writers, and especially by the author of *Njála*. One need think only of the mention of Hallgerð's thief's eyes and silken hair on the first page of the saga—to cite just one parallel for many. Other critics have emphasized the comment made by both Skarphéðinn and Flosi that Njáll was doomed to die and have suggested that it was his *feigð*, his imminent death, which precipitated his decision. Still others have unduly stressed

Njál's declaration to Flosi that he was unwilling to live in shame, or his failure to protest when Þórhalla spoke about vengeance. But I have already touched upon these arguments, and they need no further discussion here. It is perhaps difficult to find a common denominator with which all of these seemingly contradictory and disparate traits can be resolved. But we cannot get around the following facts: Njál's foreknowledge of the way in which he would die, his words of comfort to the weeping women, and the unconventional intrusion of the author into his story to underscore the significance of Njál's statement: "Such were the words of comfort he had for them, and others even more valiant." And finally, there is also the account of the removal of the bodies, which will be discussed in the following section.

Some persons probably think that there are many ideas and concepts mixed helter-skelter in Njál's thinking. It can well be said that the author is here depicting a man who is still struggling uncertainly in the dark, and who has not yet attained to a total life view, or rather, to a consistent, integrated philosophy of life. For here we see the spiritual struggle of a man who is wrestling incessantly with the realities of the external and the internal world. Here we have the opportunity to observe the manner in which broad and deep life experience together with unceasing spiritual endeavor finally bring about a new view and manner of life which are purer and more beautiful than the older ones.

VI

In Njál's concepts of providence and penance we see Christian influence. This is not to be taken to mean, of course, that these two concepts occur only in Christianity. In the writings of the pagan philosopher Marcus Aurelius, for example, there is a searching for a finer faith in providence. But here, in *Njála*, we are without doubt dealing with Christian influence. Njál's concept of penance is related to the Christian *poenitentia* as it manifests itself in the life and death of many individuals in the twelfth and thirteenth centuries in Iceland. Since I have discussed this problem in my book *The Age of the Sturlungs* (chapter 7), it will not be necessary to go into any further detail about it here. There is also Christian influence in the passage dealing with the recovery of the bodies of Njáll and Bergþóra: they are both unburned, and all present regarded this as a great miracle. Njál's body was so radiant and fair that Hjalti Skeggjason declared he had never seen such radiance in the countenance and body of a dead man before. Here too—and this is far from insignificant—we find many parallels in medieval legends. At the conclusion of *Guðmundar saga Arasonar*, to cite just one example, we read the following about the corpse of Bishop Guðmundur: "All those men who saw the body said they had never seen the flesh of a dead man so radiant and fair as his." Perhaps it would be well to refer briefly to a few further examples of how the author of *Njála* borrowed material from saints' lives and legends and freely adapted it to his own purposes. We have already seen how he took an omen from Gregory's *Dialogues* and blended it with secular elements of troll stories and tales of forebodings in Flosi's dream (chapter 133). We recall how Njál's grandson Ámundi blindi was miraculously given sight, exactly as it occurs in legendary works—and the phraseology of the passage indicates the nature of its source—so that Ámundi can perform such an unchristian act as to take blood vengeance on his father's slayer (chapter 106)! And to mention an example not previously cited, there is the dream of Gunnar's brother Kolskeggur, in which a radiant man appears and commands that Kolskeggur follow him and promises to find him a bride and to make him his knight. In the language of medieval legends the latter promise would signify that he was to become a priest or a hermit, or possibly a crusader. Indeed, a wise old man interprets the dream to mean that Kolskeggur will become "God's knight." But the fulfillment of the dream is something different: Kolskeggur marries and joins the Varangian guard, the elite troops of the emperor in Constantinople!

Now to return to our main theme. Christendom embraces a wide territory, in which we find much that is lofty as well as much that is base. Within its holy precincts thrived charity and brotherly love, but also blind fanaticism and cruelty—the Inquisition and the persecution of the Jews are only two examples in that long and sad story. The spirit of the law on the one hand and the letter of the law on the other hand were equally revered, so that it is the flock on the right hand, a flock of sheep, which is meant by the saying *misjafn sauður í mörgu fé*, which might be freely rendered "Although somewhat blemished, a sheep remains most of all a sheep." Therefore the expression "Christian influence" may be somewhat ambiguous. What seems to me most significant here is the special, personal, organic stamp of those ideas and ideals which are revealed in the saga (without regard to their origin), and the deep inwardness and earnestness with which they become part and parcel of a living human being. Here we do not find reverence for religious ceremony for its own sake, as is sometimes the case among the clergy—scarcely anything except Njál's and Bergþóra's making the sign of the cross over themselves and Kári's young son and the crosses burned on Skarphéðin's breast and back fit this category—nothing which points toward a clerical technique or the attitudes of the priestly class. Even the story of the exhumation of the bodies is to a certain extent unclerical in nature, and the same can be said about other passages in which influence from legendary writings is apparent, as we have seen above. The author of *Njála* is imbued with the spirit and not with the letter of the law, and it is from this spirit that the saga has attained its broad human validity. The saga is concerned primarily with the worth of human endeavor and good will. The author of *Njála*, not unlike Ibsen (although, to be sure, not in exactly the same theological sense) asks: "*Gælder ej et frelsens fnug mandeviljens quantum satis?*" ("Cannot the sufficiency of man's will merit a particle of redemption?") And the answer is the same: "*Han er deus caritatis*" ("He is the God of love") —or, as Njáll expressed it (and quite as well): "God is merciful."

What makes the story of Njáll so unforgettable is first of all Njál's spiritual strength, and the deep earnestness which characterizes him, and secondly, the human, diversified, complex portrait which the author created of him. He is dignified, benevolent, and honest, and yet he sometimes resorts to crafty scheming, whereby he seems more concerned with the schemes themselves than with the people affected by them. He never seeks wealth and power for himself and always displays a unique kindness and mildness; he is not meddlesome, but insists on making the decisions in matters which involve him. I do not know whether it is possible to explain his egoism better than with the words I have already used regarding his patriarchal mentality. His attitude and duties toward others can be compared with the steps of a stairway: first of all is his family, and then, in descending order, his friends, acquaintances, strangers, and lastly his enemies. But he also possesses another attitude toward people: he solves everyone's difficulties, gives without regard to the identity of his beneficiary, and he finally adopts the son of an enemy as his foster child. The former was the attitude of a family-centered society and is the more primitive one; the latter reflects a society of individual human beings, and belongs to a higher, more modern stage of development.

Njáll does not remain stationary. He is in a process of constant development, drawing nourishment into himself from all sides. His needs compel him to search and search, and the events and demands of life compel him to struggle. This character portrait is one of the clearest examples of personality development in ancient Icelandic literature.

Life events and Njál's efforts to dominate them make him one of the most dynamic forces in the saga's course of events. He endeavors to direct these events in accordance with his will, to fend off or to change his fate. But finally, after an intense struggle and broad experience he learns to free himself of his willfulness and to let providence lead him. Thus the author takes leave of Njáll: inside his flaming house, but with a spirit as serene as the evening sky.

8. Ideas and Ideals

I

Njála is a long saga, the longest of all the *Íslendingasögur*—159 chapters, or 464 pages, in the *Íslenzk fornrit* edition. Why did the author write this long saga? It will doubtless seem that I am begging the issue when I say: He wanted to tell a story. The desire to relate is the alpha and omega of all narrative art. Laxness once said, "Give me an eye to see and a tongue to tell about what I have seen." The author of *Njáls saga* had this same keen desire to see and understand human life and to relate and interpret it. His mind was assailed from all sides: love and hate, fascination and horror, grief and gladness—each following and mingling with the other, and his breast could find no peace until he had transformed this chaos into artistic form.

Could the author have had any other desire or purpose beyond that of telling a story?

The saga deals with events which occurred three centuries before the time of the author. Was his primary purpose, then, perhaps historical truth, the desire to report the events exactly as they happened? I have already touched on that question, and shall not elaborate on it here. It can be shown that although history provided the orientation for the saga, it was not its highest aim. The truth it was concerned with is, as I have already stated, truth about human life.

Some people write for the purpose of influencing public opinion or of promoting a cause or an individual—of persuading people to buy this or that product or to vote for this or that candidate. It is by no means necessary to assume that tendentious literature of this kind cannot be artistic. The purpose of such writing can be to proclaim some truth or knowledge which the author believes he has discovered. Goethe's admonition not to seek for deeper meaning beyond or behind the basic phenomena of life (*Urphänomene*) is not applicable to literature of this type, for here the phenomena are merely creations of the author as vehicles for the ideas he wishes to convey.

Although attempts have been made to interpret *Njála* as a tendentious saga, I am convinced that it was not composed for propagandistic purposes. It was not written to further a reform in the legislative or judicial system or for any other political purpose. It seems to me altogether unlikely that the episode about the establishment of the Hvítanesgoðorð (chapter 97) was created in the interests of any one individual who lived during the thirteenth century and completely out of the question that the saga as a whole was written with such a purpose in mind. The author's marked sympathy or antipathy for individuals and families was more instinctive than deliberate.

I consider it more likely that this work of narrative art is the creation of a much more complex mentality than that of a propagandist, a mentality which endeavors to fathom the mystery of reality, and we shall have to seek to comprehend this mentality if we hope to approach an understanding of its creation. Wonder at the phenomena of life is characteristic of this mentality, but it is accompanied by the desire to grapple intellectually with what the eye has seen. It is not at all farfetched to suggest that the author sought to understand life better and to make it more endurable through his literary re-creation of it. He sought to find purpose and direction in the seemingly chaotic flow of events, and it is well to keep in mind that he thought less in terms of logic and doctrine than in pictures of human life, events, and people. Imagination and empathy played a much larger part in his thinking than cold reason.

It would be easy to find in *Njáls saga* many texts to preach on, and they would doubtless last until doomsday. Much less pretentious and yet far more difficult is what I propose to undertake: to find those life attitudes and ideals of the author which have determined the mold of

his work. They must not be figments of the critic's imagination pro-
jected into the saga, but must actually be ideas inherent in it, as the
author wrestled with them. But these ideas, we must remember, need
not be in the form of logical concepts. Nor shall we attempt an exhaustive treatment of this problem: but if we proceed carefully, we
shall perhaps be able to gain an insight into it from one point of view.
To this end we shall consider two closely related groups of ideas or
sentiments in the saga. The first consists of attitudes toward man himself; the second is made up of thoughts about the struggle of man with
destiny and misfortune. The former requires no special discussion;
every literary work reveals to a certain extent the author's attitude
toward man, and *Njála*, with its pronounced sympathies and antipathies
and its judgment of men and affairs, is no exception. In regard to the
latter, it is instructive to observe that again and again the author speaks
on the one hand of fate, of that which will come to pass, of events that
take the course decided by destiny, and on the other hand of the good
and ill fortune of men, over which they have no control. It is obvious
that these matters weighed heavily upon the author's mind.

A matter of great importance in all literary criticism is the attempt
of the critic to decide what it is he should ask the work about. He must
ask the work about that with which it is concerned. I think there can
be no doubt that *Njála* is properly asked about these two matters, the
concepts of fate and of fortune.

In what follows I shall try to give an account of these ideas, but I
shall not go to the trouble of tracing each of them to its origin. It is
obvious, as has already been pointed out, that there is considerable
Christian influence to be found in the saga; and the episode of the coming of Christianity and the account of the absolution of Kári and Flosi
by the Pope, to mention just these two examples, show that the author
was not unconcerned that the reader should realize this. Christian
influence is revealed chiefly in the idea of good will and the desire for
reconciliation on the one hand and the concept of penance on the other.
But influence always implies influence *on* something. Fundamentally

the life-view of the saga is native, but it has undergone a unique development because of the warm breeze from the south. As interesting as it would be to distinguish between the old and the new, the native and the foreign, I regard it as even more important here than elsewhere in this essay to try to interpret the saga as it is. I shall therefore try to interpret those ideas of the saga which I have selected for discussion as they exist in organic connection one with the other and in the unique form they have acquired there.

II

Both *Njáls saga* and *Bandamanna saga* deal with the establishment of a new *goðorð* and with the disputes and altercations at the Assembly which result from it. Furthermore, we occasionally find in *Njála* a rather vulgar form of humor not at all unlike that in *Bandamanna saga*. But precisely where the two sagas are most similar, the difference between them is most noteworthy. Whereas *Bandamanna saga* is a bitter and biting satire on the aristocracy, there is no antiaristocratic bias to be found in *Njála*. Here the conflict is not between social classes but between individuals.

In *Njála* there is no distinct line of demarcation between the chieftains and the prominent farmers without authorities. As one example for many we might think of the descriptions of Þorgeir skorargeir and Þráinn Sigfússon. Should we, according to the saga, classify them as chieftains or simply as influential farmers? As depicted here, Icelandic society appears to be an undifferentiated entity including small landholders and tenant farmers. Similarly the household appears as a unit, as one can see most clearly in the case of Bergþórshvoll. I have repeatedly alluded to the patriarchal spirit which prevails there, in accordance with which everyone who fills his station in life is worthy of respect, whatever that station may be. The author of *Njála* could well have quoted the words of Homer about the "noble swineherd." If I were to venture a guess as to what social class the author himself belonged to, I would place him among the prominent farmers, close to the line between this class and that of the chieftains—a dividing line of which he himself, as already mentioned, seems to have been unaware. While on the one hand he had little regard for vagrants and itinerant beggars, he seems on the other hand to have had little interest in the power of chieftains and the leadership of men. He does not share Snorri's pleasure in depicting farmer-chieftains. He lacks class consciousness, but is fascinated with the individual personality.

Árni Magnússon once stated that in the *Íslendingasögur* the superiority of the Icelanders over men of all other countries in regard to merit and achievement was exaggerated to a ridiculous degree, and that the author of *Njáls saga* frequently exceeded the immodesty of all other saga writers in this regard. Árni Magnússon had in mind such episodes as those about the voyages abroad of Hrútur, Gunnar, Þráinn, and the like, in which the author indulged his fancy with little regard for the narrow limitations of reality. Here his wishful thinking is clearly revealed, and it does not require much study to discover that two motifs occur repeatedly. On the one hand there is the confrontation between the independent spirit of a member of the Icelandic Commonwealth and the power of a foreign monarch, delightful examples of which are found in the story of the Njálssons, Hrappur, and Þráinn Sigfússon in Norway, or the slaying of Gunnar Lambason by Kári at the court of the Earl of the Orkneys. One of the most striking examples of this is the story of Þorsteinn Síðu-Hallsson, following the rout of the enemies of King Brjánn in the Battle of Clontarf (chapter 157):

> King Sigtryggur fled before him (i.e., Kerþjálfaður), and at that his whole army broke into flight. Þorsteinn Síðu-Hallsson stopped running, while all the others were fleeing, and tied his shoe-thong. Kerþjálfaður asked him why he was not running.
>
> "Because," replied Þorsteinn, "I cannot reach home tonight, since my home is out in Iceland."
>
> Kerþjálfaður spared his life.[1]

1. For a discussion of this mode of thought, the independent spirit of the Commonwealth, see *Sturlungaöld* (*The Age of the Sturlungs*), chapter 3.

Another chief trait of the accounts of voyages abroad in *Njála* combines old and new elements, from the time of the Commonwealth and from the monarchal period, tinted with the color of the latter, of chivalry and romanticism, and that is the courtliness of the warriors. When these heroes return to Iceland, they often retain a shade of the foreign romantic splendor, but not, of course, their rank and position. The prevailing mode of thought in *Njála*, as in most of the *Íslendingasögur*, is that of the Commonwealth, in which the aristocratic spirit of the chieftains is blended with the independent spirit of the people. In *Njála* this attitude acquires something of the new spirit of chivalry as well as of the Church and Christianity, all of which seem to lose their specific identity. The concepts of class distinction and class values become irrelevant, and the foreign influences lose their independence. What remains is the layman's attitude toward life, which stresses human values of universal significance independent of time and place. The ideal of *Njála* is not the chieftain, or the prominent farmer, or the small landowner, or the knight, or the cleric, but the able and accomplished individual human being.

Physical abilities and accomplishments are so attractive to the author that he is sometimes in danger of being carried away by his admiration of them. He delights in showing us handsome men who are tall and strong, who can swim like seals (he uses the simile twice in the saga) and wield a sword so deftly that the onlooker believes he sees three swords flashing at one time. And yet the author does not let himself be carried away by physical accomplishments alone, for he demands more of his characters than that. He has an especial fondness for intellectual ability and the skillful use of words; he is no less delighted with a clever exchange of words than he is with the skillful interchange of arms. The entire saga is one uninterrupted witness to the author's love of the art of words and of human intelligence, a force which wields such a strong influence on men and events and enables its possessor to help his friends and confound his enemies. What is more mysterious than this power of the word and intellect, which exerts such a strong influence on people, and what does man desire more than power? The author of *Njáls saga* is entranced by this force, but he does not permit himself to be overwhelmed by it, for he demands even more of his characters.

Above all, he demands moral values. What these values are becomes evident from a consideration of the moral views of Njáll himself. Here we find in close connection two complexes of ideas which are often in opposition to each other but which nevertheless impinge upon each other and can coalesce. On the one hand, there is the concept of honor, with all that this concept entails; on the other hand, there are the qualities of good will and readiness for conciliation. These two points of view are clearly illustrated in the words of Hildigunnur the Healer about Gunnar to her brothers, the sons of Starkaður: "Gunnar may be difficult to provoke, but he is hard when cornered." This hardness (*harðdrægni*) belongs to the concept of honor, the spirit of northern paganism, which includes such qualities as manliness, will power, fortitude, and courage.

"One may expect to find honor where honor abounds," Ósvífur says in reference to Hrútur and Höskuldur (chapter 12). Honor finds its fulfillment and spreads from its source like the light from the sun. It is revealed in high-mindedness (*drengskapur*) and nobility (*göfugmennska*). It demands self-control, moderation, long-sufferance, conscientiousness, and good will. All of these peaceful attributes tend to offset the other side of honor, the demand for vengeance. "I wonder," said Gunnar after the skirmish at Hof, "whether I am any the less courageous than other men because I am so much more reluctant to kill than other men are?" And thus are added to the ideal of honor the qualities of ethical refinement and gracious deportment.

The moral views in *Njála* are not merely beautiful but unnecessary embellishments. It is obvious that they reflect the conviction, widely found in other *Íslendingasögur*, that there are values which are higher than life itself. The ideas and ideals of *Njála* represent precisely those values.[2]

2. See Sigurður Guðmundsson, "Gunnar á Hlíðarenda," *Skírnir* XCII (1918), pp. 77 ff., and Einar Ól. Sveinsson, "The Value of the Icelandic Sagas," *Saga-Book* XV (1957–59), 1–16.

moral values in Njál's Saga
reflect christeaults

Before proceeding, I should like to point out how different these life attitudes are in their entirety from medieval thought, inspired by the Church, which is characterized by the spirit of humility and asceticism; the similarity and even the relationship of individual episodes of the saga to this medieval view of life do not suffice to make a substantial change in the total picture. The nucleus of the ideas and ideals of *Njála* (and of many other *Íslendingasögur*) is faith in humanity and human virtues—a faith to which many good and wise men before and after the time of *Njáls saga* have adhered.

III

In the Proverbs of Solomon (12:21) we read: "There shall no evil happen to the just, but the wicked shall be filled with mischief." Gunnar of Hlíðarendi and Njáll—do they die of old age after a long, happy life, surrounded by their fortunate children and grandchildren? No. Gunnar was a paragon among the men of his day, yet he was drawn into misfortune and manslaughter and was finally slain himself. Njáll, the wise and benevolent seer, was brought to the point where he chose to perish in his flaming home rather than to go on living. The terrible fate of these good men seems incredible, and yet it is true to life. Virtue is no protecting shield which wards off grief and misfortune.

Like the friends of Job, some readers of *Njála* might be inclined to search for the sins of these men, large and small, which could be regarded as the cause of their misfortune—the guilt for which they were punished. This is natural and common when people attempt to understand the nature of tragedy. Now the author of the saga has confirmed the belief that everyone will be rewarded in the life to come according to his deeds in this world. In the account of the burning (chapter 129) it is stated that when the buildings at Bergþórshvoll began to burn, the women who were inside began to weep and lament. Then Njáll said, "Take courage, and speak no words of despair, for this will be only a brief storm, and it will be long before another one like it comes. Trust in the mercy of God, for He will not let us burn in both this world and the next." Suffering endured in this life will lessen the suffering in the world to come. In a similar manner the life beyond reaches into this one in the supernatural events of the battle of Clontarf, but it must be borne in mind that this episode lies outside of the mainstream of the story. The atmosphere in the incident about Gunnar in his burial mound, on the other hand, is pagan. But otherwise it cannot be said that concepts of a life to come exert any great influence in the saga.

Like many other great literary works, *Njáls saga* is a sort of microcosm with its own special laws and its own views of life. The philosophy of the prevailing belief of his time, to which the author himself subscribes, need not be the predominant philosophy of his work. During the Sturlung Age it is especially necessary to be wary in this regard, for in that turbulent era many different views of life come to the surface. And it is likely that those ideas which conflict most strikingly with the doctrines proclaimed by the churchmen are a more faithful reflection of the thoughts and beliefs of the people than the phrases they learned to repeat after the priests. But let us not take Njál's earnest words too lightly, for they must be regarded as a new vista which he won at the close of his life after having journeyed through the valley of the shadow of death. The journey through the valley of the shadow of death is the essence of the saga, and the new vista opens up at the end of that journey.

Njála is concerned with the life of man here on earth, and all of the basic ideas of the saga must revolve about this. Could it be the point of view of the saga that "*alle Schuld rächt sich auf Erden,*" that guilt always leads to misfortune? Much can be interpreted this way, and yet there are perhaps more things in the saga which point the other way. Therefore this point of view, which is somewhat related to the belief in reward and punishment on earth, cannot be dominant in the saga. Perhaps the most cogent reason for rejecting this interpretation is the fact that the author nowhere states expressly that guilt leads to misfortune. On the other hand, I will not deny that A. C. Bradley's concept of the tragic flaw in Shakespeare's tragedies applies to *Njála* to a certain degree.[3] One need merely keep in mind that the punishment is not always appropriate to the guilt. Let us turn to the text of the saga. How does the author most frequently explain events and experiences in the lives of his characters? Again and again we read about fate or destiny, which no one can withstand, and also about misfortune, which spreads from person to person like a contagious disease. It is clear that these are the matters which we must inquire about in the saga. The fatalistic view of *Njála* is well known; in the opinion of the Swedish poet A. U. Bååth, it is the basic idea of the saga. Scholars have been much less aware, however, that the concepts of good fortune and misfortune are equally important, and that they are quite different from the belief in fate even though they are connected with it.

Both of these concepts or beliefs occur widely in the ancient literature of the North, and are both old and indigenous. Since they are so remote in origin, it might seem to people of our day that they are far-fetched and of no more concern to us than old wives' tales. But I am not so sure of that. The belief in fate or destiny has grown out of deep human experience and the intellectual struggle of men to comprehend and explain it. Sometimes people have tried to make this experience more tolerable by attributing it to the will of God or the gods or to some other power which man cannot change. (A striking example of this is the Calvinistic belief in predestination.) At other times people have created philosophies of determinism. As for the concept of *gifta* and *ógifta*, it is based on the human experience of all times, which people today perhaps more than ever have tried to rationalize. Americans especially talk about the "psychology of success," and much importance is attached to the power of suggestion and to men's attitudes toward events. All of this relates to the same kinds of phenomena which appear in stories molded by the ancient concept of fortune and misfortune.

3. *Shakespearean Tragedy*, pp. 6 ff.

IV

Originally the concept of good and bad fortune was closely related to the ancient belief in wraiths, but there are hardly any signs of this in *Njála* with the possible exception of the apparition seen by Þórður leysingjason (chapter 41): the bloody male goat is the image of his waning vital force, the foreboding of his imminent death.[4] It appears as a reflection rather than as the cause of his doom. There are no instances in the saga of a connection between *gæfa* or *ógæfa* and inanimate objects, such as weapons or jewelry, nor do we find qualities of good or bad fortune associated with families rather than with individuals. In this respect *Njála* is less primitive than some of the other sagas; the author's concept of *gæfa* is more realistic and sophisticated.

This concept of good fortune has many names: in addition to *gæfa* we find the designations *hamingja*, *gipta*, and *heill*. Its origin is to be found in the ancient belief in vital force, and although the concept has changed and developed, it never completely lost its connection with its origin. *Gæfa* is a sort of spiritual and physical capacity which makes it possible for an individual to accomplish what he undertakes to do; it enables him to attain to wealth and prosperity, health of body and soul, and other natural benefits and blessings. Of chief importance is not the acquisition of things, but the enjoyment of that which is acquired. As we read in *Hávamál*:

> *Eldr er beztr*
> *með ýta sonum*
> *ok sólar sýn,*
> *heilyndi sitt,*
> *ef maðr hafa náir*
> *án við lǫst at lifa.*

[Fire is best/ for the sons of man/ and the sight of the sun/ and sturdy health/ if one can attain them/ and live without blame.]

4. To be sure, Svanur (chapter 12) is attacked by Ósvífur's *fylgjur*, and Njáll (chapter 69) sees fetches of Gunnar's enemies, but there is no connection in either case with the concept of *gæfa* or *ógæfa*.

The final line of the poem, "and live without blame," reveals a second aspect of *gæfa*, about which *Njála* has a great deal to say: moral integrity. In order to gain a better perspective of this, it is well to consider the opposite of *gæfa: ógæfa*. We see misfortune (*ógæfa*) primarily as the absence of good fortune and happiness, as mischance, bad luck, and blundering (*glöp*). Related to the word *glöp* are *glópska* (folly) and *glæpr* (crime, wickedness), and between the ethical concept of *glæpska* (a foolish evil act) and the amoral concept of *ófarnaðr* (misfortune) no clear lines of demarcation can be drawn in the saga. Thus *ógæfa* results in hostilities and manslaughter, in crimes and evil deeds.

It is said that an evil deed leaves a trail of evil behind it (*draga slóða*), and that if an evil seed be sown, evil will grow from it (*er ok illu korni sáit orðit, enda mun illt af gróa* [chapter 115]). Thus misfortune leads to more misfortune, and its growth is difficult to stop. It lives and grows as surely and as mysteriously as the grass from the earth. We come closest to the essence of *ógæfa* if we call it *mein* (hurt, harm, damage, disease, sore), a word which encompasses every aspect of this complex of ideas, including the connotation of sin in the Christian sense of the word, although, of course, its basic sense is originally different. *Ógæfa* is like an infectious disease, which is carried from one individual to another. It lives in men and in their deeds, spreading poison and infection in all directions. It is a natural phenomenon, and natural phenomena are oblivious to justice, to guilt or innocence. *Ógæfa* infects and corrupts everyone who crosses its path and does not possess a sufficient power of resistance to it.

For men are not equally susceptible to the power of *ógæfa*. Kári and Skarphéðinn both become involved in the same monstrous deed: the slaying of Höskuldur Hvítanessgoði, and both are present at the burning of Njál's home. Skarphéðinn perishes in the flames, but Kári escapes alive to avenge his kinsmen by marriage. He becomes involved in many killings and exposes himself to great dangers, yet his *hamingja*, his good fortune, never fails him, and in the end he becomes completely reconciled with his adversary, Flosi. It is almost as though these events and these deeds had no effect upon him.

People today may regard the belief in fortune and misfortune as an old-fashioned superstition, but does it not, in spite of everything, afford us an amazingly true insight into human life?

V

Whereas the concept of good fortune and misfortune presupposes an inherent dynamic force within the events themselves, belief in fate seeks explanations for these events outside the sphere of human life. During the time of paganism, the destiny of man was believed to be controlled by the norns, but in the *Íslendingasögur* this is no longer the case. Here the belief in fate appears as a sort of layman's philosophy of life in which no gods are involved. Men find themselves led or dragged into situations they had not anticipated, and they find courses of action closed which they had assumed to be open. All this is so strange and incomprehensible that it seems to them that the causes must lie beyond the world of men, in mysterious regions far removed in time and space. Dreams and prophecies reveal that all this was destined long ago, and their interpretation shows clearly that what was destined must come to pass.

The ancient belief in destiny, however, must not be thought of as a form of determinism. The events of life, to be sure, are predetermined, at least in part, but the human will is free. It is within the power of each human being to choose whether he will be led or dragged by fate; he alone decides whether he will meet it honorably or shamefully. Thus man has the possibility of gaining the victory over his destiny by not letting it defeat him, by passing through the gates of death manfully and heroically. These ideas and ideals are predominant in the *Íslendingasögur* and it is they more than anything else which bestow upon the sagas their moral elevation. *Njála* is no exception; these concepts constitute one of the foundations of the author's view of life; but he does not stop there.

It might seem that belief in destiny and the concept of good and bad luck would conflict with each other—but what contradictory views

8

4 *Njáls Saga*

are not found together in the mind of a single individual? It is safe to assert that large numbers of people today have their heads full of incongruous scraps of this and that philosophy of life, which do not collide with each other but manage somehow to exist side by side without friction. From very early times there was a connection between these two ideas, and in *Njála* they frequently coincide so closely that one cannot be distinguished from the other. A good example of this is found in the comment made by Earl Hákon Sigurðarson of Norway about Þráinn and Hrappur following his failure to find Hrappur on board Þráin's ship (chapter 88): "It was not because of lack of wisdom on my part, but rather because of this alliance of theirs, which will drag them both to their destruction." (These profound words remind me of Feuchtwanger's description of the alliance between the Duke and the protagonist of his novel *Jud Süss*). The coalescence of fatalism and the concept of individual luck is also found, to mention just one more example, in such impersonal expressions as *draga undan* "to escape" (literally, "to be drawn away") or *til verra draga* "to turn out for the worst." Here the mystery of the course of human events is admirably reflected in the idiom itself, which does not specify what it is that does the "pulling" (*draga*). These impersonal constructions convey a feeling of strangeness. Do they refer to forces outside the realm of human life, or to inclinations from within the world of men? A similar feeling of strangeness is conveyed by expressions dealing with events that are to occur in the future. The man who wrote such lines must have been profoundly aware of the wonder of *verðandi*, of that which is to be, and of the mystery of time.[5]

5. The concept of *verðandi* is illuminated by the perceptive comment of Gwyn Jones in "The Greatest of the Sagas," *Times Literary Supplement*, Dec. 24, 1954, p. 836: "For this is life itself moving before us, the moment hardly to be determined when the casual hardens into the inescapable." Some of the most masterful passages in the saga are those which depict that moment in which the "casual" and the "inescapable" are poised, so to speak, on the edge of the knife. Ludvig Holm-Olsen (*Njåls saga*, p. 131) paraphrases *verðandi* as "*dette at noe skjir*," and "*dette liv i øyeblikket*."

VI

In his tragedy *Agamemnon* (lines 174 ff.) Aeschylus expresses himself through the chorus as follows:

Whoever gladly shouts the name of Zeus in songs of victory shall gain full understanding. Zeus, who set mortals on the way to wisdom, has established as a valid law that knowledge comes through suffering. In sleep the painful recollection of suffering trickles before the heart: discretion comes to men even against their will. This is a blessing from the mighty gods, who sit upon their awful thrones.

In Greek tragedies we find various qualities which are closely related to the ideas of *Njáls saga* about the infectiousness of misfortune. The above chorus of the great pagan, who believed in the compassion of the gods and the wisdom gained from suffering, is admirably suited for comparison with those events in *Njála* to which we shall now turn our attention.

I have already referred to Njál's attempts to influence the course of events. If we examine this matter more closely, we see that this course of events to a considerable degree has its origin in Njál's own planning and counsel. He first advises Gunnar how to help Unnur win her dowry claim against Hrútur (chapter 21), and the outcome of this advice is the birth of Mörður Valgarðsson. Njáll then gives Gunnar advice about his first voyage abroad, which brings Gunnar great fame and splendor and leads indirectly to his ride to the Alþingi (despite Njál's advice to the contrary), where he wins the hand of Hallgerður and with her lifelong misfortune—misfortune which does not end with his death but manifests itself again in the enmity between Þráinn Sigfússon and the Njálssons. The fourth time Njáll gives advice, he approves the marriage of Þráinn and Þorgerður Glúmsdóttir; from the relationship by marriage of Þráinn to Hallgerður (the mother of Þorgerður) the first coolness between Þráinn and Skarphéðinn arises, and from the marriage itself is born Höskuldur. Now one piece of advice to Gunnar follows the other in an effort to help him save himself from disaster. But as one wave falls, the other rises, and it seems as though Gunnar's honor and fame incite men to enmity against him. The most important advice which Njáll gives Gunnar is never to slay more than one man in the same family and never to break the terms of a settlement, especially if he should fail to heed the first of these two warnings (chapter 55). But Mörður hatches a devilish scheme to trick Gunnar into acting against the advice of Njáll. The scheme is successful and results in the death of Gunnar. We can continue through the saga, and all of the tragic events which it relates can be connected in one way or another with the counsel of Njáll. A survey of the entire saga shows clearly that there can be no mistake about this. The author himself (chapter 20) states that Njál's "advice was sound and benevolent, always turned out well for those who followed it." His advice was indeed sound and benevolent, and it required a most extraordinary kind of inadvertence or ill luck or misfortune to bring this advice to naught. But scarcely had the words of advice left his lips, than they set off a chain reaction of events with results which no one could anticipate, not even Njáll, as wise and prescient as he was. "*Er menneskets klögt da så usel, at det ikke mægter råde over andet og tredje led af sin egen gerning?*" Ibsen has Bishop Nikulás the Bagler ask in his drama *Kongsemnerne (The Pretenders)*. Is the prudence of man so wretched that he cannot control the second and third links of his deeds? The author of *Njáls saga* would answer this question in the affirmative, and in this he would not be alone; many wise, enterprising men would agree. "That men may start a course of events but can neither calculate nor control it is a tragic fact," says A. C. Bradley in reference to the role of chance in Shakespeare's works.[6] But Njáll continues his struggle until it is absolutely certain that there is no hope of victory. Man, regardless of how wise, powerful, and benevolent he may be, is impotent against fate, against that which must come to pass.

This in itself is a significant conclusion, but the saga is not yet finished. It was known to all that fate has no power over the human

6. *Shakespearean Tragedy*, p. 15. See also Sigurður Guðmundsson, *Skírnir XCII* (1918), pp. 78–79.

will, and that man can gain the victory over destiny by not letting it crush him. He cannot escape the inevitable, but he can meet death with his eyes open and with full control of himself. This is the secret of the fulfillment of human personality, which can stand up against the entire world. But Njáll does more than this. He possesses all the manly virtues in this respect and has the greatest possible control of himself; but in addition, he comes to terms with existence. He identifies himself with his fate. He completely surrenders his independence of will and entrusts himself to providence. Then all is changed.

"Whoever shouts the name of Zeus in songs of victory shall gain full understanding. . . . This is a blessing from the mighty gods. . . ." Thus wrote the Greek poet. It is not necessary here to consider whether he had exactly the same kind of blessing in mind as the author of *Njála*. What kind of blessing did Njáll attain when he entrusted himself to providence? The blessing of penance. And Skarphéðinn, when he burned the crosses on his back and breast? Penance. Both of them succeed in transforming torment into cleansing healing.

According to the concepts of fortune and misfortune in the saga, the destruction of Njáll and his family by fire is misfortune, an outgrowth of an old, malignant sore which it had not been possible to overcome. The spirit of penance destroys the moral content of this misfortune, purges it of its pollution and corruption, so that nothing remains but empty torment, physical suffering which penance transforms into a healing balm.

Let us turn from these examples of penance, which are indisputable, to others, which are closely related. Here a similar attitude toward adversity prevails. To designate this attitude in all cases as penance would be too restrictive; sometimes it is better to refer to it as sacrifice or self-abnegation.

Hrappur brings misfortune to all people except one: Kolbeinn Arnljótarson. A close examination of the saga (chapter 87) reveals that he is made impervious to misfortune through his magnanimity toward Hrappur: he wittingly and willingly accepts Hrapp's dishonesty and disagreeable behavior toward himself, and it seems as though this weakens the infectious power of this ill-starred man.

Hrútur becomes involved in great misfortune in Norway, and this misfortune perversely influences his marriage relationship to his wife, Unnur, and afterwards leads to other serious consequences. But when it is all over, it seems as though Hrútur has a beneficial effect on everyone. Would this not result from his disposition, as it is revealed in the home of Þjóstólfur Bjarnarson at Lundur (chapter 8)? Two young lads have been holding Hrútur up to ridicule because of his marital difficulties and subsequent lawsuit, and his brother Höskuldur angrily strikes one of the boys with a stick and orders him out of the house. But Hrútur calls the boy to him, comforts him, and gives him a golden ring from his finger with the admonition: "Run along now, but never again make sport of anyone."

Another still more noteworthy example is Hallur of Síða, who lost his son in the battle at the General Assembly (chapter 145). When men attempt to discuss terms of reconciliation, everything threatens to end in brawling and abuse and discord. At this point Hallur takes the floor and declares his willingness to sacrifice his own honor by renouncing compensation for his slain son in order that a peaceful settlement might be brought about. In those days, such an offer represented an almost superhuman sacrifice.

Hallur had no way of knowing for certain, of course, that his sacrifice would have a decisive influence on the course of events, for it would not have been an easy thing to do. And yet that is what happened; this is a major turning point in the saga. From this point on, the force of misfortune subsides. A large majority of the men involved in the battle at the Assembly come to terms, and eventually those who have not yet agreed to a peaceful settlement will do so. And even Flosi, who up to this point has refused to budge an inch, is willing to make a settlement even though Kári and Þorgeir decline to enter into the agreement. "It seems to me," he says, "that the fewer good men I have against me, the better it will be." It is quite obvious to him what he has to expect from Kári, and later on he accepts with self-control the killing of many of his followers. He knows that this is the only way to a reconciliation, and the only way to efface his crime and the results of that crime. He willingly accepts the loss of his followers, the assessed compensation, and the sentence of exile, and finally receives absolution from the Pope himself. His efforts are not in vain. The saga ends with the complete reconciliation of Kári and Flosi, a reconciliation which redounds to the honor of both of them.

VII

Manly achievements and manly virtues are desirable and magnificent qualities, but they afford no protection against misfortune and evil in the conventional sense of these words. And a man's honor and renown can easily evoke envy and hatred in other men. As a matter of fact, this is what the story of Gunnar deals with to a very large degree. Good intentions per se avail almost as little against misfortune as does noble deportment. Like many of the best works of world literature, *Njála* deals with misfortune and grief—especially the misfortune and grief of good men. Strangely enough, mankind seems to have found one of its finest forms of edification precisely in this. Christians know nothing more salutary than the thought of the torture and death of a guiltless man on the cross.

The spiritual elevation which people gain from stories about grief and misfortune is doubtless of various kinds. Aristotle went to the heart of the matter when he stated that the performance of a tragedy brings about a spiritual catharsis in the onlookers. A special kind of spiritual uplift occurs when we see clearly that in sorrowful events values are created or revealed whose brightness increases in proportion to the magnitude of the events until it surpasses all the grief and misfortune. Good examples of this are found in the heroic poems of the *Edda* and in the *Íslendingasögur*, whose heroes gain a moral victory over themselves and the world at the very moment they succumb physically in the struggle against fate.

This attitude toward adversity is inborn in many of the heroes of *Njála*. In their lives and in the suffering they have to endure we get to see a variety of manly qualities: magnanimity, fidelity, integrity, benevolence, courage—qualities which appear brighter, the darker the surrounding misfortune becomes. Many heroes in *Njála* succeed in transforming their personal disaster into penance or self-sacrifice, thereby nullifying it for themselves as well as for others. In the case of most of the heroes who succeed in this, as well as in several others, we perceive a remarkable phenomenon, which cannot be a matter of chance, but obviously is a victory that they achieve. This phenomenon is a peculiar freedom and serenity of the spirit.

Think, for example, of Njáll, as he enters his home at Bergþórshvoll. He understands his past life, and is clairvoyant about the future. He is aware of everything that is at stake, and he makes his choice. He is afraid of nothing and bound by nothing, not even by the inherent desire to live. His spirit has finally achieved serenity; his words are free of the sensitivity which formerly was often noticeable. Although his mood is earnest, he even shows a trace of amusement when he speaks about his love of ease. He is exalted above joy or sorrow.

Bergþóra likewise makes a deliberate choice, and there is no doubt about the choice, nor would there ever have been at any time after her marriage to Njáll. She too has achieved serenity of spirit.

Skarphéðinn is no longer dominated by his father, nor is he in rebellion against him (this, of course, is a sort of negative domination). He loves his father as a free man. And he too makes a choice—he chooses to be burned to death with his father "to please him," as he says. He knows what his decision will cost; he is no longer controlled by the instinctive desire to live. He sees through this desire to live and through his entire life; all is transparent and clear and serene.

In the case of Gunnar we have a similar phenomenon, yet the motives for his decision to return home are less clear. In the background we are aware of the view (expressed in the verse he recites in his burial mound as well as in Skarphéðin's words about him to his son Högni) that he was unwilling to yield to his enemies. If this passionate desire was the basis for his decision to turn back, it is at variance with the freedom of spirit we have been discussing. In the prose narrative of the events themselves, however, a different motive is dominant: Gunnar makes his choice with the full knowledge that it will cost him his life. But his choice was influenced by his love for his native land. Thus he was not in control of his feelings, but rather was controlled by them.

This spiritual freedom and serenity renders even death itself insignificant. Indeed, from the example discussed, it might be assumed that this quality was merely a preparation for death, but other examples show that this need not be the case. Men can attain this spiritual freedom long before the end of their days.

More than anyone else Flosi was keenly aware of what he was doing, and what the consequences of his actions would be. He knew how much each deed would cost. He was a man of action with an iron will, who performed whatever deeds he considered necessary, even if it might be an enormous crime and a great responsibility before God. Despite this awareness, his deeds were accompanied by storms of passion which did not abate until he was able to forget the bloody cloak which Hildigunnur threw around his shoulders at her home, Vorsabær. After the burning of Njáll he harassed Ásgrímur Elliða-Grímsson (chapter 136) almost beyond endurance, and at the Assembly he resorted to extreme measures, including all sorts of chicanery and finally a trial of force. But at the very moment in which Hallur offered to forego compensation for his slain son, a change came over Flosi. He saw things in their proper perspective, measured one course of action against the other, and then made his decision: he chose penance for his crime, and good will and conciliatoriness rather than excessive zeal. And he now showed the same iron will as when he took vengeance for the slaying of Höskuldur. He became a free man. With stoic serenity he accepted everything which was demanded of him: the payment of compensation, banishment, the pilgrimage to Rome, and the loss of his followers at the hands of Kári. After all this, he became reconciled with his opponent.

Flosi never boasted about burning Njáll and his family to death. Far from speaking ill of Kári, he never ceased praising his valor. When his difficulties with Kári were at their worst, the saga states that "Flosi was a most cheerful man and a splendid host." When he went abroad on his final voyage and people found fault with his ship, he replied that it was quite good enough for an old man doomed to die. He was a genial man, always prepared to pay the price which life demanded.

> So when at last the Angel of the drink
> Of Darkness finds you by the river-brink
> And, proffering his Cup, invites your Soul
> Forth to your Lips to quaff it—do not shrink.[7]

Flosi's adversary, Kári, appears as a completely free and independent man from the very beginning. He comes sailing into the saga from far off in the distance. He is a seagoing merchant, a royal retainer, a man of the world, who likes to be on the move, but really has no great love for distant countries. He is at home everywhere and nowhere. He travels throughout the lands and realms of the earth alone and completely independent, and even when he becomes involved in matters, he never becomes enslaved to them. He is liked by all, is quick to make friends, to whom he is true and faithful, but finds it just as easy to take leave of them as to make their acquaintance. And when he does take leave of them it is with cordiality and the hope of meeting them again somewhere. On his expedition eastward into Skaftafellssýsla with Björn of Mörk, his loneliness resembles that of Skarphéðinn but lacks its torment.

Kári is well endowed with desirable physical and spiritual qualities: he is handsome, stately, accomplished, high-minded, and courageous; and none of these good qualities is the source of tragedy, as is so often the case with saga heroes. His magnanimous treatment of the Njáls-sons and later on his friendship and relationship by marriage to them repeatedly get him into danger, yet it seems as though nothing can

7. Verse XLVI of the *Rubáiyát* of Omar Khayyám in the translation (1869) of Edward FitzGerald.

harm him. He knows how much or how little everything is worth, and on the basis of this he makes his choice. He does not hesitate to risk his life. Here too he makes a choice, and he chooses things other than his own personal safety—noble behavior, deeds of prowess, virtue —since he finds them of higher value than life itself.

Kári grieves constantly for Njáll and Skarphéðinn, and for them alone, as it seems, and he never forgets them. He is filled with thoughts of vengeance and yet, as strange as it may seem, his mind loses none of its lucidity because of this. He bears a deep grudge against the arsonists, but has a high regard for Flosi. The desire for vengeance abates, but the vengeance itself continues. He seems to be above the deeds he performs, free and independent, as we see best in the account of his expedition with Björn of Mörk, when the seriousness and dangers of life and even life itself and its value seem to dissolve in the mirage of his unique sympathetic irony.

Hans E. Kinck, who in my opinion has written most perceptively about Kári (although I am unable to agree with his basic hypotheses), made the following statement about the reconciliation between Flosi and Kári: "*En höjere form for lidenskapernes renselse er ikke ofte fundet i kunstens verden.*" ("A loftier form of catharsis of human passions is seldom found in the world of art.")[8] All of the examples mentioned above reveal a strange and wonderful purification of emotion. Over all there prevails a sort of late-summer serenity—everything is clear and bright and transparent. Life has lost the belief in itself as the highest good which it possessed during the growing time of spring, and death has lost its terror. Some things are of greater and others of lesser value, but life itself is not the greatest. This view of life possesses an intimation of infinity; it signifies complete freedom and independence.

8. *Mange slags kunst*, p. 57.

Appendix A

The Old Norse translation of Gregory's *Dialogues* has been preserved in more or less fragmentary form in four MSS: (1) AM 667, xiv, 4to is a fragment of two leaves from ca. 1400. (2) AM 239 fol. is an Icelandic MS from the latter part of the fourteenth century, which has a very free reproduction of the original. C. R. Unger's text of the story of Anastasius in his *Heilagra manna sögur* (Vol. I, p. 189) is based on this MS. (3) The Icelandic Kálfafell Fragment, AM 677, 4, 4to, dates from ca. 1200. In this MS the Anastasius story is lacking because of a lacuna. (4) RA 71, 72, 77 are MS fragments housed in the Riksarkivet in Oslo. The text of this MS includes the passage in question, but is difficult to read because it has been damaged.

The text of MSS 3 and 4 is close to the original. In order to get a correct impression of the text known to the author of *Njála* it is necessary to have the original for comparison. This reveals great verbal similarity with the text of *Njála*. In my presentation (p. 14) I have followed the Latin text more closely than the Icelandic MS (AM 239), and I have also taken the Norwegian fragments into consideration.

The Latin text is as follows (J. P. Migne, *Patrologia Latina*, lxxvii, col. 185):

Quo videlicet in loco (Suppentonia) ingens desuper rupes eminet, et profundum subter præcipitium patet. Quadam vero nocte cum jam omnipotens Deus ejusdem venerabilis viri Anastasii labores remunerare decrevisset, ab alta rupe vox facta est, quæ producto sonitu clamaret, dicens: Anastasi, veni! Quo vocato alii quoquæ septem fratres vocati sunt ex nomine. Parvo autem momento ea quæ fuerat emissa vox siluit, et octavum fratrem vocavit. Quas dum aperte voces congregatio audisset, dubium non fuit quin eorum qui

voćati fuerant obitus appropinquasset. Intra paucos igitur dies primus ven-
erandus vir Anastasius, cæteri autem in eo ordine ex carne educti sunt, quo
de rupis vertice fuerant vocati. Frater vero ille ad quem vocandum vox parum
siluit, atque eum ita nominavit, morientibus aliis, paucis diebus vixit, et tunc
vitam finivit; ut aperte monstraretur quia interjectum vocis silentium parvum
vivendi spatium signaverit.

(A steep mountain towered high above the monastery {Suppentonia], and a
deep chasm lay beneath it. When omnipotent God had decided to reward
the venerable Anastasius for his labors, a voice was heard one night crying
out from the top of the cliff in prolonged tones saying: "Anastasius, come !"
And when this had been said, seven other monks were likewise called by
name. For a short while, however, the voice which had been heard fell silent,
and then it called the eighth monk. Since the community had clearly heard
this, no one doubted that death was approaching those whose names had been
called. Thus within a few days first the most revered Anastasius passed away,
and the others also in the same order in which their names had been called
from the top of the mountain. That brother whose name had been preceded
by a moment of silence lived on for a few days after the others had died and
then he too passed away. Thus it was clearly shown that the silence which
interrupted the voice signified a brief period of life.)

Appendix B

Hans E. Kinck's article "Et par ting om ættesagaen, skikkelser den ikke forstod," which first appeared in the volume in honor of Gerhard Gran (1916), pp. 32–58, was reprinted in his *Mange slags kunst* (1921), pp. 1–58, and again in his *Sagaenes ånd og skikkelser* (1951), pp. 9–46. This article has exerted a far-reaching influence, traces of which can be detected, for example, in Sigurður Guðmundsson's article "Gunnar á Hlíðarenda," *Skirnir* XCII (1918), 63–88, 221–51; in the radio address by Séra Ólafur Ólafsson (first printed in *Jörð* and again in *Lögberg*, 1933), although the influence here may have been indirect; in the stage play *Nial den vise* by Thit Jensen, 1934; and in Hallvard Lie's treatise, *Studier í Heimskringlas stil*, 1937, pp. 14–15. It should be mentioned that before Kinck published his article there were people in Iceland who were eager to take Hallgerð's part, a question which has been discussed somewhat by Matthías Jóhannesson in the first chapters of *Njála í íslenzkum skáldskap*, Reykjavík, 1953. It is difficult to say whether Kinck's article directly influenced Magnús Sigurðsson's article "Hallgerður í Njálu," *Tímarit Þjóðræknisfélagsins* XIII (1931), 75–88. Hallgerður has been discussed widely. The conventional interpretations of her (generally characterized either by neutrality or antipathy) are found in such major literary histories as those of Rosenberg, Finnur Jónsson, and Elster (who declares that Hallgerður is not worthy of the defenders who plead her cause); in C. Hauch's *Afhandlinger og æsthetiske Betragtninger*, 1885, pp. 428 ff.; in Friðrik Bergmann's article "Gunnar á Hlíðarenda," printed in *Vafurlogar*, Winnipeg, 1906, pp. 1–72; in A. Rittershaus, *Altnordische Frauen*, 1917; and in the article by Einar Hjörleifsson (Kvaran), "Skapstórar konur," in *Skirnir* (1908). More independent is the view of Hermann Jónasson as set forth in his *Draumar*, 1919, p. 43. Here he writes as follows:

> He (the dream man) stressed, for example, that I thought that the saga was very disparaging of Hallgerður langbrók, but that I was wrong for the most part. It was the magic power of derangement in her eyes which shackled Þjóstólfur with fiendish fetters, so that even though he knew she was giving him Loki-counsel, he could not resist her, but straightway rode west to Dalur and let Hrútur slay him, "the killer and overbearing man," without putting up any real defense.—But after that Hallgerður was never really in her right mind for the rest of her life, and that is why it seems so difficult to understand her.

Close to this point of view is G. Á. in "Faein orð um Hallgerði langbrók," *19. júni* V (1921), 44–45. A. Heusler is also independent in his views in *Die Geschichte vom weisen Njál*, 1914, pp. 13–14. Heusler is critical of Hallgerð's portrait as it appears in the saga, and in this respect he is in agreement with Kinck.

Appendix C

Complete consistency in the treatment of Icelandic proper names is practically impossible to achieve. For the most part I have used modern orthography except for a few names (such as Gizur) whose modern forms might seem strange to readers familiar with the Old Icelandic forms. I have also retained the older spelling in a few quotations in which modern orthography seemed inappropriate. The nominative singular form has been retained for all cases except the possessive, which is usually formed by the addition of *s* to the stem: Njáll, Skarphéðinn, Höskuldur, Auður; Njál's, Skarphéðin's, Höskuld's, Auð's, etc. In a few names, however, *s* is added to the nominative: Grettir's, Sverrir's, etc., since such possessive forms are familiar to English readers.

The pronunciation of Icelandic is rather complicated, and the following simplified rules are designed to help the reader achieve a comfortable approximation of the pronunciation of personal and place names as well as of brief quotations.

Main stress regularly falls on the first syllable, but stress is distributed somewhat more evenly throughout the word than in English.

Except for a strong tendency toward unvoicing, consonants in Icelandic are similar to their English counterparts. *S* is never voiced as in *has*, but is always pronounced as in *this*. *R* is an apical trill, as in Italian or Spanish, and *j* is a glide somewhat like *y* in *yes* or *j* in German *ja*. Thorn (þ) and edh (ð), which were borrowed from the Anglo-Saxon alphabet shortly after the year 1000, correspond to the initial fricatives in *thin* and *then* respectively. The character *g* stands for a number of sounds. In initial position it is a voiced palatal or velar stop as in *give* or *go*. In medial or final position it is a voiced palatal or velar fricative.

The vowels *i* (*y*), *e*, *a*, *o*, *u* are qualitatively similar to the radical vowels in *mid, feather, father, not* (British), and *stood*. The tense vowels *í* (*ý*) and *ú* are like those in *feed* and *food*. The letters *á*, *é*, and *ó* and the ligature *æ* represent diphthongs similar to those in *house, yes, boat*, and *mine*. Vowels and diphthongs are long when followed by one consonant and short when followed by two or more consonants.